Henry VIII's Quest for an Heir

Henry VIII's Quest for an Heir

The King's Great Matter

Helene Harrison

PEN & SWORD
HISTORY

First published in Great Britain in 2026 by
Pen & Sword History
An imprint of Pen & Sword Books Limited
Yorkshire – Philadelphia

ISBN 978 1 03610 487 0

A CIP catalogue record for this book is available from the British Library.

Typeset by Mac Style
Printed in the UK by CPI Group (UK) Ltd, Croydon, CR0 4YY.

MIX
Paper | Supporting responsible forestry
FSC www.fsc.org FSC® C013604

The Publisher's authorised representative in the EU for product safety is Authorised Rep Compliance Ltd., Ground Floor, 71 Lower Baggot Street, Dublin D02 P593, Ireland.
www.arccompliance.com

For a complete list of Pen & Sword titles please contact:

PEN & SWORD BOOKS LIMITED
47 Church Street, Barnsley, South Yorkshire, S70 2AS, England
E-mail: enquiries@pen-and-sword.co.uk
Website: www.pen-and-sword.co.uk
or
PEN AND SWORD BOOKS
1950 Lawrence Road, Havertown, PA 19083, USA
E-mail: uspen-and-sword@casematepublishers.com
Website: www.penandswordbooks.com

To my beloved grandparents,
On the very special occasion of their
70th wedding anniversary,
With many congratulations and much love
xxx

Contents

Acknowledgements

It is still a pinch-me moment that this is my fourth book. Sometimes it feels like it has all happened in no time at all! Thank you so much to everyone at Pen and Sword, including Sarah-Beth Watkins, Laura Hirst, Travis King, and Rosie Crofts and the social media team. Also, to my lovely editor, Sarah Hodder, for all of your hard work.

A massive thank you has to go to my friend and editor, Laura, who manages to pick up my crazy typos for me and makes sure that what I have written actually makes sense. You are the first to read all of my work, and you do a great job. Huge thanks to Mark, I honestly do not know where I would be without you, your unconditional support keeps me going, talking me down when I am stressed and worried, helping me handle deadlines, and giving me the best emotional support a woman could ask for. You are amazing. Big thanks also to Hattie for being a constant boost in morale and a sounding board when I need it and for bringing lots of McDonalds to my door. And to Ben for supporting me and letting me babble on about history without even making sense all of the time!

Thank you also to my family – mum, dad, and Matilda. To my grandparents who have always unconditionally loved and supported me, even from 300 miles away, always thinking of me and wishing me the best. To Auntie Jackie, Auntie Kate, and Uncle Gerard for letting me come and stay, and giving me a relaxing break from the writing. Also, to Uncle Brian, Auntie Marie, and Auntie Krystyna for buying and reading my books, listening to podcasts and the general support I get from you all, thank you so very much. And to my godson and cousins – James, Thomas, and Fred – who are not overly invested in the history, but I know are proud of me anyway, as I am of them.

To all of those podcasters who have interviewed me over the last few years, let me talk about my research and have promoted my books – Natalie Grueninger (Talking Tudors), Adam Pennington (The Tudor Chest), Rebecca

Larson (Tudors Dynasty and Beyond), Emma Holbrook (The Ill-Fated Wives of Henry VIII), Claire Ridgway (The Anne Boleyn Files), Jess Faulkner (Herstory) and Carol Ann Lloyd (Royals, Rebels, and Romantics). You are all great hosts and ask some fascinating questions to help your listeners to engage in the subject being discussed. Thank you also to all of the lovely bloggers and Instagrammers who have featured my books over the years, too many to name!

To my history girls on social media who all support each other in all kinds of ways – Amy McElroy, Rebecca Batley, Carol Ann Lloyd, Sharon Bennett Connolly, Aimee Fleming, Beverley Adams, and Laura Adkins. To anyone I've missed, I apologise! Thanks also to The Tudor Trio (Owen Emmerson, Kate McCaffrey, and Nicola Tallis), now Owen & Kate History, for providing so many interesting points of research through their videos and events and providing opportunities to ask historians and writers questions and hear about their research as well. It has opened my eyes and encouraged me to read and engage with more different things.

Lastly, thanks to you, the reader, for buying this book. I hope you enjoy it!

Illustration Credits

1. Arthur Tudor, Prince of Wales, *c.*1500 by Meynnart Werwyck. Located at Hever Castle and Gardens. Photograph: Author's Own.
2. Henry VIII, *c.*1520 by an unknown artist. Located at the National Portrait Gallery. Photograph: Author's Own.
3. Katherine of Aragon miniature, *c.*1526 from the Horenbout family workshop. Located at the National Portrait Gallery. Photograph: Author's Own.
4. Cardinal Thomas Wolsey, Archbishop of York, 1738 by Jacobus Houbraken. Yale Center for British Art, Yale University Art Gallery Collection, B1998.14.403.
5. Henry Fitzroy, Duke of Richmond and Somerset, *c.*1533 from the Horenbout family workshop. Kept in the Royal Collection. Photograph: Author's Own.
6. Priory of St Lawrence at Blackmore. Photograph with kind permission from Rebecca Batley.
7. Mary Boleyn by an unknown artist. Located at Hever Castle and Gardens. Photograph: Author's Own.
8. Engraving of Katherine of Aragon pleading with Henry VIII, 1794 by William Ward after Richard Westall. Rijksmuseum, Amsterdam, RP-P-1918-2123.
9. Woman thought to be Catherine Carey Knollys, daughter of Mary Boleyn *c.*1562 by an unknown artist, Yale Center for British Art, Paul Mellon Collection, B1974.3.22.
10. Anne Boleyn, Hever Rose portrait, *c.*1583 by an unknown artist, based on a lost original. Located at Hever Castle and Gardens. Photograph: Author's Own.
11. Hever Castle. Photograph: Author's Own.

12. Thomas Cromwell, Earl of Essex, 1739 by Jacobus Houbraken. Yale Center for British Art, Paul Mellon Collection, B1977.14.11796.
13. Statue of John Fisher, Bishop of Rocester. Located at Rochester Cathedral. Photograph: Author's Own.
14. Burial place of Katherine of Aragon in Peterborough Cathedral. Wikimedia Commons: Dave Hitchborne, CC BY-SA 2.0.
15. Site of the scaffold on Tower Hill. Photograph: Author's Own.
16. Engraving of the beheading of Anne Boleyn, 1699 by Van Eeghen. Rijksmuseum, Amsterdam, RP-P-1896-A-19368-1726.
17. White Tower at the Tower of London. Photograph: Author's Own.
18. Tomb marker for Anne Boleyn in the Chapel of St Peter ad Vincula in the Tower of London. Wikimedia Commons: AloeVera95, CC BY-SA 4.0.
19. Jane Seymour miniature, *c.*1536 from the Horenbout family workshop. Located at Sudeley Castle. Photograph: Author's Own.
20. Tomb of Henry Fitzroy, 1st Duke of Richmond and Somerset, at St Michael's Church, Framlingham. Photograph: Author's Own.
21. Engraving of Henry VIII, Jane Seymour, Henry VII, and Elizabeth of York, *c.*1743 engraving by George Vertue after Remigius van Leemput, after Hans Holbein. Wellcome Collection, 570451i.
22. An Allegory of the Tudor Succession, *c.*1590 by an unknown artist. Yale Center for British Art, Paul Mellon Collection, B1974.3.7.
23. Henry VIII, Will Somers, Edward VI, Mary I, and Elizabeth I, 1800 by Francesco Bartolozzi. Yale Center for British Art, Paul Mellon Collection, B1977.14.19606.
24. Edward VI, 1550 by an unknown artist. Rijksmuseum, Amsterdam, SK-A-980.
25. Mary I, 1554 by Hans Eworth. Located at the National Portrait Gallery. Photograph: Author's Own.
26. Elizabeth I, late 16th century by an unknown artist. Rijksmuseum, Amsterdam, SK-C-1466.

Preface

Writing about what is often today known as 'The King's Great Matter' is difficult because there are so many strands to it, and it is very complex to unravel at times. The first question is, when do you start in the chronology, and when do you end? How much of the religious division which pulled England apart at this time needs to be covered and in how much detail? It cannot be denied that the annulment of Henry VIII's marriage to Katherine of Aragon and the English Reformation were closely intertwined. Then there is the enigmatic figure of Anne Boleyn who many think they know and understand, but there is so much more to her and her role in the 'Great Matter'. At the heart of the story are women whose lives were completely upturned by the events of these years – Katherine of Aragon, Anne Boleyn, Jane Seymour, and the future Mary I and Elizabeth I. How were these women affected by the events and how much evidence do we have for how they felt about these things? There are also the ministers who came from humble beginnings to feature at the centre of political life in England – Thomas Wolsey and Thomas Cromwell, the sons of a butcher and a blacksmith respectively. What roles did they play and how far did one influence the other? These are all questions I try and cover in this book, though many do not have certain or complete answers.

What drove me to write this book in the first place is the two women at the heart of the story – Katherine of Aragon and Anne Boleyn. I am fascinated by women's history, and the position of women in stories we traditionally see from the male point of view. And it is the women in the 'Great Matter' whose lives are most affected. Katherine of Aragon was demoted from a queen to a dowager princess of Wales and died in exile. Anne Boleyn was raised from the daughter of a knight to a marquess, a traditionally male title, then to queen, yet ended under an executioner's sword. Jane Seymour presided over a court where her predecessor, Anne Boleyn, was barely cold in her grave before she married Anne's husband, the king, having also served Katherine of Aragon, before providing the much-desired son and promptly dying. Princess Mary, later Mary I, had gone from being the feted and beloved daughter of a king, heir apparent to the throne, to being pushed out and replaced by the daughter of the woman who supplanted her adored mother. Princess Elizabeth, who would one day be Queen Elizabeth I, was not yet 3 years old when her mother died, and would have heard about the events leading up to her own birth as she grew up; she must surely have been affected by the fate of her mother at the hands of her father.

This period of English history has been my favourite since I first started researching the Tudors, because there are strong women at the heart of the story. But there is also an interesting psychological component in that this is the period where we most clearly see the development of Henry VIII from the handsome and feted young king into the tyrant that we most often view him as today. It is the 'Great Matter' that helps to shape Henry, and it is fascinating to study and try and understand how that came to be, even though trying to understand Henry VIII often seems like a losing battle. The psychological state of the women in the story is also interesting, with their huge changes in status, both up and down, and how they coped with it, which I think is also a huge part of why their stories endure and captivate us today.

It is people who are at the centre of this story, so although this book will examine the politics and religious changes that happened during this period, as is necessary to get a fuller understanding of the events of the 'Great Matter', the focus is very much on the people – Henry VIII, Katherine of Aragon, Anne Boleyn, Princess or Lady Mary, Thomas Wolsey, and Thomas Cromwell. The 'Great Matter' is often seen as the catalyst for the huge religious changes which swept England, which in a lot of ways it was, as the upheaval split apart families, ended lives, and left a huge emotional toll in its wake on the people at the centre of the maelstrom.

Helene Harrison, July 2025

Introduction

Henry VIII's 'Great Matter', or 'The King's Great Matter' is an often-used term for the period during which Henry VIII attempted to annul his marriage to his first wife, Katherine of Aragon, so that he could marry Anne Boleyn. The king was unwavering in his belief that a woman could not rule England and that he needed a son to succeed him. Katherine of Aragon had failed in this regard by the mid-1520s, providing Henry VIII with only a single daughter, Mary. This simple fact was the driving force behind the 'Great Matter'.

Centuries before, Empress Matilda had been declared 'Lady of the English', rather than queen, during the period known as the Anarchy, in 1141. When she attempted to get to Westminster Abbey in London to be crowned, she faced bitter opposition and was denied entry to the city. This was the only time prior to the Tudor dynasty that a woman had endeavoured to be crowned in her own right in England. With this being the only example of female rule in England before Henry VIII in the sixteenth century, it is understandable why he believed that he needed a son. Henry VIII did not have the examples of Elizabeth I, Queen Anne, Queen Victoria, or Elizabeth II to prove that a woman could rule in England.

Despite this, the Tudor dynasty would be unique, seeing two crowned regnant queens one after the other – Mary I and Elizabeth I – and that was after a contentious reign of a thirteen-day queen, Lady Jane Grey. Those two crowned regnant queens were two of the women at the centre of the 'Great Matter':

> It might have been possible to dismiss one regnant queen as a blip in the tradition of male monarchy. Together these two women [Mary and Elizabeth] reigned for fifty years. The reality of female rule couldn't be undone.[1]

It was Henry VIII's 'Great Matter' which allowed this to come to pass. Neither of his first two wives produced a surviving son, leaving only a daughter apiece. And when Henry's son by his third wife, Edward VI, died young and without an heir of his own, all of the potential candidates were women. The 'Great Matter' had eventually provided a son, though he would not be the long-reigning and successful monarch of the dynasty that his father had hoped he would be. Henry VIII believed that his son would reign and have sons of his own and that neither of his daughters would wear the crown when he died in 1547, despite him returning his daughters to the succession in 1544. It would, in fact, be the executed Anne Boleyn's daughter, Elizabeth, who would be the longest-reigning monarch of the Tudor dynasty, though her childless state would bring the dynasty to an end in 1603, paving the way for the son of the executed Mary, Queen of Scots to succeed to the throne, and unite England and Scotland.

The 'Great Matter' is often claimed to span the period circa 1526 to 1533 – from the time Henry VIII decided to annul his marriage to Katherine of Aragon, until he married Anne Boleyn. However, this short a period has been debated in recent years. This book will argue that the 'Great Matter' was over a more extended period of time, from the birth of Henry Fitzroy in 1519 up to the birth of Edward VI in 1537. It was bookended by the births of two sons to Henry VIII, one illegitimate and one legitimate, both of whom would die young. But it is also important to look further back to Katherine of Aragon's first marriage to Prince Arthur in 1501 and the implications this had on her marriage to Henry VIII. Had Katherine of Aragon given Henry VIII a living son, this first marriage would likely not be remembered in history, but she did not produce a son and so it became the crux of the annulment case. However, it is not right to say that the 'Great Matter' stretches back so far, even though that is when the seeds of it were sown. With the birth of Henry Fitzroy in 1519 and Katherine's failure to produce a son and heir (her final pregnancy was the year before), this was the crucial moment.

It is interesting at this point to consider the ages of death of those young men around the throne. Henry VIII's brother, Prince Arthur, died in April 1502 at the age of 15 years and seven months. Henry's illegitimate son, Henry Fitzroy, died in July 1536 aged 17 years and one month. Edward VI,

Henry VIII's only legitimate surviving son, died in July 1553 aged 15 years and nine months. The three young men of the Tudor dynasty closest to the throne, aside from Henry VII and Henry VIII, all died before attaining their majority, between the ages of 15 and 17. Perhaps there was, in fact, a curse on the male Tudor heirs. It has been said that Katherine of Aragon claimed that 'she had not offended, but it was a judgment of God, for that her former marriage was made in blood, meaning that of the Earl of Warwick'.[2] Katherine was referring to an event that enabled her marriage to Prince Arthur in 1501. Her mother and father, Isabella I of Castile, and Ferdinand II of Aragon, refused to send Katherine to England for her marriage until there did not remain 'a drop of doubtful Royal blood' in England.[3] The royal blood referred to was that of Edward Plantagenet, 17th Earl of Warwick, who was executed in 1499 by Henry VII. Warwick was the closest remaining claimant from the house of York, a nephew to both Edward IV and Richard III, and was executed for his supposed involvement with the pretender, Perkin Warbeck. Warbeck had claimed to be Richard of Shrewsbury, Duke of York, the younger of the Princes in the Tower and allegedly plotted with the Earl of Warwick in the Tower after his arrest. How much of this involvement was real or manipulated is still questioned today. But this did seem to be the start of a series of incidents which led to the 'Great Matter'.

By the mid-1520s, Katherine of Aragon had only a single living daughter, Mary, though she had suffered multiple infant deaths, miscarriages, and stillbirths. Henry VIII also had an illegitimate son, Henry Fitzroy, with his mistress, Elizabeth 'Bessie' Blount, but he did not have a legitimate son to succeed him on the throne. When Henry had 'deliberately withdrawn' from Katherine in 1525, he made his illegitimate son the Duke of Richmond and Somerset.[4] The Richmond title had belonged to Henry VIII's father, Henry VII, before he was king, though as an earldom rather than a dukedom. It still had huge significance in terms of Fitzroy's elevated status – he was effectively granted a royal title. Did this mean that Henry VIII was looking to Fitzroy to succeed him on the throne? It is possible, though he soon turned his mind to other ways of having a legitimate son. When the king fell in love with the alluring Anne Boleyn who refused to become his mistress, Henry started to consider making her his queen. Anne was young enough to give the king a son and heir to succeed him. Anne herself was not the reason for the divorce, but she, and the lure of a legitimate son, was the catalyst for the king to act. Henry VIII could now see his future, and he would stop at nothing to make the fantasy and dream come true.

The historian Herbert Thurston writing in 1904 said that the divorce had been investigated with 'quite extraordinary thoroughness' already, but that the 'question is one rather of canon law than of history'.[5] At the time, it was certainly a question of both canon law and theology, but investigating it nowadays, it is a historical question as well, as it is important not to look at the 'Great Matter' through twenty-first century eyes. We cannot apply today's thinking to what was happening and what people were thinking 500 years ago; it will give us an inaccurate perception and understanding of how things were and what was important at the time it was occurring. We cannot completely eradicate bias and how we think today, as everything we think and write is informed by the times in which we live, but it is important to acknowledge that expectations, thoughts, and perceptions, were very different 500 years ago, especially when it came to divorce, or annulment, and ending a marriage. The importance of male succession in the eyes of English monarchs was all-encompassing. It is easy to forget that it was only in 2013 that the law of male primogeniture was overturned with the Succession to the Crown Act, meaning that, for the first time, a female sits above her younger brother in the line of succession. That did not happen until 500 years after the birth of Mary I, England's first queen regnant and Henry VIII's eldest daughter.

One important thing to consider in the 'Great Matter' is whether Henry VIII intended this to be a divorce or an annulment. The king did not want a divorce; he wanted the marriage annulled on the basis that it was never valid in the first place. It is often referred to as a divorce, but that is not what it was in reality. Later chapters will deal with the basis for the annulment, but Henry VIII believed in the statement in the book of Leviticus in the Bible, chapter twenty, verse twenty-one (Leviticus 20:21), which said:

> And if a man shall take his brother's wife, it is an unclean thing: he hath uncovered his brother's nakedness; they shall be childless.[6]

Henry VIII believed that to be without a son was to effectively be childless. He did not believe that a woman could rule saw a son as a necessity. Thus, Henry believed that his marriage to Katherine of Aragon was condemned by God. However, there is an opposing text to Leviticus in the book of Deuteronomy:

> If brethren dwell together, and one of them die, and have no child, the wife of the dead shall not marry without unto a stranger: her husband's brother shall go in unto her, and take her to him to wife, and perform the duty of an husband's brother unto her.[7]

Henry VIII believed firmly in the Leviticus text and his interpretation of it, but the Deuteronomy text could be used to oppose his main argument. There were those who would not argue with the king or disagree openly with his point of view, but Katherine of Aragon was not one of them. She would assert that her marriage was legal and valid until her dying day. Many people did side with Katherine during the annulment case, but 'to side with [Katherine] was, of course, to stand against Henry'.[8] This was dangerous and could, as will be seen, result in execution.

The Papacy also needs a brief mention at this point, as they were central to the story. The Papacy was critical of the king's 'Great Matter' and how the English Reformation came about. There are two key Popes related to the annulment case, and they are Clement VII (1523–1534) and Paul III (1534–1549); both had their roles to play in the progress of the English Reformation as a result of the annulment case. There were also international implications relating to the Papacy, from Francis I of France, and Charles V, the Holy Roman Emperor.

This book will focus less on the legalities and how laws changed, parliament developed, and the mechanism of what happened, and more on the people involved. From Katherine of Aragon to the Boleyns, and Thomas Cromwell to Princess Mary, these are their stories during one of the most tumultuous periods in English history.

Chapter 1

Roots of Dissatisfaction

To understand Henry VIII's 'Great Matter' and his quest to annul his marriage to Katherine of Aragon in pursuit of the all-important son and heir to the English throne, it is crucial to look backwards to see what led to this decision on Henry's part. Was it simply that he fell in love with the alluring Anne Boleyn, or were there deeper origins of this momentous choice? What were the roots of dissatisfaction which would lead to England being torn apart in Henry's quest for an heir? Henry VIII had already decided to investigate a way to annul his first marriage by the time that things became serious with Anne Boleyn. She was the catalyst that gave Henry VIII something to work towards, but the annulment began with Henry's history with Katherine of Aragon.

Henry VIII married Katherine of Aragon on 11 June 1509 in the Church of the Observant Friars at Greenwich. The ceremony was a private one. Henry and Katherine were then crowned together at Westminster Abbey on 24 June 1509. However, the roots of annulment were sown even further back, in November 1501, when Katherine of Aragon had married Henry VIII's elder brother, Arthur, Prince of Wales, at St Paul's Cathedral. It was Arthur who was supposed to be king of England as the elder son, not Henry. This first marriage would provide the excuse Henry VIII needed in the 1520s to assert that his own marriage to Katherine was not valid.

Katherine of Aragon, christened Catalina, was born on 16 December 1485 as the youngest child of Isabella I of Castile and Ferdinand II of Aragon. Her parents' marriage had united Spain into a European power. Prince Arthur Tudor was born on either 19 or 20 September 1486 as the eldest child of Henry VII of England and Elizabeth of York. The marriage of Henry and Elizabeth united the warring houses of Lancaster and York, but the Tudor dynasty was still only a year old at the time of Arthur's birth, and there would be several attempts to unseat Henry VII.

The Treaty of Medina del Campo was agreed on 26 March 1489, signed the following day by the Spanish, but not ratified by Henry VII until September 1490. It was this treaty, in clause seventeen, which agreed the marriage between Prince Arthur and Katherine of Aragon as part of a treaty between England and Spain:

> In order to strengthen this alliance the Princess Katharine is to marry Prince Arthur. The marriage is to be contracted per verba de futuro as soon as Katharine and Arthur attain the necessary age.[1]

'*Per verba de futuro*' meant a promise to marry in the future. Unlike '*per verba de praesenti*' vows, '*de futuro*' vows could be dissolved and were not binding as they were future vows as opposed to present ones. Marriages were often used as a way to strengthen or solidify alliances, as it meant the two families making the alliance were tied together by blood. It does not necessarily work, as is seen in the alliance between England and Scotland when Henry VIII's sister, Margaret Tudor, married James IV of Scotland to cement the partnership in 1503 – ten years later, in 1513, Henry VIII's forces would kill James IV at the Battle of Flodden after he invaded England.

The necessary age that two parties needed to reach for the betrothal was 14 for boys and 12 for girls.[2] This meant that the betrothal became official in 1500, when Arthur reached the age of 14 and the marriage could go ahead. The eighteenth clause in the Treaty of Medina del Campo declared that:

> The marriage shall be contracted per verba de praesenti and consummated as soon as the Prince and the Princess attain the necessary age for it. Henry and Ferdinand and Isabella shall swear to employ all their influence with their children that the marriage be contracted as stipulated.[3]

Once Katherine reached the age of 12 and Arthur age 14, then the betrothal would be made '*per verba de praesenti*', making it effectively a valid marriage at the time. These were vows made in the present and were difficult to dissolve, and almost impossible if followed by consummation. Arthur and Katherine's betrothal at this time was made by proxy and their parents were to do their utmost to make sure the marriage went ahead. It is interesting to note that Elizabeth of York, Arthur's mother, is not named, though both of Katherine's parents are. This is possibly because Ferdinand and Isabella were both monarchs in their own right, whereas Elizabeth of York was a queen consort not a regnant queen.

A further agreement to the marriage of Katherine and Arthur was signed in London on 1 October 1496 and it was then sent to Spain where Ferdinand and Isabella signed it along with, for the first time, Katherine of Aragon. It was 'a symbolic act, a rite of passage for a young girl indicating that she was leaving her childhood behind'.[4] Rodrigo Gonzalez de Puebla was formally empowered to take Katherine's role in the proceedings in England which would solidify her coming marriage. The formal betrothal took place at Woodstock Palace in Oxfordshire on 15 August 1497 where de Puebla stood in for Katherine as her proxy, speaking the words to make the betrothal binding. The marriage by proxy, again with de Puebla standing in for Katherine, took place at Tickenhill Manor in Worcestershire on 19 May 1499, which was one of Prince Arthur's residences. From that moment, when the '*de praesenti*' vows had been spoken, Katherine of Aragon was officially styled as Princess of Wales, and she and Arthur were officially married, though they had not yet met and were still in separate countries.

Katherine of Aragon left her home of the Alhambra in Spain on 21 May 1501 to begin her journey to England. It had to have been emotional for her, as she must have realised that she likely would not see her parents or her homeland again; she was only 15 years old, though had known she was going to be Princess of Wales and then queen of England for many years already. Many of the ladies and gentlemen who accompanied her would soon be sent back to Spain upon her arrival in England, possibly leaving her feeling even more isolated and homesick in a foreign country. There were delays as she travelled overland, and then storms at sea delayed her sailing, but the fleet arrived in Plymouth harbour on 2 October 1501.

Katherine was accompanied by English nobles as she travelled towards London, arriving at Dogmersfield House on 6 November, where she would, for the first time, meet her husband and her father-in-law, Prince Arthur and Henry VII. There was a clash of English and Spanish customs, as the Spanish informed the English royals that a Spanish Infanta could not entertain her husband or father-in-law until the full marriage ceremony had been completed as her virtue would be under threat. But the king was not pleased and demanded to see his daughter-in-law, to see what she was like, and that she was as reported to him.[5] Katherine seems to have reacted calmly, despite the worries and panic of her attendants, worried about breaking Spanish custom, and she got ready to meet the king. It must have been an awkward meeting as neither could speak the other's language. It is strange that Ferdinand and Isabella, despite having negotiated a treaty in 1489 that would see Katherine become queen of England in the future, did not think in the following twelve years before she left for England that she might like to learn English, despite her speaking many other languages. Katherine met Henry VII first, and then prepared to meet her husband, Arthur. They spoke in Latin for a while and then there was a small party where both Katherine and Arthur danced, though not with each other. The next morning Katherine set off for London and her official wedding. Henry VII and Prince Arthur had gone on ahead to meet her there.

Katherine of Aragon and Prince Arthur married at St Paul's Cathedral on 14 November 1501. The young Prince Henry, later Henry VIII, walked Katherine into the cathedral and down the aisle to hand her over to his brother. Katherine wore a white satin dress over a farthingale, with a white silk veil over her face. Arthur was also dressed in white satin. There was much celebrating, feasting, and dancing after the ceremony before the consummation needed to take place. This consummation is perhaps the most talked about royal bedding in English history and it would be at the centre of Henry VIII's case for an annulment over twenty-five years later. Katherine of Aragon always maintained that the marriage was never consummated and that she was a virgin when she married Henry VIII in 1509. However, Henry would come to believe that Katherine's first marriage was in fact consummated, thus making his marriage to her null and void. As Herbert Thurston describes it, the question of consummation later became a matter of 'unpleasant controversy'.[6] It was debated openly in a legal court, with witnesses called – nothing, it seems, was private in this matter of the king's annulment case. However, at the time of the wedding there did not seem to have been any questions raised over whether the marriage was consummated, though only Katherine and Arthur know the truth of exactly what happened.

Historian Julia Fox writes that at the time 'it was uncritically assumed that sexual intercourse did take place'.[7] Fox goes on to say that the following morning Arthur seemed to be 'full of the joys of marriage' but that he would not have risked losing face with his gentlemen if he had failed to consummate the marriage.[8] This is understandable, so we cannot assume from Arthur's own comments and demeanour that the marriage was definitely consummated. Amy Licence backs up Fox's logic, stating that there was a need for Arthur to prove himself as a man – 'his duty was to achieve intercourse, and definitions of his masculinity, his prowess and fitness to rule rested upon his success or failure' in his marital bed.[9] Juan de Gamarra, a 12-year-old boy at the time of the wedding in Katherine of Aragon's service, said that he had remained in Katherine's antechamber during the wedding night and that Arthur got up early in the morning, which surprised everyone. He also said that one of Katherine's ladies, Francesca de Cáceres, told the other ladies that 'nothing had passed between Prince Arthur and his wife, which surprised everyone and made them laugh at him'.[10] Katherine's lady, Dona Elvira, claimed that Katherine was as pure as when she left her mother's womb, and told this to Katherine's father, Ferdinand, who seems to have believed her.[11] Arthur would have no doubt been embarrassed had he failed to consummate the marriage, and would have hoped that he could make it good on successive nights. Being aged 15 and surrounded by young men of the court who probably had more experience than him, it would be no wonder if he evidenced a little bravado.

The later depositions given in 1529 at Blackfriars have George Talbot, 4th Earl of Shrewsbury, who was part of the group who conducted Prince Arthur to the marital bed the night of the wedding, saying that he 'supposed that the Prince consummated the marriage'.[12] Thomas Grey, 2nd Marquess of Dorset, said that he had also accompanied Arthur on the night of his wedding and that he 'thinks that he used the princess as his wife, for he was of a good and sanguine complexion, and they were commonly reputed as man and wife during prince Arthur's life'.[13] The third deposition comes from Sir Anthony Willoughby who testified that, the morning after the wedding, Prince Arthur said to him 'Willoughby, bring me a cup of ale, for I have been this night in the midst of Spain' and that 'Masters, it is good pastime to have a wife', so he could only assume that the marriage had been successfully consummated.[14] Willoughby in addition claimed that Katherine and Arthur lived together as man and wife for the rest of Arthur's life. How accurate these testimonies are is unclear, but Henry VIII and his councillors had certainly done their best to try and prove that the marriage between Katherine of Aragon and Prince Arthur had been consummated, and thus that the marriage between Henry VIII and Katherine was null and void as a result.

Soon after the wedding, it was time for Prince Arthur to return to Ludlow Castle, in the Welsh Marches, which is where his household had been set up for him as Prince of Wales. There appear to have been some questions as to whether his new wife, Katherine, would accompany him. There were some worries that Katherine might struggle to adjust even more to the damp and cold of Ludlow than the English court at Richmond or Greenwich. There also appear to have been concerns that the young Arthur and Katherine might over exert themselves in bed. Giles Tremlett records how Henry VII asked Katherine whether she would prefer to stay in London or accompany Arthur to Ludlow, but that she avoided answering him, stating that she 'did not have any will but his', and would be 'content with what he decided'.[15] Katherine did end up accompanying Arthur to Ludlow, leaving in December 1501. Little is known about their time in Ludlow as a married couple, although we do know that Katherine would form a lasting friendship with Lady Margaret Pole, later Countess of Salisbury in her own right. Margaret would play a crucial role later on in the early upbringing of Katherine's daughter, Mary.

Prince Arthur sadly died at Ludlow Castle on 2 April 1502, having only been married for less than five months. Katherine of Aragon was also very ill at this time, although she survived. Several theories have been suggested as to the reason for Arthur's death at this time. Historian Amy Licence describes how Arthur's physician, Dr Alcarez, diagnosed his condition as 'tisis' or 'phthisis', pulmonary tuberculosis, which also presented with similar symptoms to the sweating sickness. Licence goes on to explain that Katherine and Arthur did not both have tuberculosis, but if Arthur had already contracted it and then a strain of sickness swept through Ludlow, Arthur may have been too weak to fight it off as well as Katherine did.[16] Giles Tremlett quotes the same term as Licence – 'tisis' – but explains that it was a 'Spanish catch-all word' covering everything from pulmonary tuberculosis to any kind of wasting disease producing ulceration of the organs.[17] Patrick Williams says that the illness was described as the sweating sickness but that it may have been pulmonary tuberculosis.[18] It is always difficult to diagnose something at a distance of over 500 years, and so it is with Prince Arthur, and the physicians at the time did not have the same knowledge of the body and medicine as professionals do today. The consensus, however, seems to have been that Arthur died from something affecting his lungs, quite possibly tuberculosis.

On hearing of Arthur's death, Katherine of Aragon's parents, Isabella and Ferdinand, wrote to their ambassador in England, de Puebla, to say that they had:

> read with profound sorrow the news of the death of Prince Arthur. The affliction caused by all their former losses has been revived by it. But the will of God must be obeyed. Have heard that the Princess of Wales is suffering. She must be removed, without loss of time, from the unhealthy place where she now is.[19]

Giles Tremlett writes about how Katherine and her ladies had spent time since Arthur died writing to Spain, complaining about the 'unhealthy' and 'doom-laden' castle at Ludlow.[20] This explains the reference in the letter from the Spanish monarchs to the 'unhealthy place where she now is'. Katherine would not remain there for long.

After Katherine had recovered from her illness, she returned to London in a litter covered in black velvet and was settled at Durham House on the Strand. The first thing to do was to establish if Katherine was pregnant, as it was not immediately clear whether the marriage had been consummated. Prince Henry was not immediately declared to be Prince of Wales in case Katherine was pregnant as, if it was a son, then he would be the new Prince of Wales, and Katherine the mother of the future king of England. It was fairly quickly discovered that she was not pregnant and so Prince Henry, age 10, was declared the new Prince of Wales. Discussions seem to have begun almost immediately between Henry VII and Katherine's parents, Isabella and Ferdinand, over Katherine's future; it seems they all still wanted to maintain the Anglo-Spanish alliance. Isabella and Ferdinand, however, sent instructions to their new envoy in England, Hernán Duque de Estrada:

1. To reclaim from the King of England the 100,000 scudos which have been paid as the first instalment of the marriage portion of the said Princess of Wales.
2. To demand that the King of England should deliver to the Princess of Wales those towns, manors, lands, &c. which have been assigned to her as her dowry, which is to amount to one third of the revenues of Wales, Cornwall, and Chester.
3. To beg the King of England to send the Princess Katharine to Spain in the best manner, and in the shortest time possible, and, if necessary, to superintend himself the arrangements for her departure.[21]

It is a mixed bag of instructions, and it seems like the Spanish monarchs were covering their bases in a sense. The first instruction relates to the return of the first instalment of Katherine's dowry, which Ferdinand and Isabella wanted repaid as Arthur was dead. The second is in relation to Katherine being given her dower lands as Arthur's widow, and the third is Katherine's parents asking Henry VII to allow her to return to Spain. This was not what Henry VII wanted. He was determined to maintain the Spanish alliance which offered dynastic support to his fledgling dynasty, and to keep Katherine's dowry as well. It was probably these considerations which led to the agreement whereby Katherine of Aragon was betrothed to her dead husband's brother, Prince Henry. It is possible that Katherine and her parents believed that it was Katherine's destiny to be queen of England, and what they wanted all along was a new marriage.

Queen Isabella I of Castile wrote to her ambassadors in England on 11 April 1503, taking charge of the future of her daughter, Katherine. She was obviously angry that what had been agreed had not been done, 'in order to delay the fulfilment of his promise to us and the Princess of Wales, our daughter' and asks that 'preparations must be made for the return hither of the Princess of Wales, our daughter, for there must be no delay about her departure'.[22] In a separate letter written the same day, Isabella hints at a different motive for pushing for Katherine's return to Spain, that 'it would not be right that the Princess should stay in England during the period of mourning for the Prince of Wales. Much greater also will be the necessity and obligation of her coming hither if the betrothal between her and the Prince of Wales should not be immediately concluded'.[23] It seems that there were some political manoeuvrings going on with Katherine as the pawn, in order that both the English and the Spanish could get the most out of a difficult situation. It does not seem at all fair on Katherine, mourning her husband, and unsure of exactly what her future would look like.

After the death of Elizabeth of York in February 1503, Henry VII appears to have suggested to Isabella and Ferdinand that he could marry his daughter-in-law, the young, widowed Princess of Wales, Katherine of Aragon, himself and she would immediately become queen of England. When news of this proposal reached Spain, Isabella was horrified and said that:

> … concerning the marriage of the King of England with the Princess of Wales, our daughter, saying that it is spoken of in England. But as this would be a very evil thing – one never before seen, and the mere mention of which offends the ears – we would not for anything in the world that it should take place. Therefore, if anything be said to you about it, speak of it as a thing not to be endured.[24]

Had Katherine married Henry VII she would have been queen of England for just a few years, and her children would not have succeeded to the throne with Prince Henry as the heir. In terms of Katherine being a part of creating an English dynasty, it was not a sensible move, and that was without considering the age gap – in February 1503 when Elizabeth of York died, Katherine of Aragon was just 17 years old, whereas Henry VII was 46 years old. That cannot have been a nice thought for any parents and, as can be seen in the above letter, Isabella and Ferdinand strongly objected. There were also other contenders for Henry VII's second wife – Philip, Duke of Burgundy (Katherine of Aragon's brother-in-law) proposed his sister, Margaret of Austria, dowager Duchess of Savoy (who had previously been married to Katherine's brother, Juan). The French king, Louis XII, put forward his cousin, Marguerite of Angoulême, and Ferdinand of Aragon suggested his widowed niece, Juana, queen of Naples.[25] In the end, though, Henry VII would not remarry, and would outlive his wife by just six years.

Henry, Prince of Wales, later Henry VIII, would be betrothed to his brother's widow, Katherine of Aragon, on 23 June 1503. But Katherine's widowhood while she waited to marry Prince Henry was not easy. As the waiting continued, she wrote to her father and begged to be allowed to return to Spain and enter a convent, 'unless, and that is necessary, you send for me so that I may conclude my few remaining days in serving God. That would be the greatest good I could have in this world'.[26] This seems a little ironic given that during the later annulment proceedings of her marriage to Henry, it was suggested as a solution that Katherine could enter a convent to allow Henry to remarry. Earlier in the same letter, Katherine complains about the way she is being treated in England:

> … for as things here become daily worse, and my life more and more insupportable, I can no longer bear this in any manner … It is impossible for me any longer to endure what I have gone through and still am suffering from the unkindness of the King and the manner in which he treats me … To tell the truth, my necessities have risen so high that I do not know how to maintain myself. For I have already sold my household goods, as it was impossible to avoid it, and I do not know whence I can have anything else.[27]

This letter was written in March 1509. The following month, Henry VII would die at Richmond Palace, on 21 April, and just two months after that, Katherine would marry her Prince Henry, now Henry VIII, and become queen of England. It must have seemed like a dizzying turn of events for a young woman who it sounded like had given up all hopes of being queen.

Katherine of Aragon's wedding to the new king, Henry VIII, would be much quieter than her first wedding to his brother, Prince Arthur. No big ceremony in St Paul's Cathedral this time, but a private ceremony in the Church of the Observant Friars at Greenwich on 11 June 1509. Henry VIII was just over two weeks away from his eighteenth birthday, while Katherine was 23 years old. She had been a widow for over seven years. The formal words pronounced at the wedding of Henry and Katherine were 'Most illustrious Prince, is it your will to fulfil the treaty of marriage concluded by your father, the late King of England, and the parents of the Princess of Wales, the King and Queen of Spain; and, as the Pope has dispensed with this marriage, to take the Princess who is here present for your lawful wife?' to which Henry replied 'I will'.[28] The deed was done and Katherine of Aragon was queen of England. Henry and Katherine were then crowned together at Westminster Abbey on 24 June 1509, nearly two weeks after their wedding. This was a celebration big enough to make up for the small and intimate wedding ceremony.

There is a record of those ladies called upon to serve Katherine of Aragon at the coronation, and these included Maria de Salinas, one of her ladies who had accompanied her from Spain, along with Margaret Pole, who had served her since the days in Ludlow. Also on the list is the name of Elizabeth Boleyn, the mother of Anne Boleyn who, two decades on, would unseat and replace Katherine on the throne.[29] But that was in the future. For now, Henry and Katherine were celebrated as the new king and queen of England with hopes that they would produce a nursery of children and heirs to follow their father on the throne. Just after the coronation, Henry VIII wrote to Margaret of Austria, Duchess of Savoy, the former sister-in-law of Katherine of Aragon, to say that he 'was charged by Henry VII., on his death bed, among other good counsels, to fulfil the old treaty with Ferdinand and Isabella of Spain by taking their daughter Katharine in marriage; now that he is of full age, would not disobey' and that 'they were both crowned in Westminster Abbey in presence of all the nobility. The realm is in as good peace as in the late King's time'.[30] England was at peace with a young king and queen on the throne, and plenty of hope for the future.

Almost immediately on her marriage to Henry VIII in 1509, Katherine of Aragon fell pregnant. This was a positive omen for the newly married couple – Katherine had conceived quickly. However, the pregnancy would end on 31 January 1510, thirty-three weeks after her wedding, when she birthed a stillborn daughter. Her pregnancy had been announced to the court on 1 November, which probably meant the child had quickened, or moved in the womb, prior to this announcement, which usually happened at around four- or five-months gestation.[31] The news of the stillbirth was not passed on to Katherine's father, Ferdinand, until her confessor, Diego Fernandez, wrote to him on 25 May. Fernandez wrote that he 'did not dare to write to your Highness of the condition of the Queen my Lady, in order not to annoy her, and because all the physicians deceived themselves until time was the judge of the truth'.[32] He reports that Katherine felt nothing beforehand but a pain in her knee the night before.

The physician had said that Katherine was still pregnant of a twin of the first baby as her belly did not shrink, so the loss was kept quiet, with only the king, Fernandez, the physician, and two Spanish women knowing about it.[33] It is 'little surprise' that Katherine 'allowed herself to be convinced' she was still pregnant.[34] She was so desperate to have a child and provide the king with an heir, that Henry VIII's hopes, and the assertions of her physician combined to convince her, even if she doubted. However, once she entered her lying-in and the time for the birth passed, it was realised that Katherine was not in fact still pregnant, and she was probably embarrassed and ashamed to have to re-enter the court without a baby. It was, nevertheless, only her first pregnancy and there was no reason to think she would not go on to birth a healthy son. She had proven quickly that she could fall pregnant. Katherine herself wrote to her father two days after Diego Fernandez's letter to tell him about her stillborn daughter, but that she and Henry were 'cheerful' and she thanks God 'for such a husband'.[35] However, it was then realised that, despite the difficulties with the first pregnancy, Katherine was already again pregnant: 'she is already, by the grace of our Lord, very large, so much so that all the physicians know and affirm it'.[36] It seems Henry and Katherine had been intimate during her lying-in or very shortly afterwards. This pregnancy would go to term.

Katherine of Aragon birthed a live son, Henry, Duke of Cornwall, on 1 January 1511 at Richmond Palace. He was christened four days later, on 5 January, with Louis XII of France, William Warham, Archbishop of Canterbury, and Margaret of Austria, Duchess of Savoy, as his godparents. Richard Foxe, Bishop of Winchester, stood in for the French king, and Anne of York, Countess of Surrey, stood in for the Duchess of Savoy.[37] Foreign royals were unlikely to attend a christening and instead a churchman or peer would stand in for them, so this was not unusual. Tradition said that boys should have two godfathers and one godmother, while girls should have two godmothers and one godfather.[38] Prince Henry had two foreign godparents' and the other was the most senior churchman in England at the time. Later, when Princess Mary was born, her godparents were selected from within England. This perhaps demonstrates the level of importance placed on a son when compared to a daughter.

A tournament was held at Westminster Palace on 12 and 13 February 1511 to celebrate the birth of Prince Henry, who was expected to also be created Prince of Wales and to eventually succeed his father on the throne.

Had this son lived, he may well have become Henry IX, and the 'Great Matter' would not have happened. The tournament to celebrate the birth is illustrated in the Westminster Tournament Roll kept at the College of Arms in London. It is almost sixty feet long and features, among other things, an image of Henry VIII tilting in front of Katherine of Aragon. There were four challengers, or knights, leading groups of gentlemen. The challengers were Henry VIII as 'Ceure Loyall', Sir Edward Nevil as 'Valliaunt Desyre', William Courtenay, Earl of Devon, as 'Bone Valoyr', and Sir Thomas Knyvet as 'Joyous Panser'. The other gentlemen included: Sir Thomas Boleyn, later Earl of Wiltshire; Sir William Parr; Thomas Howard, Earl of Surrey and later 2nd Duke of Norfolk; Henry Stafford, 1st Earl of Wiltshire; Charles Brandon, later 1st Duke of Suffolk; and Edmund Howard.[39] Many of what we would recognise as the most important families in the country under Henry VIII are represented in this tournament. Unfortunately, this celebration was premature.

Henry, Duke of Cornwall, first son of Henry VIII and Katherine of Aragon, died at Richmond Palace, aged 52 days, on 22 February 1511, and was buried in Westminster Abbey. As John Dewhurst puts it, 'a gathering of nobles for the celebration of a triumphant birth became one of lamentation for a tragic death'.[40] Black cloth was ordered for the funeral, 186 yards worth, along with a canopy, banners, and over 5000 lb of wax for torches. The mourners were listed as: Thomas Grey, 2nd Marquess of Dorset; Henry Bourchier, 2nd Earl of Essex; Henry Stafford, 1st Earl of Wiltshire; William FitzAlan, 8th Baron Maltravers; and 'lord Howarde', likely one of the sons of Thomas Howard, Earl of Surrey, though which one is unclear. Hall's Chronicle described the king and queen thus:

> The kyng lyke a wyse prynce, took this dolorous chaunce wonderously wisely, and the more to comfort the Quene, he dissimuled the matter, and made no great mourning outwardly; but the Quene lyke a naturall woman; made much lamentacion, how be it, by the kynges good persuasion and behaviour, her sorowe was mytigated, but not shortlye.[41]

This was shattering news for Katherine of Aragon, after a miscarriage or stillbirth the year before, then thinking that she had done her duty and provided the king with a son and heir, to have him ripped from her. Later on, we see how devoted Katherine was to her only surviving child, Princess Mary, so it is easy to imagine she would have been just as devoted to her son. Henry VIII seems to have comforted his wife who struggled more with the death, though this is attributed to her being a woman, who feel things more keenly than men according to the views at the time. To Katherine it was 'the shattering of what seemed to be perfect happiness' but, as a Catholic, she probably viewed it as the will of God.[42] This was only the second year of their marriage, and it was now known that Katherine could carry to term and birth what seemed to initially be a healthy son. In 1511, like after the stillbirth in 1510, there was no reason to think that she would not be able to carry and birth a healthy second son who would survive.

There is much debate over the precise number of miscarriages and stillbirths that Katherine of Aragon suffered during her marriage to Henry VIII. There have been figures suggested from around five pregnancies up to eight or nine. Some authors just say 'several' miscarriages which leaves the exact figure open to interpretation. Scarisbrick writes that Katherine had 'several miscarriages, three infants who were either stillborn or died immediately after birth (two of them males), two infants who had died within a few weeks of birth (one of them a boy) and one girl, Princess Mary'.[43] John Dewhurst summarises that Scarisbrick suggests nine pregnancies with 'several' miscarriages meaning at least three.[44] A. F. Pollard has Katherine with 'various' miscarriages, and John Bowle describes Katherine as having six pregnancies while Hester Chapman has seven pregnancies.[45] It is obvious that there is little agreement over Katherine of Aragon's pregnancy and birth history, except for the fact that she had multiple miscarriages or stillbirths during her marriage. Theresa Earenfight states that Katherine's family history 'does not suggest any abnormalities'.[46] Her sisters Juana and Maria had six and ten children each respectively, and their mother, Isabella, showed no signs of struggling to conceive or carry.

Katherine of Aragon's next confinement we can be sure of for an expected birth was in 1513, although it is unclear what exactly happened. There were accounts of a son having been born, with one Venetian reporting that, 'a male heir was born to the King of England, and will inherit the crown, the other son having died'.[47] If a son was born alive, he did not live long.

There are no English sources which suggest a live son was born in 1513, so it lends weight to the argument that, if born alive, he must have died very soon after birth. By summer 1514, Katherine of Aragon was again pregnant. During a celebration of the marriage of Mary Tudor, Henry VIII's sister, to Louis XII of France, it was reported that, 'after the King came the Queen (who is pregnant) clad in ash-coloured satin, with chains and jewels, and on her head a cap of cloth of gold, covering the ears in the Venetian fashion'.[48] However, this pregnancy would also end in tragedy. The Venetian ambassador, Andrea Badoer, reported that 'the Queen had been delivered of a still-born male child of eight months, to the very great grief of the whole Court'.[49] Holinshed reported that 'in November the queen was delivered of a prince which lived not long after'.[50] It was another devastating blow for Henry VIII and Katherine of Aragon who must have begun to see a pattern emerging of disappointment and sorrow.

But it seemed things were changing. Katherine of Aragon gave birth to a healthy child at Greenwich Palace at 4:00 am on 18 February 1516. But it was not the son and heir that she and Henry so desperately wanted. It was a daughter who they named Mary, possibly after Henry's sister, Mary, the former queen of France and now Duchess of Suffolk. The Venetian ambassador, Sebastian Giustinian, wrote that he had congratulated the king on the birth of his daughter, and the health of the queen:

> … adding that the State would have been yet more pleased had the child been a son. The King returned thanks, saying 'We are both young; if it was a daughter this time, by the grace of God the sons will follow'.[51]

The baby was christened two days later in the Church of the Observant Friars at Greenwich, where Henry VIII and Katherine of Aragon had been married nearly seven years earlier. The church was 'hung with cloth of needlework garnished with precious stones and pearls', and Princess Mary was held by the Countess of Surrey, later the Duchess of Norfolk, Elizabeth Howard née Stafford, under a canopy borne by four men.[52] Mary's godparents were Cardinal Thomas Wolsey, Agnes Tilney, Duchess of Norfolk, Margaret Pole, Countess of Salisbury and Catherine Courtenay, Countess of Devon.[53] Her godparents were illustrious. Thomas Wolsey, although rising from humble beginnings, was the king's chief minister and a cardinal of the Roman Catholic Church. Agnes Tilney was wife to Thomas Howard, 2nd Duke of Norfolk, one of the premier peers in the realm, though the dukedom had only been restored in 1513 after his victory at the Battle of Flodden Field. Margaret Pole was Countess of Salisbury in her own right, one of only two women under the Tudors to hold this distinction (the other being Anne Boleyn when she was created Marquess of Pembroke in 1532 in preparation for her marriage to the king). Margaret was also the daughter of George Plantagenet, Duke of Clarence, and the niece of both Edward IV and Richard III. Catherine Courtenay was the daughter of Edward IV and Elizabeth Woodville, and thus a sister to Henry VII's queen, Elizabeth of York and aunt to Henry VIII. These were some of the highest and best-connected women in the land who became godmothers to the new princess. The Venetian ambassador wrote that he believed the choice of godparents was made 'because the King did not wish to make any distinction between the representatives of the Holy Roman Emperor, France, Spain, and Venice … an act of prudent impartiality'.[54] As we saw earlier with the christening of Henry, Duke of Cornwall, godparents were often foreign royalty, but this was not the case with Princess Mary – whether for the reason the Venetian ambassador suggested, or because she was a daughter rather than a son, is unclear.

Katherine of Aragon would fall pregnant one more time. She seemed to have no trouble falling pregnant, but she did in carrying the baby to term. Henry VIII wrote to Cardinal Wolsey on 1 July 1518 to announce the pregnancy, saying that 'two things there be which be so secret that they cause me at this time to write to you myself; the one, is that I trust the Queen my wife be with child'.[55] There was a lot of hope and perhaps it is only with hindsight that we can see just how much was resting on this final pregnancy. Katherine could not have known that she would not conceive again. This pregnancy would, like several times before, also result in a stillbirth. The Venetian ambassador, Guistinian, reported on 10 November 1518 that 'in the past night the Queen had been delivered of a daughter, to the vexation of everybody. Never had the kingdom so anxiously desired anything as it did a prince'.[56] Without a living male heir, Henry would see Katherine as having failed at what was expected of her as his wife and queen. The sources we have suggest a minimum of six pregnancies over the nine years from 1509 to

1518, and only a single surviving daughter. Historian Amy Licence suggests that it was this final failure in pregnancy which led to Katherine adopting a hair shirt worn under her clothing as an act of penance.[57] She probably knew that Henry saw her failure to produce a son as her fault and although she may have hoped she would again fall pregnant, by the beginning of 1519, Katherine was aged 34 and considered old at the time to be birthing children.

The hopes of Henry VIII, that a son would follow with Katherine of Aragon, would not come to fruition. This is a big part of why the marriage ended in the way that it did. It is 'more than probable' that had Katherine birthed a son who survived, that the marriage 'would have survived until death parted them'.[58] Henry VIII would not have risked sullying the legitimacy of a son born to his queen by divorce or annulment and so the 'Great Matter' would not have happened, and we would not remember Henry as we do today, as the much-married king who broke with Rome. Katherine of Aragon would soon go through the menopause and by the mid-1520s it seems Henry had ceased sleeping with her. Katherine's failure in Henry's eyes to produce a son would be the catalyst for the king's 'Great Matter' which dominated the 1520s and 1530s. A son would come for Henry VIII in the late 1510s – Henry Fitzroy – not born of a marriage, but an affair.

Chapter 2

The Mistress and the Son

The year 1519 was a turning point in Henry VIII's relationship with Katherine of Aragon and planted the seeds of the 'Great Matter'. Katherine was 'wise enough' to understand that kings took mistresses 'with whom they lived parallel lives'.[1] Such affairs were 'generally regarded as an appropriate response to what were seen as the natural sexual needs of a husband'.[2] The same understanding was not given to wives who were unfaithful. Henry VIII's contemporary and rival king, Francis I of France, was known to keep a succession of mistresses on whom he lavished attention. His best-known mistress is probably Françoise de Foix, Countess of Châteaubriant, who had the title 'maîtresse-en-titre', meaning that she was the official mistress of the French king. Henry VIII is often said to have been incredibly promiscuous with scores of mistresses and a litany of bastard children but he was seemingly much more discreet, and we do not have the evidence to support this for Henry, unlike with Francis.

There are only two mistresses that Henry VIII is known with absolute certainty to have had a relationship with outside of his wives and the women he would go on to marry – Bessie Blount and Mary Boleyn – both during his marriage to Katherine of Aragon. There are plenty of rumours about others including a sister of the Duke of Buckingham, and a Shelton cousin of Anne Boleyn, but little concrete evidence. The relationship with Mary Boleyn we only really have evidence of because of Henry VIII's later marriage to her sister, Anne. As will be discussed in chapter 3 there have been suggestions that Mary Boleyn's children, Henry and Catherine Carey, were in fact fathered by Henry VIII, but there is no real evidence of this being the case. The only illegitimate child that Henry VIII acknowledged and that we can be absolutely certain was his, was the child that Bessie Blount gave birth to in 1519 – Henry Fitzroy. Beverley A. Murphy says that 'there can be no doubt that Richmond was Henry's son … the distinctive red hair and wilful

Tudor personality were merely secondary considerations'.[3] Fitzroy seems to have taken after Henry VIII, but there was no need to make physical or personality comparisons with the king as he acknowledged his son without any complaint or doubts.

In June 1519, Elizabeth Blount, most often known as Bessie, gave birth to her son at the Augustinian priory of St Lawrence at Blackmore in Essex. But this was not an everyday birth. The boy would be christened Henry Fitzroy – 'Fitz' was from Norman French meaning 'son of' and 'roy' was also from the French, meaning 'king'. Henry Fitzroy was the son of King Henry VIII, not by his wife, but by his mistress. Cardinal Thomas Wolsey, Archbishop of York and England's Lord Chancellor, was one of the godfathers.[4] Fitzroy was acknowledged and accepted as the king's son and with the most powerful man in England aside from the king himself as his godfather, it seemed he was being groomed as a potential heir, but certainly at least to take a prominent role in the future. Fitzroy's succession to the throne, had that been the intention, would have needed the agreement of the Papacy as he was illegitimate, and it could still have been challenged even with the Pope's backing. Princess Mary, born in 1516, was popular as the legitimate child of Henry VIII and Katherine of Aragon and would probably have had the backing to oppose the succession of Henry Fitzroy, had that come to pass.

At the time when Bessie Blount was conceiving the king's child, his wife, Katherine of Aragon, was also pregnant. This pregnancy would result in the birth of a stillborn daughter in 1518. It must have been even more devastating for Katherine, after having giving birth to a stillborn daughter, knowing that her maid-of-honour had birthed a live son for the king, something that she had so desperately wanted for the decade of her marriage to this point. This would also end up being Katherine's final pregnancy, and it was probably very difficult for her in later years that her last pregnancy had ended in heartbreak at the same time as her husband was conceiving a son with another woman. Antonia Fraser describes Fitzroy's conception as 'more of a happy accident in a light-hearted career than the symbol of any great and torrid love affair'.[5] The implication is that, as Katherine of Aragon was pregnant at the time, Henry VIII almost saw it as his right to share a bed with another woman while his wife was unable to, while not forming a long-lasting attachment. We are not sure how long Henry and Bessie's relationship was, whether they met only once or a couple of times, or had a longer liaison lasting months or even years. Taking a mistress was almost typical in the elite and royal families during a wife's 'perceived sexual unavailability' when she was pregnant and for a period after childbirth as well.[6] It was thought to be harmful to the health of mother and child to indulge in intercourse during pregnancy. But intercourse was also, at this time, supposed to be for the conception of children rather than enjoyment, so once a woman was pregnant, the couple would abstain with the primary goal of intercourse and conception having been achieved. Of course, a mistress was taken for pleasure rather than conception.

There have been suggestions that Henry VIII had several other illegitimate children both before and after Fitzroy was born in 1519. However, Henry had 'remarkably few mistresses by the standards of the time' and was not the 'libidinous predator he is often painted as'.[7] In a letter dated April 1538, when Henry VIII was in negotiations to take a fourth wife, he referred to Fitzroy, who had been dead for nearly two years at this time, as 'our only bastard son'.[8] This would seem to rule out Henry Carey, 1st Baron Hunsdon, who is discussed in the following chapter, along with Sir John Perrot. Perrot was born circa 1526, placing his birth around the same time that time Henry VIII was beginning his pursuit of Anne Boleyn. There were rumours at the time that Perrot was illegitimate, but there is no evidence to link him to the king.[9] It seems to have been his looks which put him in the frame for an illegitimate child of Henry VIII:

> If we compare his picture, his qualities, his gesture and voice with that of the King, whose memory yet remains among us, they will plead strongly that he was a surreptitious child of the blood royal.[10]

Perrot went on to serve all three of Henry's children, Edward VI, Mary I, and Elizabeth I, dying in 1592. Perrot's birth is also thought to be around the time that Henry Carey was born. As we will see in chapter 3, there is no real evidence that Carey was Henry VIII's son either and, in fact, there is evidence to the contrary. But Henry VIII's comment only rules out other illegitimate sons, not daughters and Henry Carey's sister, Catherine Carey Knollys, is interesting and of the two siblings, she is the more likely to be the child of Henry VIII, as the probable elder sibling (see chapter 3). Another suggested illegitimate daughter of Henry VIII is Ethelreda or Audrey Harrington, the child of Joan Dingley, who was said to be a royal laundress, though there is no suggestion of this liaison in the contemporary sources.[11] Daughters were probably even less likely to be acknowledged by the king than sons, as they were less valuable in terms of the succession, though could still have been useful in terms of alliance through marriage. Beverley A. Murphy, Fitzroy's biographer, points out that it does not really matter whether Henry Fitzroy was the king's only illegitimate child or not, 'what is most important is that he was the only one that Henry was prepared to acknowledge and employ on the wider political stage'.[12] It does seem likely, though, that Fitzroy was the king's only illegitimate issue, certainly his only illegitimate son, as why only acknowledge one?

We do not know the date of birth for Henry Fitzroy's mother, Bessie Blount, and even the year is debated, meaning that we are not sure of her age when she gave birth. Her age could have a bearing on the likelihood of when her relationship with the king began. Historians have suggested anywhere from 1498 to 1502, so she was a similar age probably to Anne Boleyn. The historian David Loades suggests that Henry VIII began to 'dally' with Bessie Blount in around 1515, but he then says that Bessie was the king's mistress for two years before giving birth to her son in 1519.[13] The dates do not seem to add up. Karen Lindsey suggests that Henry's affair with Bessie began in 1514.[14] Jerry Rabow concurs with Lindsey's viewpoint.[15] Antonia Fraser has Bessie Blount coming to the English court in 1513, and says that she became a favoured dancing partner of the king.[16] If Bessie's relationship with the king did begin somewhere around 1513 to 1515, she would only have been a teenager, anywhere from age 12 to 17, depending on which date of birth you favour for her. Age 12 seems a little young, especially given the experience of Henry VIII's grandmother, Margaret Beaufort, who became pregnant at the age of 12 with the future Henry VII, which her grandson would have been aware of. Margaret Beaufort would not conceive again after the birth of Henry VII, and it is quite possible that she suffered some irreparable damage as a result of pregnancy and giving birth at such a young age. Margaret would later advocate for her granddaughter, Margaret Tudor,

Queen of Scotland, not to be sent north too early, in case she suffered similarly. It seems unlikely that Henry VIII would risk that with Bessie Blount and would wait until she was older before pursuing her sexually.

Both Bessie Blount and Mary Boleyn were maids-of-honour in Katherine of Aragon's household when they caught the king's eye. Similarly, Anne Boleyn would be serving in Katherine of Aragon's household when she came to the king's attention, and later, Jane Seymour would serve in Anne Boleyn's household when she was noticed by the king. Henry VIII, it seems, did not like to look very far for his female companions. The households of his queens were full of ladies. The chronicler, Herbert of Cherbury, describes Bessie Blount as being considered for 'her rare ornaments of nature, and education, to be the beauty and mistress-piece of her time'.[17] Cherbury goes on to describe Blount's son, Henry Fitzroy, as 'so equally like to both his parents' and:

> ... very personable and of great expectation, insomuch as he was thought, not only for ability of body but mind, to be one of the rarest of his time; for which reason he was also much cherish'd by our king, as also because he had no issue male by his queen, nor did, perchance, expect any.[18]

From this description, the sense is that Fitzroy was almost the prodigal child, perfect in every possible way. His perfection was a foil to Katherine of Aragon's failure. No doubt it seemed like that to Henry VIII anyway, who must have begun to despair of ever having a son, having been married for a decade by the time of Fitzroy's birth, with only a single surviving daughter. The only problem with Fitzroy was that he was illegitimate. This description has Fitzroy being a rare jewel, intelligent, and cherished by the king who had been so desperate for a son. Herbert of Cherbury suggests that, by the time of Fitzroy's birth in 1519, Henry VIII despaired of having any other children by Katherine, which would in fact prove to be true. However, this was written with hindsight as Cherbury was not born until well into the reign of Elizabeth I, so he would also have been aware of Fitzroy's and Katherine's eventual fates. In 1519, Henry VIII and Katherine of Aragon could not have known that the queen would not fall pregnant again, and it is unlikely that Henry gave up hope at this time, as there is no movement towards a divorce or annulment for another seven years, as far as we know.

Either shortly before or after the birth of Henry Fitzroy in June 1519, Bessie Blount was married. Her husband was Gilbert Tailboys, 1st Baron Tailboys of Kyme. The couple would have several children of their own – a daughter, Elizabeth, and two sons, George and Robert. Tailboys died in 1530, leaving Bessie a widow after eleven years of marriage, and both of their sons as well as their daughter would succeed to the barony in turn. Bessie Blount then remarried to Edward Clinton, 1st Earl of Lincoln, though he was not an earl in Bessie's lifetime, but a baron. They had three daughters together – Bridget, Katherine, and Margaret. Bessie did not vanish entirely into obscurity after Fitzroy's birth, we still find references to her in the contemporary sources. One of the charges against Cardinal Thomas Wolsey in 1529 was that under his governance:

> … We have begun to encourage the young gentlewomen of the realm to be our concubines by the well marrying of Besse Blont, whom we would yet by sleight have married much better than she is, and for that purpose changed her name.[19]

The implication was that Wolsey had encouraged the women of the court to act inappropriately and endeavour to reach higher than they ought, either by sleeping with the king for material advantage or hoping for a better marriage than they might otherwise have achieved. The words 'by sleight' suggest that there was some kind of manipulation which resulted in an unfair advantage for Bessie, and that Wolsey may have had a hand in it. More dangerously in the case of Anne Boleyn, who was queen-in-waiting by the time of Wolsey's fall, women could reach for the crown itself, by refusing to become a mistress. The only other possible prior example of this in England was Elizabeth Woodville who, it was said, claimed she was too simple to be the king's wife but too good to be his concubine.[20] Edward IV married her in 1464.

Elizabeth Woodville's situation was different from Anne Boleyn's though, as Edward IV was not married so did not need an annulment to marry her. However, this would later be called into question and Elizabeth's royal marriage declared invalid in 1483. This understanding, that a woman could become queen by refusing to be a royal mistress, would help to end Anne Boleyn's life in 1536. If a woman of Anne's birth could supplant a royal

Spanish princess like Katherine of Aragon, then she could also be undone. The wording of this comment against Wolsey demonstrates a fear by the men in power that they could be ruled by women, which is exactly what Henry VIII hoped to avoid in his desperate quest for a male heir to succeed him.

In June 1519, around the time of Henry Fitzroy's birth, two Venetian ambassadors in France wrote that Francis I of France had claimed Henry VIII 'has an old, deformed wife, while he himself is young and handsome'.[21] At this time, Katherine of Aragon was aged 33, and Henry VIII aged 28, so it was only a five-year age difference, but it seemed to be very obvious to onlookers. Perhaps the pregnancies and grief of losing so many children had aged Katherine prematurely. But it is also slightly ironic that it was probably, at least in part, Katherine falling pregnant and hoping to produce a son, that drove Henry into the arms and the bed of Bessie Blount in the first place. As has been seen in chapter 1, Katherine was pregnant in July 1518 and seems to have lost the child that November. Given that Henry Fitzroy was likely born in June or July 1519, it is probable that he was conceived sometime between August and October 1518, when Katherine was pregnant for the final time and the king would not have been sharing her bed as a result.

It is thought that Henry VIII ended his relationship with Bessie Blount once she fell pregnant. As previously discussed, it was normal for a king to take a mistress once his wife was with child as it was thought to be detrimental to the health of the mother and unborn child to continue having intercourse during pregnancy. So, it is safe to assume that Henry would also have ceased sleeping with his mistress at this time. Bessie also does not seem to have resumed her duties at court after the birth of Henry Fitzroy. She was not present at the Field of the Cloth of Gold summit in 1520 when you might have assumed she would be in attendance on the queen, and there was speculation that she had been replaced in the king's bed, though this is uncorroborated and 'seems doubtful'.[22] It is just possible that in 1520, Henry VIII had begun a sexual relationship with Mary Boleyn, though there is no evidence for this and she would only just have been married to William Carey. Bessie Blount's second child, a daughter, was born in 1520, but there is no suggestion that she was fathered by Henry VIII, so it does seem likely that the king's relationship with Bessie ended with the discovery of her pregnancy and the birth of Henry Fitzroy in 1519.[23] She then appears to have been sleeping with her husband, Gilbert Tailboys, and conceived his child not long afterwards. As Bessie seemed to conceive quickly with her husband and Katherine of Aragon seemed to have little trouble conceiving a child with the king, perhaps Bessie's relationship with the king was not a long one after all. This could have been because she quickly conceived the king's child and was then married off after the birth. It is interesting to consider, though very far from being conclusive.

Historian Lucy Wooding describes how Fitzroy was 'raised with as much care as if he was a legitimate prince'.[24] Henry Fitzroy was living proof that Henry VIII could produce a living son. In this way it made sense to treasure him. His birth and survival could be used as evidence that the lack of a living son in their marriage was the fault of Katherine of Aragon, or some kind of divine punishment for something they had done. Fitzroy's birth 'focused Henry's anxieties even more on Katherine's inadequacies'.[25] This must have been a really difficult time for Katherine. She grieved for her lost children over many years and retreated into prayer in her desperation to conceive and birth a living son. She could not, however, have guessed what the king would do or the lengths he would go to in order to get a legitimate son. Katherine would not conceive again, and Henry Fitzroy would be raised high.

We know little of Henry Fitzroy until he was suddenly catapulted into the public gaze when, on 7 June 1525, he was created a Knight of the Garter, marking his first entry into the public sphere. He had been elected on 23 April, but the installation was not made until June, when he was about to celebrate his sixth birthday. Fitzroy was given the second stall on the king's side of St George's Chapel at Windsor.[26] This was quite possibly a demonstration of his closeness to the king and Crown, and a suggestion that he was potentially being considered as a contender for heir to the throne. Later that same month, on 18 June 1525, Fitzroy was created the Duke of Richmond and Somerset as well as the Earl of Nottingham. Richmond was a notable title, as Henry Fitzroy's paternal grandfather, Henry VII, had been Earl of Richmond before he took the throne and crown of England. The title of duke was often given to those of royal blood. It was a name 'full of resonance' and demonstrates Henry VIII's desperation over the succession, the fact that he seemed to be contemplating a move 'so fraught with danger' – to make his illegitimate son his heir, rather than his legitimate daughter.[27]

Fitzroy was then sent to the north of England, to Sheriff Hutton, with the title of lieutenant, and a large household, to run the council of the north, at least nominally. Letters patent gave Fitzroy precedence over all other dukes already created, or created in the future, except for sons legitimately born to the king.[28] He was catapulted to the top of the English nobility, second only to the king and royal princes.

His elevation could be seen to give him the same 'symbolic importance as a legitimate prince'.[29] Katherine of Aragon was 'mortified' and believed that Fitzroy's elevation was a threat to Princess Mary's position. Mary had been sent to Ludlow Castle in the Welsh Marches to act nominally as Princess of Wales, though this title was never officially given to her. However, it may have been part of Wolsey's own scheme to elevate Fitzroy in order to consolidate his own plans for power.[30] If Wolsey could somehow gain control of Fitzroy's household, and many people in the household had already been appointed by him, then he might have a great deal of influence over the future heir to the throne. Henry Fitzroy was appointed to important posts, and given a household and a council, all within a couple of months of being made a duke.[31] Perhaps he was being groomed potentially for the throne, but certainly for a prominent role in the future. There was a rule that bastard children could not inherit from their parents' wills, but bastards of princes were exceptions.[32] It was a meteoric rise in a short space of time, but Fitzroy was the king's only son, even if he was illegitimate.

Katherine of Aragon was reported to resent the elevation of her husband's illegitimate son, and she expressed her anger to the king. It seems to be one of the only times we hear of Katherine speaking against her husband prior to the 'Great Matter', and he dismissed three of her ladies as a result of their support for her.[33] Katherine seems to have chosen her battles carefully in order to fight the ones that really mattered – to protect her own position as queen, and her daughter's position as the king's legitimate heir. Katherine had a legitimate daughter and could not understand why that daughter could not become queen of England in her own right one day. Katherine's own mother, Isabella of Castile, had ruled Castile as a regnant queen. On the death of Isabella in 1504, Katherine's sister, Juana, became queen of Castile also in her own right, though her son did lock her away, claiming she was insane and ruled in her stead. Juana also became queen of Aragon on her father's death in 1515. Katherine's former sister-in-law, Margaret of Austria, Duchess of Savoy, ruled the Low Countries as regent. Katherine's successor as queen, Anne Boleyn, served in the household of Margaret of Austria as a maid of honour for around eighteen months between 1512 and 1513, and would have witnessed Margaret wielding power on behalf of the Holy Roman Emperor. There were plenty of examples in Katherine's own family of women in power, and she could not understand why her daughter could not join their ranks. However, Henry VIII believed firmly that he needed a son to succeed him and rule England. Henry publicly recognising Fitzroy as his son may have been 'an attempt to keep open the possibilities for Tudor male succession if needed'.[34] To Katherine, Fitzroy's elevation was likely seen as the first step to disinheriting Mary and replacing her as heir with her illegitimate half-brother. Katherine would do everything she could to protect the rights and position of her daughter.

There was a suggestion made to resolve the succession dispute, by marrying Princess Mary to her half-brother, Henry Fitzroy, in the 1520s. It was against canon law, as the two shared a father, but 'it seems to have received tacit papal approval'.[35] The Pope seems to have been willing to allow the marriage if Henry VIII gave up all thought of a divorce or annulment of his marriage to Katherine of Aragon, which he was pursuing at the time. Cardinal Lorenzo Campeggio, who was in England to try the annulment case for the king as a representative of the Pope, wrote that 'they have thought of marrying the Princess, by dispensation from his Holiness, to the King's natural son, if it can be done. At first, I myself had thought of this as a means of establishing the succession, but I do not believe that this design would suffice to satisfy the King's desires'.[36] It is possible that the 'they' who thought it up was Henry VIII and Cardinal Wolsey. Even had the succession been resolved in this way, Campeggio evidently did not believe that Henry VIII would drop his annulment case, so determined was he to marry Anne Boleyn and father a legitimate son. Henry was not interested in workarounds and wanted Anne as his wife and queen. Henry VIII's annulment case rested on the line in Leviticus which said that if a man married his brother's wife, they would be childless. The king believed that 'childless' meant a lack of sons from the marriage. He believed that Anne would give him a son which would resolve the succession without having to marry his daughter to her half-brother, which would have created the same kind of affinity as the king being married to his brother's widow. The idea seems to have been quietly dropped, and we do not have Henry VIII's thoughts on the plan. Katherine of Aragon likely would have been outraged at the suggestion and fought it with everything she had, had she been aware of it, and we have to assume that she heard rumours about the proposal at the very least.

In 1527, just as Henry VIII was getting ready to request an annulment of his marriage to Katherine of Aragon from Pope Clement VII, a rumour spread that Henry VIII and Cardinal Thomas Wolsey intended to make Henry Fitzroy the king of Ireland. It seems it was timed to coincide with a time when the king was looking to make a marriage for his illegitimate son, and this would perhaps enhance his desirability on the marriage market.[37] However, there were concerns in England that this could make Ireland as much of a threat in the west as Scotland was in the north, despite Fitzroy being the king's son. It was the king's nephew, James V, who was causing problems in Scotland, so familial ties were no protection. How seriously this plan was considered is unclear, though it does not seem to have advanced in any concrete way. The only move made with regards to Fitzroy and Ireland was to make him Lord Lieutenant of Ireland in 1529, an office he held until 1534. However, there is no evidence that he ever actually set foot in Ireland and things there were handled by others in his name.

Henry Fitzroy, Duke of Richmond and Somerset, and the king's illegitimate son, could be a commodity on the marriage market. Despite being illegitimate, he did have royal blood, enhanced by the suggestion that he could be king of England if Henry VIII failed to produce a legitimate son. Alliances with the Holy Roman Empire, and even the Medici family were proposed. Charles V's niece, the Infanta Mary of Portugal was suggested, as was Catherine de Medici, later queen of France. These negotiations were occurring alongside negotiations for the marriage of the Princess Mary, whom Henry VIII and Wolsey hoped to marry into France. The English ambassadors assured Charles V that if there was an appropriate Habsburg prince for Princess Mary to marry, then that was what they would be negotiating rather than a French match.[38] A foreign match for Henry Fitzroy, however, would never come to pass. Neither would it for Princess Mary. Events would overtake them in the form of the 'Great Matter' as

Henry VIII's focus turned to annulling his marriage to Katherine of Aragon and marrying Anne Boleyn in his quest to get a male heir who would displace both Princess Mary and Henry Fitzroy in the line of succession.

In 1532, Henry Fitzroy accompanied Henry VIII and Anne Boleyn to Calais to meet with Francis I of France and gain approval for their upcoming marriage. After the summit, Fitzroy would remain in France along with his friend, Henry Howard, Earl of Surrey. The Earl of Surrey was the eldest son and heir of Anne Boleyn's uncle, Thomas Howard, 3rd Duke of Norfolk. The Howards were keeping as close to the throne as they could, aware that if Anne failed to produce a son, there was still a possibility that Fitzroy could become king. Fitzroy and Surrey spent time with Henri, Duc d'Orléans, later Henri II of France.[39] The pair, along with their household, remained in France for just under a year before Henry VIII recalled them. The Pope finally issued his declaration that Henry VIII's separation from Katherine of Aragon was unlawful on 11 July 1533, that the king should return to her, and that any children born to Henry and Anne Boleyn would thus be illegitimate and it was at this time that Fitzroy and Surrey were recalled to England.[40] It is unclear exactly when Fitzroy and Surrey arrived back in England, but they were certainly back by November 1533.

Henry VIII married Anne Boleyn in January 1533 (see chapter 7) and she gave birth to Princess Elizabeth that September. On 25 or 26 November 1533, Henry Fitzroy, 1st Duke of Richmond and Somerset, married Lady Mary Howard, the daughter of Thomas Howard, 3rd Duke of Norfolk. Mary was a first cousin of the new queen, Anne Boleyn and Anne herself likely had a role in arranging the marriage. Fitzroy was a claimant to the throne until Anne produced a son of her own, so it made sense for her to marry him into her own family, to prevent him being married to a foreign princess with foreign support for his claim. By November 1533, Anne had given birth to a daughter, Elizabeth, but had no son. Fitzroy was aged 14, and Mary was thought to be around the same age. Eustace Chapuys relegates the marriage of Mary and Fitzroy to a footnote in his letter of 24 November 1533 where he says that 'there is no other news except that the duke of Richmond is to be married tomorrow to the duke of Norfolk's daughter'.[41] It is this letter which is given as evidence that the marriage took place on 25 November, though many historians today seem to agree that it actually took place a day later, on 26 November, including Henry Fitzroy's biographer, Beverley A. Murphy. Murphy argues that the marriage was a political match, but that Henry VIII did not make a foreign alliance for his illegitimate son because, although the 1527 negotiations had proved there was 'scope' for a diplomatic marriage, Henry was otherwise preoccupied in the period between then and 1533 with his 'Great Matter'.[42] Perhaps Henry VIII was also influenced by Anne Boleyn in this, hoping to tie the king's only son into her own family and influence.

However, the marriage is thought to have remained unconsummated on Fitzroy's death in July 1536, less than three years after the wedding. Perhaps sexual intercourse was thought to be 'too taxing for one of doubtful health'.[43] Mary was left a young widow who had to fight for her widow's jointure – a settlement that a widow was entitled to when her husband died in order to support herself. For the nobility, this was usually a package of lands and holdings from which she could draw rents to pay her expenses and bills. As the marriage between Mary Howard and Henry Fitzroy allegedly remained unconsummated, it could be argued that the marriage was not in fact valid, and therefore Mary was not entitled to a widow's jointure, though she continued to be referred to as the Duchess of Richmond and Somerset. There is also the possibility that her connection to Anne Boleyn prejudiced the king against her. By the time of Fitzroy's death, Anne had been recently executed, so perhaps this execution of her cousin contributed to the king's reluctance to provide Mary's widow's jointure. Mary Howard would not remarry, and would live into the reign of her sister-in-law, Mary I, dying in 1557.

In a letter dated 19 May 1536, the very day of Anne Boleyn's execution, the Imperial ambassador, Eustace Chapuys, reported that on the evening of Anne Boleyn's arrest, Henry Fitzroy went to see his father, the king, 'and ask[ed] his blessing after the English custom, the King began to weep, saying that he and his sister, meaning the Princess, were greatly bound to God for having escaped the hands of that accursed whore, who had determined to poison them'.[44] Whether this was Henry's paranoia talking, or whether he truly believed this of Anne, is unknown. But Henry was determined to paint Anne in the worst possible light with her as the villain and him as the saint and wronged man who had been manipulated by a woman who slept with his friends. He was willing to believe that Anne Boleyn would have done whatever it took to keep power and to ensure that her child and no other would succeed to the throne, even murdering rivals to her child's claim, including her own stepson and stepdaughter. How Fitzroy must have felt on hearing this is difficult to know; we have no real record of his personality, so it is difficult to judge. But it does seem that Fitzroy's relationship with Anne Boleyn was not a particularly positive one. She was likely too afraid of his position in relation to her daughter's, to treat him with kindness or respect.

Henry Fitzroy was kept largely out of the limelight, rarely appearing in public before his ennoblement at the age of 6 and attending few public functions. He did, however, attend the execution of Anne Boleyn in May 1536 at the Tower of London. Fitzroy died at the age of just 17 on 23 July 1536, two months after Anne's execution, at St James's Palace. He 'departed this world as he had entered it, in quiet obscurity' and it is 'difficult to find any enduring legacy'.[45] It has been suggested that he had been in poor health, possibly since his marriage in 1533.[46] However, there is little evidence of this in the surviving sources and, as he attended Anne Boleyn's execution just two months before his death, it suggests he was certainly well up to that point. Fitzroy's death has also been blamed on poison administered by Anne Boleyn or her brother, George, before their deaths but, again, there is no real evidence except the suggestion of a king willing to believe anything of his executed second wife.[47] Fitzroy left behind his widow, Mary Howard Fitzroy, but no children. His father, Henry VIII, was said to be devastated at his death, deprived of the only son he had at that time. His only legitimate son, the future Edward VI, would be born in October 1537, but for this brief period, July 1536 to October 1537, the succession seemed to be in real peril, with only two illegitimate daughters, and everything resting in the belly of the king's new wife, Jane Seymour.

But what if Fitzroy had not died in June 1536? We know that Edward VI died at the age of just 15 in 1553. If Fitzroy had been alive in 1553, he would have been aged 34 and, as a male, may have been a preferred candidate for the throne to either Mary I or Lady Jane Grey. The Second Act of Succession of 1536 made both of Henry VIII's daughters illegitimate and, as the king had no son at the time, there was a clause that would allow Henry VIII to choose his own successor if he had no legitimate heir to succeed him.

This would have paved the way for Henry Fitzroy to potentially have been declared the heir to the throne, had he still been alive. Civil lawyers and those versed in canon law agreed that a king had 'inherent power' to dispense his regal right but that he could not utilise it 'without constitutional provisions embodying the people's consent'.[48] Essentially, if the king decided to make Fitzroy his heir, his decision would need to be authorised by parliament or a body with equal weight to make it legal.[49] The weight of a king's word alone was not enough to make it legal, as would be seen later with the *Devise for the Succession* written by the dying Edward VI.

Whether the people would have chosen Henry Fitzroy above Princesses Mary or Elizabeth in 1553 is unclear, but the people certainly chose Princess Mary over Lady Jane Grey. Thomas Fuller explored the possibility that neither Mary I nor Elizabeth I would have sat on the English throne had Fitzroy survived:

> Very much of his own arbitrariness appears in this will of king Henry, entailing the crown according to his own fancy, against all right and reason … If Mary and Elizabeth were not his lawful children, how came they by any right to the crown? … Well it was for them that Henry Fitzroy his natural son, (but one of supernatural and extraordinary endowments,) was dead; otherwise (some suspect) had he survived King Edward the Sixth, we might presently have heard of a King Henry the Ninth, so great was his father's affection and so unlimited his power to prefer him.[50]

The interesting comment on Henry VIII about how arbitrary his decision on something as important as the crown and succession was, seems at odds with what the king really wanted – to pass the crown to a legitimate son of his own. He was desperate to do so. That was the crux of the 'Great Matter'. Anne Boleyn was the catalyst, but the perceived need for a male heir was the driving force. The suggestion that Henry VIII may have made Henry Fitzroy King Henry IX after Edward VI is an interesting one. The king considered both of his daughters illegitimate but still restored them to the line of succession by the Third Act of Succession 1544. The difference is that he had been married to their mothers, even if he later annulled the marriages. Would an illegitimate son whose mother he never went through a wedding ceremony with have triumphed over two illegitimate daughters whose mothers he had a wedding with and a coronation for? Beverley A. Murphy explains it as 'any consideration of what might have been, is always a matter of conjecture' but, had Fitzroy lived, the history of England would have been very different.[51] It is a question that will never be answered.

Had Bessie Blount never birthed the king's son, she would have 'left no imprint on the swept sands of history'.[52] We might barely know her name. Like Mary and Anne Boleyn, her name is known because of her connection to Henry VIII. But unlike many other mistresses of kings, her name is also known because she gave Henry the son he could not have with his wife. The problem is that he was illegitimate. Bessie proved to Henry that he could have a son, and that the blame for his lack of a legitimate son did not lie with him. In his eyes, the fault was with Katherine of Aragon. The birth of Fitzroy, along with Katherine's seeming inability to birth a healthy son, pushed the king into action.

Henry Fitzroy was a boy who never really got the chance to emerge fully into the light of day. Because he was illegitimate, he did not take part in many of the formalities that later Prince Edward would. Perhaps, had he grown into a man, we would have more of a sense of who he was, and what he might have been capable of. Would English history have changed had he survived? Unlikely. Henry VIII may have included him in the Third Act of Succession in 1544, just as he did with his illegitimate daughters, Mary and Elizabeth. But it is a great unknown as to who the adult Henry Fitzroy, Duke of Richmond and Somerset, might have been. We get so few glimpses of him as a child and teenager that it is difficult to form any view of him at all. However, it is interesting to consider what kind of effect he might have had on politics and religion later in the reign, and into the reigns of his half-siblings.

Bessie Blount and Henry Fitzroy in 1525, at the time when the latter was created Duke of Richmond and Somerset, would soon be overtaken by events which would change England forever. Henry Fitzroy could have taken the English throne, only if the king did not marry again, or if he married again and produced only daughters. It certainly gave Fitzroy and his friends and supporters a vested interest in the events which followed. Bessie Blount was replaced at some point as Henry VIII's mistress by Mary Boleyn, and Mary would be supplanted by her own sister. The Boleyn family did not just suddenly appear at court, but now they moved centre stage.

Chapter 3

Enter the Boleyns

Anne Boleyn was not the first member of the Boleyn family to share King Henry VIII's bed. Her sister, Mary Boleyn, preceded Anne as Henry's mistress. There has been a suggestion that Mary's two eldest children, Henry and Catherine Carey, were possibly fathered by the king during this relationship. Legally, the pair were considered to be the children of Mary's first husband, William Carey, but there have been numerous observations made of how much Catherine – probably the elder of the two – resembled Henry VIII and, later, Elizabeth I. In the portrait we have which is suspected to be Catherine Carey, although it is not confirmed, you can see how much the woman depicted does resemble Henry VIII. However, there is no certainty that the portrait does in fact depict Catherine at all. We do not actually know how long the relationship between Henry and Mary Boleyn lasted, whether it was a short-term or longer-term liaison. There is actually no real evidence of it happening at all in contemporary sources. Possibly the only reason we know of the liaison between Henry and Mary is because of the king's later relationship with Mary's sister, Anne, which meant that he needed a dispensation to marry her, being within the forbidden degrees of affinity. Ironically, this was similar to the relationship between Henry VIII and Katherine of Aragon.

Henry VIII's relationship with Anne's sister, Mary Boleyn, is recorded in a letter from George Throckmorton, after Anne's death. He recalled a conversation with the king before his marriage to Anne Boleyn, where he thought the king's conscience might be troubled if he married her 'for it is thought ye have meddled both with the mother and the sister', but Henry replied, 'never with the mother'.[1] This is a tacit confirmation of some kind of relationship between himself and Mary as he never denied that connection, only that with their mother Elizabeth Boleyn. Whether this relationship with Mary was what would later be used to annul the king's marriage to

Anne Boleyn is unclear, as we only know that the marriage was annulled in May 1536, but there is no record as to the reason that was used to justify it. It could have been the relationship with Mary, or Anne's prior relationship with Henry Percy, although Percy denied any betrothal took place when he was questioned in May 1536.

There is no certainty over when Henry VIII and Mary Boleyn's relationship began, or how long it lasted. It is often assumed that it happened over an extended period, but there is no evidence for this at all. Jerry Rabow says that 'during the period of her relationship with the king', Mary gave birth to two children, in 1524 and 1526.[2] This would suggest that the relationship lasted at least two years in order to conceive the two children. Rabow also states that Mary Boleyn became the royal mistress for six years.[3] Kelly Hart suggests that Henry and Mary's relationship began around 1522, as this is when we begin to see increased grants to Mary's husband, William Carey, which continued regularly until May 1526, after the birth of Henry Carey either earlier that year or the previous year, but before William's death in 1528.[4] Philippa Jones suggests that, as soon as Henry VIII declared his interest in Mary, she was found a husband, and that their relationship continued until she had her first child.[5] This implies that the relationship began around 1520 and ended circa 1524. Josephine Wilkinson acknowledges that it is difficult to pinpoint Henry and Mary's relationship, though she does say that it was a long relationship, and that the duration would exceed some of the king's later marriages, based on the grants that William Carey received between 1522 and 1525. The affair had probably begun by February 1522 but when it ended is unclear, although William Carey received his last grant in 1526.[6] This concurs with both Kelly Hart and Philippa Jones, that the relationship was over by the end of 1526. Alison Weir states that going on the 'sparse surviving evidence', Mary's relationship with Henry VIII likely began after her marriage to William Carey in 1520, though he 'probably' did not begin pursuing her until 1522.[7] The relationship had to have been over by 1526, as that is likely when Henry VIII began pursuing Mary's sister, Anne Boleyn. The evidence suggests it happened sometime between 1520 and 1526 though the duration is unclear.

There is no concrete evidence that either of Mary's Carey children were fathered by Henry VIII. The eldest was Catherine Carey, born around 1524, who later became Catherine Knollys as the wife of Francis Knollys. The younger was Henry Carey, later 1st Baron Hunsdon, who was born in 1525 or 1526. The king's patronage of Mary's husband, William Carey, and father, Thomas Boleyn, is often cited as evidence that her children were fathered by Henry VIII, but this is likely to just be a reward to these men for not interfering in his relationship with Mary. In Thomas Boleyn's case, these may have been rewards or a thank you for his diplomatic skills which appear to have been very much in demand prior to either of his daughters sleeping with the king. It does not necessarily follow that these rewards were related to Mary's children. Beverley A. Murphy claims that Henry and Mary's relationship began after Mary's marriage to William Carey in February 1520.[8] We have already seen that this is suggested by other historians, too. So, did the king organise Mary's marriage to Carey in order to cover up the fact that he wanted to sleep with her? Bessie Blount had been unmarried, so it was perhaps more of a scandal for the king to sleep with her than a married woman, and Henry had likely learnt from this. If Mary was married, the paternity of any children could also be attributed to her husband.

Henry VIII never acknowledged paternity of either of Mary Boleyn's Carey children, unlike with Henry Fitzroy. It seems likely that the king would have at least acknowledged a son, if not a daughter, even if just to prove that he was capable of fathering children, specifically sons. However, the timing of Henry Carey's birth is interesting in terms of the king's relationship with Anne Boleyn. It is thought that Henry Carey was born in March in either 1525 or 1526; both have been suggested. If it was 1526, then this may have been around the time of the beginning of Henry VIII's relationship with Anne, the baby's aunt. Although the king may not have been considering marriage with Anne at this point, it could explain why, if Henry Carey was the king's child, the king did not acknowledge him. It has been suggested that the first indication of Henry Carey being the king's son was when Katherine of Aragon's supporters were trying to slander the Boleyns by suggesting Anne Boleyn's nephew was in fact the king's son.[9] If true, this would have made Anne not only the boy's aunt, but also his stepmother on her marriage. People would drag up anything they could to slander Anne and try and prevent the annulment and her marriage to the king. There does not seem to have been a suggestion at the time of his birth that Henry Carey was anything other than the son of Mary and William Carey.

Catherine Carey is certainly the more likely of the two Carey children to have been fathered by Henry VIII. She is generally considered to be the elder of the two, and it seems entirely possible that the relationship between Henry VIII and Mary Boleyn had ended by the time of Henry Carey's conception, quite possibly with Catherine's conception around 1523, if we take her birth date as 1524. Wendy J. Dunn argues that Mary Boleyn and William Carey lived together for the first two years of their marriage, from 1520, but remained childless, and that the children only began to come when Mary started sleeping with Henry VIII. After her royal relationship ended, Mary did not conceive again until her second marriage to William Stafford in 1534.[10] The problem with this theory is that we do not know when Henry VIII and Mary Boleyn's relationship was, or how long it was. There is no evidence in the contemporary sources, only later rumour and supposition on which to base theories.

As Jerry Rabow points out, Henry VIII settled lands on Bessie Blount when he ended his relationship with her, and arranged a marriage for her, but he made 'little or no provision' for Mary Boleyn at the end of their relationship and failed to initiate any financial assistance for her when her first husband died of the sweating sickness in 1528.[11] However, Mary Boleyn was likely married either before or around the time of her relationship with Henry VIII, so he could not offer her a marriage as a settlement at the end of their relationship. There were some grants made to Mary's father and husband, Thomas Boleyn and William Carey, as previously explained, that are possibly linked to the king's relationship with Mary. But these are nothing like the recompense that Henry VIII gave to Bessie Blount, perhaps as a reward for providing him with a son, and to provide for the boy's early upbringing. As Henry VIII 'was not exactly overendowed with legitimate issue', it could be argued that it is reasonable to assume he would want to lay claim to any children he could in order to prove his virility.[12] Wendy J. Dunn suggests that the grants made to William Carey by Henry VIII were for the care of his own illegitimate daughter, Catherine Carey, rather than as a thank you to William himself.[13] Laying claim to any illegitimate living children he could would confirm the king's own virility and, in his eyes, prove that their lack of sons was Katherine of Aragon's fault, and not his own. This was the crux of the annulment – Henry wanted to remarry to produce a male heir to continue the succession, and the fault was with his wife.

Mary Boleyn's history is often used as a reason to explain why she would have become the mistress of Henry VIII; namely that she earned a 'special reputation' in France for the number of her sexual encounters.[14] As John Guy and Julia Fox have argued however, there is no proof that Francis I ever used the words 'una grandissima ribalda, et infame sopra tutte' meaning 'a very great bawd, and infamous above all' to describe Mary Boleyn. Francis was simply said to have used these words during a 'vitriolic smear campaign' in March 1536, more aimed at Anne Boleyn than Mary and that without better evidence 'the question of Mary's morals must be left open'.[15] The phrase about Mary Boleyn being a 'great bawd' appears in the *Letters and Papers of Henry VIII*, though it is dubbed a 'modern copy' and Guy and Fox say that this summary letter 'obliterates the context' of the original kept in the Vatican Archives.[16] Marie Louise Bruce claims that Francis I called Mary his 'English mare' in reference to the number of times he had 'ridden' her, but there does not seem to be any contemporary evidence to back up this claim.[17] Josephine Wilkinson asserts that Mary Boleyn was 'used simply as a sex object' and that she had a series of short-lived sexual encounters, first with the king and then with his favourites when he tired of her.[18] Francis Hackett describes Mary Boleyn as a 'light-hearted and easy-spirited girl, the sort of being who is soon in intimacy with men, knows the morose valleys between the heights of their ardour and the heights of their disdain, and is aware that she must inveigle or humour the beasts, or be beaten'.[19] Wendy J. Dunn says that Mary returned to England from France 'under a dark cloud' and that her family 'probably knew she was a virgin no more'.[20] But it is largely speculation. There is not really any evidence about Mary's behaviour in France except for these later comments, so perhaps her behaviour was not all that remarkable after all as we have no contemporary evidence of it. Alison Weir states that 'according to the historical evidence, Mary never incurred notoriety or infamy as a royal mistress'.[21] Weir agrees with this author's assessment that, if Mary Boleyn had been so scandalous, there would have been reports of it. She notes that Francis I would have been unlikely to have called Mary 'a very great whore, and infamous above all' as that was 'certainly saying something, for the French court was reputed to be the most scandalous in Christendom'.[22] It seems unlikely that Mary could have become so scandalous, more so than any of Francis's official mistresses, and yet not incited any comment in the contemporary sources. Perhaps she did sleep with Francis I, but it is highly doubtful that she was passed around the whole court as some historians suggest, and it would likely not have been a very long affair if it happened, as there is no evidence.

It is uncertain exactly when Mary Boleyn returned to England. It is possible that she returned with Mary Tudor in 1515 after the death of her first husband, Louis XII of France, and Mary's second, secret, marriage to Charles Brandon, Duke of Suffolk. Mary Boleyn was certainly back in England by 1520 when she married William Carey, thus returning before her sister, Anne, who likely did not return until 1521, with her first recorded appearance at the English court in early 1522, alongside her sister, Mary, and future sister-in-law, Jane Parker, later Jane Boleyn, Viscountess Rochford. There do not seem to be reports of Mary Boleyn being in France after Mary Tudor leaves.

Anne Boleyn, when she returned to England in around 1521 or early 1522, was seen as exotic, and her attraction was not in her looks but in her wit and intellect. She had been sent to the court of Margaret of Austria, Duchess of Savoy, at Mechelen in the Low Countries in 1513, when she was only around 12 or 13 years old. The following year, Anne moved to the French court to serve the new queen, Mary Tudor, Henry VIII's sister, who married Louis XII of France. Louis only lived a few months into the marriage, and Mary returned to England, having secretly married Henry VIII's close friend, Charles Brandon, 1st Duke of Suffolk. Anne Boleyn remained at the French court rather than returning to England with the Suffolks and moved into the service of the new French queen, Claude, wife of Francis I. Anne was exposed during her time on the continent to many women exercising power, which seems to have had a huge influence on her during her formative years. Margaret of Austria was Regent of the Netherlands for her father, Maximilian I, and presided over a cultured court where she raised her nieces and nephew, the future Charles V. Although Claude of France did not appear to exercise a huge amount of power, spending a lot of her time pregnant, Francis I's mother, Louise of Savoy, was said to have been the power behind the French throne. Marguerite of Angoulême, also known as Marguerite of Navarre, Francis' sister, was another powerful and outspoken woman at the French court who the young Anne would have witnessed and been around.

While at the court at Mechelen serving Margaret of Austria in 1513, the young Anne Boleyn wrote home to her father to say that she hoped she would be:

> … a worthy woman when I come to the Court and you inform me that the Queen will take the trouble to converse with me, which rejoices me much to think of talking with a person so wise and worthy. This will make me have greater desire to continue to speak French well and also spell, especially because you have so enjoined it on me, and with my own hand I inform you that I will observe it the best I can.[23]

Anne was looking forward to serving the queen, Katherine of Aragon, on her return to England, hoping that she would be a credit to her father and her family. She was well-educated, and versed in dancing, singing, embroidery, and the etiquette of courtly love, which was a Renaissance chivalric tradition. The French language was thought to be important, both in the language of courtly love and often of diplomacy as well; Anne would put it to good use in later years. It was thought that Thomas Boleyn would be able to get his daughter a place in Katherine of Aragon's household in a few years' time. The letter is written in 'poor, scattered French for which the young Anne apologises'.[24] She hoped to improve her French but was proud to have written the letter in her own hand with her own spelling and grammar rather than copying one written for her. The fact that the letter survives today tells us that Thomas Boleyn kept it and demonstrates 'just how proud he was of his daughter and of the impression she made in Brussels'.[25] Anne Boleyn seemed to be a very intelligent and sharp young woman, and these characteristics would develop through her adolescent years, and on her return to England would catch the king's eye.

In addition to Anne's own letter written from the Low Countries, we also have a letter written by Margaret of Austria to Anne's father, Thomas Boleyn. Margaret says that she hopes to 'treat her in such a fashion that you will have reason to be content with it', and that they will need no intermediary other than Anne in the future. She goes on to say that she found her 'of such good address and so pleasing in her youthful age that I am more beholden to you for having sent her to me than you are to me'.[26] Margaret seemed to relish educating the young people in her charge, and it appeared that Anne was no different, as was evident in her own letter – she was determined to improve her French in both speaking and writing the language. Margaret also seemed to take pleasure in Anne, and she was thankful to Thomas Boleyn for sending his daughter to her court. It is testament that, even in her youth, Anne could catch people's eyes and seemed almost extraordinary for her time. It is little wonder that she caught the eye of the king of England on her return to her home country.

There is little evidence of Anne Boleyn in France, in contrast to the evidence from the Low Countries. It is thought that she returned to England around 1521 or early 1522 because a marriage was being arranged for her. Her return also coincided with a change in Anglo-French relations. At the Field of the Cloth of Gold in 1520, Henry VIII and Francis I of France signed an alliance treaty. Anne was quite possibly present in the train of Queen Claude, and likely was reunited with the rest of her family who probably accompanied Henry VIII. However, the alliance quicky broke down, and Henry turned to Charles V and the Holy Roman Empire instead. It was politic for Thomas Boleyn to arrange his daughter's return from France, even without the proposed marriage. The suggested marriage for Anne Boleyn in 1521 was to James Butler, the son of Piers Butler. The Butlers had effectively claimed the earldom of Ormond, but Anne's father, Thomas Boleyn, also had a claim to the earldom through his mother, Margaret Butler, who was the joint heiress of her father, Thomas Butler, 7th Earl of Ormond. Piers Butler had the backing of the Irish to take the earldom, but Thomas Boleyn had the backing of King Henry VIII.[27] An idea was proposed to resolve the problem, by marrying James Butler to his cousin Anne Boleyn, thus uniting the two claims to the earldom, and the matter of the inheritance. It is unclear exactly what happened and why the marriage did not go ahead, but perhaps the couple themselves were not keen, or Thomas Boleyn wanted the earldom for himself and was not willing to let it pass him by.

While negotiations rumbled on over the proposed marriage, Anne Boleyn made her first recorded appearance at the English court. This was in March 1522 at the Chateau Vert pageant held at Wolsey's house of York Place (later Whitehall Palace). Legend has it that Anne played the role of Perseverance, with her sister, Mary Boleyn, in the role of Kindness, and her soon to be sister-in-law, Jane Parker, later Jane Boleyn, Viscountess Rochford, in the role of Constance. However, there is no direct evidence that these were the roles played by the young women. Dr James Taffe appears to have first asked the question as to where this knowledge came from as there is no contemporary source that confirms it. Dr Owen Emmerson and Natalie Grueninger have investigated and the earliest source they revealed that they could find was in Eric Ives' study of Anne Boleyn.[28] The chronicler Edward Hall gives a detailed account of the pageant, describing that the ladies kept in the castle were called Beauty, Honour, Perseverance, Kindness, Constance, Bounty, Mercy, and Pity, and that the ladies wore gowns of white satin with their names embroidered in gold and bonnets of gold.[29] Hall does not, however, specify which lady played which part. In a record of payments at the time, made by Richard Gibson, he describes how the outfits were created and paid for, that they were delivered and 'these things remain with the French queen, the countess of Devonshire, Mistress Anne Boleyn, Mistress Karre [Carey], Mistress Parker, Mistress Browne, Mistress Danet and Mistress_'.[30] It seems that the list of the parts in Hall's account has been matched with the list of ladies in Gibson's account by Eric Ives and the order assumed to be the same, rather than there being an explicit account or reference.[31] This means that we cannot be sure that Anne Boleyn did in fact play the role of Perseverance and Mary Boleyn did in fact play the part of Kindness, despite these being, as Eric Ives said, 'roles of historic appropriateness'.[32] It is a legend that appears to have become fact without the contemporary evidence to back it up, perhaps because, with hindsight, they do seem to have been appropriate roles.

We know that Henry VIII was not Anne Boleyn's first romantic attachment. She has been connected to both Henry Percy, later 6th Earl of Northumberland, and to the poet Sir Thomas Wyatt prior to the king's interest in her, on her return to England. Evidence of the Percy affair comes largely from Cardinal Thomas Wolsey's gentleman usher, George

Cavendish, who was there at the time. There was also an enquiry made to Henry Percy in May 1536 after Anne's arrest, as to whether he and Anne had been betrothed, as that would have given the king an excuse to annul his marriage to her. However, Percy responded to Cromwell saying that:

> I perceive by Raynold Carnaby that there is supposed a pre-contract between the Queen and me; whereupon I was not only heretofore examined upon my oath before the archbishops of Canterbury and York, but also received the blessed sacrament upon the same before the duke of Norfolk and other the King's highness' council learned in the spiritual law, assuring you, Mr. Secretary, by the said oath and blessed body, which afore I received and hereafter intend to receive, that the same may be to my damnation if ever there were any contract or promise of marriage between her and me.[33]

He does not deny that there was a relationship or connection of sorts, but he does deny, on the damnation of his soul, that there was any formal arrangement, betrothal, marriage, or long-lasting connection between them. Percy's wife, Mary Talbot, had already tried to claim that her marriage to Percy was invalid because of Percy's prior relationship with Anne Boleyn. This was in 1532, before Anne married Henry VIII. According to Eric Ives, Mary Talbot told her husband, Henry Percy, that he neglected her, to which he replied that they were not married anyway as he had previously been contracted to Anne Boleyn. The countess told her father, the Earl of Shrewsbury, who reported it to Anne's uncle, the Duke of Norfolk. Anne took the letter to the king herself and demanded an investigation.[34] Percy was questioned, but the case was thrown out and the Percys remained married, though often lived apart. With Percy's denial of any betrothal, this probably was not the reason Henry and Anne's marriage was annulled in 1536 as he is very clear in his letter about it. Instead, it is possible that it was Henry's former relationship with Anne's sister, Mary Boleyn, which was the reason, but we cannot say this with any certainty as there is no surviving evidence or record.

In George Cavendish's account of the relationship between Anne Boleyn and Henry Percy, he reports that Henry VIII began to 'kindle the brand of amours' for Anne on her return from France, but that she was involved with Percy at the time and did not know of the king's affections.[35] We have no evidence that Henry VIII fell for Anne Boleyn immediately on her return from France, at this time, the king may in fact have been involved with Mary Boleyn. Cavendish claims that Percy fell:

> … in dalliance among the queen's maidens, being at the last more conversant with Mistress Anne Boleyn than with any other; so that there grew such a secret love between them that, at length, they were ensured together, intending to marry.[36]

Anne Boleyn was serving in the household of Queen Katherine of Aragon at the time, and Percy was in Wolsey's household, so the pair were frequently together at court. Cavendish was also present at court at the time, as part of Wolsey's household like Percy, but the work was written decades later in the reign of Mary I. It is plausible that notes for the account were written earlier, only cementing it in its final form in the 1550s. Writing and publishing the book under Mary I, it would have been prudent to disparage Anne Boleyn, and write in favour of Katherine of Aragon, Mary's mother.

It was Cardinal Wolsey, according to Cavendish, who ended the relationship between Anne Boleyn and Henry Percy on Henry VIII's orders, as the king wanted Anne for himself. Wolsey is alleged to have called Percy to him and said that 'I marvel not a little … of thy peevish folly, that thou wouldest tangle and ensure thyself with a foolish girl yonder in the court, I mean Anne Boleyn'.[37] Wolsey chastised Percy in Cavendish's account, that he should aim higher and marry where his father decrees. Percy, however, declared that 'in this matter I have gone so far, before many so worthy witnesses, that I know not how to avoid myself nor to discharge my conscience'.[38] This suggests that perhaps there was some kind of binding agreement between Anne Boleyn and Henry Percy, whatever Percy later swore. It may have been love and the fact that he had given his heart to her meant that he was not willing to give her up, rather than an actual precontract. Whatever the reality, it made no difference. The couple were separated. Percy was sent north to marry Mary Talbot, daughter of George Talbot, 4th Earl of Shrewsbury, and Anne Boleyn was sent to rusticate at her family home of Hever Castle in Kent. Wolsey's opinion of the Boleyns is made quite clear – he did not believe that Anne Boleyn was good enough to marry into one of the premier noble families in

England. Anne Boleyn is often thought to be a commoner, and that her story is almost a rags to riches tale, however, she was descended from the Dukes of Norfolk on her mother's side, and the Earls of Ormond on her father's side, so she did have good, noble blood. It seems ironic that Wolsey did not think Anne was good enough for a future earl, but he would fall from power and die in disgrace as she reached for, and won, a king.

It is also from Cavendish's account that we get the idea that Anne Boleyn swore revenge on Wolsey for the break-up of this relationship. Wolsey had lost Anne the chance to be a countess, as well as a man she may well have loved. Cavendish records 'the grudge, how it began, that in process of time burst out to the utter undoing of the cardinal' as Anne 'was greatly offended, saying, that if it lay ever in her power, she would work the cardinal as much displeasure; as she did indeed after'.[39] The historian Eric Ives, however, doubts the veracity of this account, describing Anne Boleyn's reaction as 'improbable'. Making threats against Cardinal Wolsey as early as 1522 or 1523, which is likely when the Percy affair happened, was 'both unwise and childish, and Anne was neither'.[40] It does not really make sense for Anne to be voicing her opinions of someone still very much in the king's good graces who wielded a lot of power and influence – it could have jeopardised her position at court and her future prospects. But we also know from the historical record that Anne could be impetuous, especially when angry or fearful, so perhaps she did make some kind of threat, without knowing whether she would ever be able to back it up. It could equally have been something that Cavendish added to his account later with the benefit of hindsight, having seen that Anne did go on to play a role in the cardinal's undoing.

It seems possible that it was around this time at Hever Castle that Anne Boleyn may have become involved with the poet Thomas Wyatt. He would also be arrested alongside Anne in May 1536 and sent to the Tower of London, where he would be imprisoned in the Bell Tower, although he would survive, be released, and reinstated at court, unlike other men caught up in those awful events. Anne's relationship with Wyatt has attracted more popular attention than her relationship with Henry Percy, though there is less corroboration for it in the contemporary sources. Wyatt's poetry is often given as evidence of a relationship between them, though there is no justification of this assumption in any of the poems and Anne is never named. This poetry, combined with Wyatt's arrest and incarceration in May 1536 alongside Anne and her 'lovers', has people supposing that the pair were in love and may even have had sexual relations prior to Anne's royal marriage. There was a possible family connection as the Boleyn family home at Hever Castle was close to the Wyatt family home at Allington Castle. Wyatt's poem *Whoso List to Hunt* has the line '*noli me tangere*; for Caesar's I am', highlighting the moment when Anne Boleyn made it clear that she chose Henry VIII over Wyatt.[41] Whether this was a true event, or a complete figment of Wyatt's imagination is unclear. It could have been a case of unrequited love on Wyatt's part. 'Noli me tangere' translates as 'do not touch me'; Anne is telling Wyatt that she belongs to someone else and that he had no right to touch her any longer. It does suggest a kind of intimacy between them, or that Wyatt was fantasising about what he wanted to happen with Anne, but that it was not possible any longer because she had been claimed by another, more powerful, man.

Another Wyatt poem which seems to have a concrete relation to Anne Boleyn is *If Waker care; if sudden pale colour*. There was a later change of line in the poem, with the changed line reading 'Brunet, that set my wealth in such a roar', but the original being 'Brunet, her that did set our country in a rore [*sic*]'.[42] The change of line may have been made after Anne's execution to avoid it being so controversial, about a woman Henry VIII did not want to be reminded of, whom he believed had cheated on him. It is difficult to think of any other woman who set the country in a roar in this period that Wyatt could have written about. Anne Boleyn's relationship with the king forever changed England because of what was undertaken to make the marriage happen, and then the tragedy that ended it. The poem begins on a note of longing or yearning: 'if many sighs with little speech to plain'.[43] This suggests that Wyatt could only watch from afar as Henry VIII took the woman that he wanted. He could wish and sigh but could not speak out for what he yearned for. It gives a sense that Wyatt was pining after what he had lost, whether real or imagined, and now what he could never have. Anne Boleyn did have more agency than many women of the period – she refused to become the king's mistress. But, in the end, she could not get away from him and choose another man, even if she had wanted to. The king had set his eyes on her and he continued to pursue her until she married him.

There is no real agreement as to when Henry VIII's eye first fell on Anne Boleyn. He likely did not initially intend to marry her, he probably saw her as another mistress as her sister had been. But Anne was very different to Mary Boleyn. She would not surrender herself to the king on his request. Looking at the evidence, it seems that Henry's attention may have first turned to Anne sometime in 1526, with the pair committing to each other in 1527, which is when we really begin to see the 'Great Matter' gathering pace. Henry now had something – or someone – tangible to move towards, not just something to escape from. That gave him something worth fighting for. Perhaps Anne's commitment to Henry came in 1527 because she could see that he had already pledged himself to proceedings which would annul his marriage to Katherine of Aragon.[44] It is plausible that Anne waited until Henry had put things in motion before she would commit to become his wife and queen. As we have already seen, George Cavendish places Henry VIII's interest in Anne much earlier, to around 1523 or 1524, at the time of her relationship with Henry Percy.[45] If Henry had fallen for Anne this early on, why did he not appear to act until 1526 or 1527? It does not seem like Henry was reluctant to act with any other woman in his life, though perhaps Anne was at her family home of Hever Castle and thus unavailable to the king for a while. It is possible he began to pay attention to her on her return to court after the Percy affair, though if she was at Hever, it is unclear as to how long she was there or when she returned to court in Katherine of Aragon's household.

Amy Licence dates Henry VIII's interest in Anne Boleyn to beginning at some point in 1526, quite possibly to February of that year. Anne seems to have resisted him for about a year, before she capitulated in 1527 and agreed to marry him. Henry 'was the driving force in their relationship, not her'.[46] Henry would have been aged 34, and Anne around 25, if we take her birth date as circa 1501. Anne was fifteen years younger than Katherine of Aragon, who was at this point past childbearing, and very much of an age to be able to give the king sons. The 1526 Shrovetide jousts were held at Greenwich and the king dressed in gold and silver with the motto 'declare, I dare not', suggesting a new affection.[47] This could well be the moment when Henry VIII began pursuing Anne Boleyn with the initial intention of making her his mistress, rather than as his future wife and queen. It was her denial of the king which made him rethink her position. John Guy and Julia Fox have Henry falling for Anne at the same moment, with this pageant being his declaration that there was someone he was interested in – 'all he can have wanted was a sexual adventure with a passionate Francophile' but he 'came to love her with an ardour and intensity he never found elsewhere'; she would be the love of his life.[48] Tracy Borman also cites this moment as an important one, and that Henry's love for Anne 'developed gradually out of a charade of courtly love'.[49] The king was not captivated by Anne's looks or beauty, but she was 'a charismatic and accomplished young émigré from the French court … unlike any other woman Henry had met. He was captivated by her sharp mind and quick wit, her unshakeable self-confidence'.[50] Anne Boleyn seemed unique in England at the time, so it is little wonder that the king's eye was drawn to her. He could converse with her – she was witty, well-educated, musical, and intelligent; all things that the king appreciated. But these aspects of Anne's character along with Henry's need for control and his expectations of women would lead the pair into a relationship of sunshine and showers with stormy arguments and passionate reconciliations.

Henry VIII's relationship with Anne Boleyn is nowhere better illustrated than in the love letters he wrote her in the mid to late 1520s. Seventeen of them survive in the Vatican Archives, supposedly because they were secretly taken from England by Cardinal Lorenzo Campeggio after the 1529 Blackfriars legatine trial. The letters are available to view online in the Vatican Archives.[51] David Starkey wrote that the love letters were a testament to Henry VIII's grand passion for Anne Boleyn which tore England apart at the seams.[52] Henry's love for Anne was certainly the catalyst for the annulment of his marriage to Katherine of Aragon, but it was not the deciding factor. He wanted to remarry and produce a male heir, which Katherine was unable to provide. Anne's greatest power lay in her role as emotional mistress to Henry VIII as he confided in her as in no one else. As we have seen, factors in the annulment go back much further – to the birth of Henry Fitzroy in 1519, and Katherine of Aragon's failure to have a son, with roots in Katherine's first marriage to Henry's elder brother, Prince Arthur. Henry VIII knew that he could impugn his marriage to Katherine before Anne Boleyn came to court as a decree of nullity was allegedly considered as early as 1514. It remained a practical thought until Charles V's influence in Rome through

1527 and 1528 provided an obstacle.[53] When Henry first noticed Anne, it brought all of these worries to the fore, and he realised that he could marry her, and she could produce the son he so desperately craved.

None of the letters Henry wrote to Anne Boleyn are dated, and we do not know what order they fall in. We also lack Anne's replies to Henry's letters. David Starkey and Karen Lindsey date the earliest letters to 1524 with Lindsey specifying that they began just after the end of Anne Boleyn's relationship with Henry Percy.[54] Joanna Denny and David Loades date the first letters to 1526.[55] Retha Warnicke, however, dates the earliest letters to 1528.[56] The earlier date of 1524 is largely rejected because there is no real evidence of a relationship between Henry VIII and Anne Boleyn before 1527 though the earliest letters are likely to have begun in 1526. A letter often assumed to be from the earliest batch claims that Henry had 'been for the whole year stricken with the dart of love'.[57] The fact that Henry claims he was struck for a year by love does not mean that his feelings were at this time reciprocated or even known about. Henry may have admired Anne from afar before acting, we do not know or have the evidence to tell us exactly when Henry told Anne of his feelings for her, let alone when those feelings began. G. W. Bernard suggested that Henry VIII first explored an annulment of his marriage to Katherine of Aragon in May 1527, which means that the latest he and Anne could have committed to each other was August of that year.[58] August 1527 was when Henry VIII drafted a dispensation to be submitted to the Pope to allow him to marry Anne Boleyn despite being within the forbidden degrees of affinity. The affinity due to the king's prior relationship with Anne's sister meant that the Pope needed to issue a dispensation in order for Henry's marriage to Anne to be considered valid and their children legitimate. It does make sense to date their commitment to sometime in the first half of 1527.

One of the most important letters in the sequence describes a gift Anne sent to Henry, thought to symbolise her acceptance of his marriage proposal (see chapter 4). Anne Boleyn's gift to Henry may give an insight into the relationship, imbued as it was with symbolism. However, the letter Henry wrote to Anne to thank her for the gift, and which describes it, is also undated. The gift personified Anne's acceptance of Henry VIII's proposal to become his wife and queen. Anne Boleyn's meteoric rise had begun.

Chapter 4

Agreement to Marry

At the beginning of 1527, there was a major turning point in the 'Great Matter', despite the usual considerations that the 'Great Matter' had barely begun. Anne Boleyn agreed to marry Henry VIII. There had not previously been a solid reason for Henry to annul his marriage, other than the vague hope that he would remarry and produce an heir, but no future wife had yet presented herself. Until now. This arrangement between Henry and Anne was the catalyst for the gathering pace of the annulment case. Anne's agreement to become Henry's wife was signalled by a letter and gift she sent to the king, probably around New Year 1527, though as previously discussed, it is difficult to date many of the letters. Claire Ridgway and Owen Emmerson state that 'at some point during that Christmas [1526] at Hever Castle, Anne made her decision'.[1] Tracy Adams states that the popular narrative of Anne being harassed by a lustful king who fails to get what he wants so proposes marriage, might not be so prevalent if it was not for the surviving love letters.[2] It is an interesting thought, as the love letters do appear one-sided because we are missing Anne's replies. We only have Henry's quite lust-filled and almost desperate letters to her. Perhaps if we had Anne's, or none at all, there might be a more balanced picture emerging, even if only from supposition and inferences of other surviving accounts and sources. John Guy and Julia Fox wrote that 'Anne had bowled [the king] over, flinging open the doors of his perception', allowing him to think about what he could do rather than what he should do.[3] Anne Boleyn was what Henry wanted, and he would do what was necessary to have her.

This particular letter is quite possibly the most significant of the batch of surviving love letters sent from Henry VIII to Anne Boleyn. It describes the gift Anne had sent to the king and how pleased he was with her submission to him and, we assume and can infer, agreement to marry once he gained his annulment. Henry did not expect the granting of an annulment of his marriage to Katherine of Aragon to take too long. The gift was 'one of those trinkets concealing a meaning that Tudor people loved'.[4] Historian Joanna Denny writes that the gift was 'poignantly symbolic of the terrible situation in which she found herself'.[5] It must not have been an easy decision for Anne to make, to accept the king's proposal. Yes, she would be queen, but it would not be an easy road to get there, and she would replace a popular and admired queen in Katherine of Aragon. She could not have been certain how she would be received. This gift that Anne sent to Henry does not survive today, so this is the best idea we have of how Anne signalled her agreement, and it is quite a detailed description:

> For a present so beautiful that nothing could be more so (considering the whole of it), I thank you most cordially, not only on account of the fine diamond and the ship in which the solitary damsel is tossed about, but chiefly for the fine interpretation and the too humble submission which your goodness hath used towards me in this case.[6]

It has been said that this was the gift which signalled Anne's acceptance of Henry VIII's proposal of marriage, to make her his wife and queen and, hopefully, mother to his heirs. This is what the 'fine interpretation' is said to be, as the ship represents protection, like the ark that protected Noah in the Bible, with the maiden aboard being protected by the ship while the storm rages around her. Henry VIII was the ship, to protect Anne from the people who wanted to undo her. He could only truly protect her through marriage, though marriage would also prove Anne's undoing. The diamond symbolises steadfastness and faithfulness, Anne's devotion to the king and determination to follow it through, no matter what the obstacles or difficulties, and there would be plenty. *The Romaunt of the Rose* by Geoffrey Chaucer describes a 'herte as hard as Diamaunt, Stedfast, and naught pliaunt' meaning a 'heart as hard as a diamond, steadfast and never-changing'.[7] Anne had submitted to Henry, and agreed to become his wife, no matter how difficult that path to the throne might be. Neither of them could have seen just how long or arduous Anne's path to the crown would actually be at that time. It would irrevocably change England's political and religious life and affect how Henry VIII, in particular, would be seen for the next 500 years and more.

The historian Carolly Erickson suggests that the ship was an 'allegory of Anne's own tempest-tossed life'.[8] Her life had never been what was considered 'normal' for a woman of the time – being educated abroad for so many years was an immense privilege for her and not afforded to many of her class and background. Perhaps Anne was destined to have a life that was not plain sailing precisely because she was an unusual woman for the time. She certainly seemed to have ambition and dedication to seeing something through once she made up her mind.

Tracy Adams claims that Henry VIII never actually intended to make Anne Boleyn his mistress, but that marriage was in fact his goal all along. This is not an entirely convincing argument, but it is worth examining in more detail as the assumption is often made that initially Henry intended to make Anne his mistress, and he does use this word in his letters to her. However, Adams argues that this claim is based on a modern understanding of the word 'mistress', meaning a 'long-term extra-conjugal sexual partner', but that it meant something different in the sixteenth century.[9] She explains that during Henry and Anne's lifetimes, the English word 'mistress' referred to a woman a man loved and/or intended to marry, and that the meaning only changed around the beginning of the seventeenth century to have among its definitions a woman with whom a man was having an adulterous affair.[10] It is an interesting thing to consider – did Henry VIII intend to marry Anne from the beginning of his attachment to her and did he hold off making it official until he had set the wheels in motion for his annulment? It is possible that Henry asked Anne to marry him earlier than the end of 1526 or early 1527 when her acceptance is symbolised by the gift described at the beginning of this chapter. Maybe she demurred over it, perhaps unsure if the king would actually be able to successfully annul his marriage to Katherine of Aragon and was serious about marrying her and perhaps even whether it was what she really wanted. Though whether she could in fact have said no without repercussions is another question entirely. To Anne, it may have been a surprise to realise that the king of England not only wanted to marry her but would go to such lengths to do so.

Anne Boleyn's refusal to become the king's mistress, and agreement to be his wife, stemmed in part from her sister's experience as she shared her father's and brother's ambition and 'was not therefore content to join the ranks of the king's discarded mistresses, and then be married off to whichever gentleman of the court was prepared to turn a blind eye to her indiscretions'.[11] Anne wanted to control her own future so, if we believe the traditional narrative, she said no to being the king's mistress, which led to a greater destiny for herself. It seems that Anne 'had either fallen for the king's charms or been worn down by his constant pursuit'.[12] Anne 'cleverly gave [the king] just enough encouragement to stoke his interest even further, telling him that although she loved him in spirit, she could not love him in body unless they were married'.[13] It is possible that Anne was encouraged by her father, Thomas Boleyn, and uncle, Thomas Howard, 3rd Duke of Norfolk, to take this tack, although we have no evidence either way to confirm this. It is doubtful that Anne's father would have wanted her to be a king's mistress with her sister's example before her, and with the excellent education she had been afforded, and her obvious intelligence, wit, and charisma. Being discarded by a king would have had a detrimental effect on her marriage prospects. We have a letter from 1533, where Chapuys writes that 'I must add that the said earl of Wiltshire has never declared himself up to this moment; on the contrary, he has hitherto, as the duke of Norfolk has frequently told me, tried to dissuade the King rather than otherwise from the marriage'.[14] This suggests that Anne's father was not hugely enthusiastic about her proposed marriage to the king, perhaps doubting that it would ever really happen and that Anne would be ruined. This was a new situation that Anne found herself in – betrothed to a king who was already married and whose wife was fighting back.

This agreement to marry between Henry VIII and Anne Boleyn marked a turning point in the 'Great Matter'. Henry could look forward to a future with a younger and more attractive woman who would hopefully give him a son and 'it would be quite out of character for Henry not to act immediately Anne had yielded'.[15] From 1527 we see the case for the annulment gathering pace, and Anne Boleyn and her family gaining power and influence. Anne's father, Thomas Boleyn, was an accomplished diplomat and courtier already, but we see him gaining more power and titles, first Viscount Rochford then Earl of Wiltshire and Ormond in 1529, with his son, George, getting the Rochford viscountcy. By 1527 when Anne accepted the king, Thomas Boleyn had become one of the wealthiest men in England. Owen Emmerson and Claire Ridgway state that, in a subsidy on lands, the average peer was found to be worth between £300 and £600 while Thomas Boleyn was worth £800.[16] However, things were still unsettled for Anne. We know that she retreated multiple times back to her family home at Hever Castle, and the king continued sending letters to her when she was away from court, refusing to take no for an answer. Perhaps, and completely understandably, the pressure was too much at times and she needed to decompress away from the eyes of the court who must have been constantly watching her for any sign of weakness.

Anne rejoined the court having accepted the king's marriage proposal, but it was important that this did not become public knowledge. Anne returned not as a queen-in-waiting, but to serve Henry's current wife, Katherine of Aragon. Anne 'understood well that public knowledge of her agreement with Henry could undermine his case for an annulment from his marriage'.[17] That would in turn jeopardise her own future with the king. By August 1527, however, rumours were beginning to spread about how Henry VIII intended to annul his marriage to Katherine of Aragon. This would have put more pressure on Anne with her link to the king being made public and his intentions towards her. However, for a time, the knowledge that Henry intended for Anne to replace Katherine was not widely known.

Cardinal Wolsey wrote that a rumour, 'somehow or another, has sprung up in England that proceedings are being taken for a divorce between the King and Queen, which is entirely without foundation, yet not altogether causeless; for there has been some discussion about the Papal dispensation, not with any view to a divorce, but to satisfy the French, who have raised the objection on proposing a marriage between the Princess and their Sovereign'.[18] This question was raised over a potential French marriage for Princess Mary, whose legitimacy was being questioned in negotiations. On his way to France in 1527, Wolsey tantalisingly wrote that he:

> … was met by the Archbishop, with whom he communicated on the King's secret matter;—what had been done in it;—how displeasantly the Queen takes it;—what the King has done to pacify her,—declaring that hitherto nothing had been intended by the King, except to discover the truth, on occasion moved by the bishop of Tarbe.[19]

Henry VIII almost tried to reframe the annulment case as being a result of the discussions regarding a French marriage for Princess Mary, rather than from his own desires and at his own instigation. The Bishop of Tarbes was one of the negotiators for that French treaty. Melita Thomas records that 'it seems unlikely that Henry would have invented the claim entirely' of the French questioning Mary's legitimacy, but that it seems 'hardly feasible' that Tarbes was in London from 26 February to 8 May 1527 and Wolsey swiftly convened his secret court on 17 May.[20] It is possible that Tarbes raised the question as some kind of negotiation technique as things dragged on.

By the middle of 1527 the annulment rumours were not entirely without foundation as Henry VIII had already instigated an investigation with a view to annulling his marriage so that he could marry Anne Boleyn. Henry VIII requested a dispensation from Rome in order to marry Anne within months of receiving her agreement to marry him. Henry was wasting no time. He had previously had an affair with Anne's sister, Mary Boleyn, meaning that he and Anne were related within the forbidden degrees of affinity. The Pope received the king's request for a dispensation on 23 December 1527:

> Proposed bull of dispensation for Henry VIII., in case his marriage with Katharine, his brother's widow, be pronounced unlawful, to marry another, even if she have contracted marriage with another man, provided it be not consummated, and even if she be of the second degree of consanguinity, or of the first degree of affinity, ex quocumque licito seu illicito coitu; in order to prevent uncertainty in the succession, which in past times has been the occasion of war.[21]

This is phrased as a potential bull, only to be used if the first marriage was annulled, and it makes it sound like there is no guarantee it will be, despite Henry VIII's assertions of his surety in his case and his determination, or bullheadedness. The wording is interesting, as it covers the idea that the woman may have contracted marriage with another man, but that it would not be valid as long as it was not consummated, which surely must relate to Anne's supposed relationship and possible secret betrothal or marriage with Henry Percy, heir to the earldom of Northumberland. The Latin 'ex quocumque licito seu illicito coitu' means whether from a lawful or unlawful union or intercourse. The reason for the dispensation, and annulment on which it depended, is set out clearly to give the best reason for the Pope to grant the annulment – the succession and prevention of civil war. It almost seems manipulative and backhanded to ask for a dispensation to remarry before the annulment of the existing marriage is granted and then to state that it, and said annulment, are needed for the protection of the realm. There is a note in the margin of a copy of this draft bull to say that the dispensation should be unconditional and not dependent on the annulment.[22] The Pope would not have granted this, as it would basically mean sanctioning bigamy. If it was not dependent on the annulment, Henry may well have taken it for granted that his first marriage would be declared null and void and jump the gun to marry Anne Boleyn in hopes of quickly producing an heir. The Pope ensured that Henry would legally need to have his marriage annulled or a divorce granted before he could remarry. Ironically, it was Katherine of Aragon being related to Henry in forbidden degrees of affinity, which was the basis for his annulment case, and now Henry wanted to marry another woman in a similar position. But then again, Henry VIII was related to all of his six wives.

Reginald Pole, the king's cousin, later wrote a treatise called *Pro ecclesiasticae unitatis defensione*, commonly known in English as *Defense of the Unity of the Church*, which he completed in June 1536, just a month after Anne Boleyn's death. He described the king's relationship with Anne, directly to Henry himself:

> You, a man of your age and with such experience, are miserably burning with passion for the love of a girl. She, indeed, has said that she will make herself available to you on one condition alone. You must reject your wife whose place she desires to hold. This modest woman does not want to be your concubine! She wants to be your wife. I believe that she learned from the example of her sister, if in no other way, how quickly you can have your fill of concubines. She, however, was anxious to surpass her sister by retaining you as a lover.[23]

Pole sees that Henry's desire for an annulment of his marriage has been driven solely by his infatuation with Anne and her refusal to be his mistress; she had learned from her sister's example and would not submit. Anne is seen to be taking advantage of the king's weakness as a result of his sexual desire.[24] Describing Anne as 'modest' appears to be an insult, insinuating that she is not worthy of being Henry's wife and queen. Anne is portrayed as ambitious and scheming to replace Katherine of Aragon, where it actually seems likely she did not welcome the king's advances, or did not trust his intentions, at least at the beginning.

In May 1527, another major event happened which, this time, looked to be halting the annulment case before it could really start. Troops of Emperor Charles V sacked Rome. This horrifying event saw Imperial soldiers running amuck through Rome, looting, killing, and holding people to ransom. It shocked Christendom and the Pope initially took refuge in the Castel Sant'Angelo within Rome when his guard was slaughtered. Charles V was Katherine of Aragon's nephew and the Pope, Clement VII, was now entirely in his power, trapped in the citadel, and then allowed to escape to become almost a refugee, living in Orvieto with a very reduced court. There was also an uprising at the same time which expelled his family, the Medicis, from Florence.[25] It was to Orvieto that the emissaries from England, Stephen Gardiner and Edward Foxe, went to try and get the dispensation for the king to marry Anne Boleyn. The Pope tried to make concessions to Henry VIII as far as he could without angering the emperor by deciding, or seeming to decide, that the case would be tried and judgement made in England rather than in Rome.

Stephen Gardiner and Edward Foxe were sent by Cardinal Wolsey to see the Pope about the annulment case. It seems that Henry VIII instructed that they stopped en route to the Continent to visit Anne Boleyn at Hever Castle in February 1528 to keep her updated on what was happening with regards to the 'Great Matter'.[26] She was definitely an active player, not just a passive spectator waiting for the king to grant her desires. In a letter written to Anne which seems likely to refer to this visit, Henry VIII said that:

> Darling, these shall be only to advertise you that this bearer and his fellow be despatched with as many things to compass our matter, and to bring it to pass as our wits could imagine or devise; which brought to pass, as I trust, by their diligence, it shall be shortly, you and I shall have our desired end, which should be more to my heart's ease, and more quietness to my mind, than any other thing in this world.[27]

The 'bearer and his fellow' likely refer to Gardiner and Foxe, who were on their way to the Pope with the king's hopes that the annulment would be granted, hence his hope for the 'desired end' which was his marriage to Anne and their expected happily ever after with lots of children, including sons. Henry expresses how unsettled he has been in heart and mind as this case dragged on, though he could not know it would still be many more years and a lot of difficulty before he could have his 'desired end'.

Henry VIII and Anne Boleyn's relationship was one of sunshine and storms, with blazing arguments and passionate reconciliations. Before their marriage, they were working towards a common goal and this made them strong, though frustrations over delays and the amount of time it was taking inevitably caused some friction. We know that Henry sent Anne gifts in the early part of their relationship from the love letters he wrote her, one of those was 'my picture set in bracelets, with the whole of the device, which you already know, wishing myself in their place, if it should please you'.[28] In another, 'I send you by the bearer of this a buck, killed late last night by my own hand, hoping that when you eat it you may think of the hunter'.[29] As well as sending her gifts, Henry expresses his uncertainty prior to their betrothal, that 'I have been told that the opinion in which I left you is totally changed, and that you would not come to court either with your mother, if you could, or in any other manner'.[30] This is a big contrast with letters which must fall later in their relationship which are more explicit 'but that I would you were in mine arms, or I in yours, for I think it long since I kissed you'.[31] Or, probably one of the most well-known, 'wishing myself (especially an evening) in my sweetheart's arms, whose pretty dukkys, I trust shortly to cusse'.[32] 'Dukkys' referred to Anne's breasts, and 'cusse' to kiss, so there was some kind of physical contact between them prior to marriage, though it likely stopped short of full consummation.

In 1528, there was an outbreak of the sweating sickness in England. Anne Boleyn, her brother, George, and their father, Thomas, all fell sick. It is where we find some of Henry's most desperate letters which demonstrate his passion for and devotion to Anne. We know that Henry was terrified of disease, and he fled London in the face of the contagion. One of the love letters Henry VIII wrote to Anne Boleyn we can date to this period as Henry wrote that:

> … when we were at Walton, two ushers, two valets de chambre, and your brother, fell ill, but are now quite well; and since we have returned to your house at Hunsdon, we have been perfectly well, and have not, at present, one sick person, God be praised; and I think, if you would retire from Surrey, as we did, you would escape all danger. There is another thing that may comfort you, which is, that, in truth, in this distemper few or no women have been taken ill, and, what is more, no person of our court, and few elsewhere, have died of it.[33]

Henry was obviously worried about his own health, and that of his mistress and future wife, Anne Boleyn. In the letter, he tells Anne of her brother's illness, but that he has also now recovered, so he does not seem to have suffered too badly. Henry seems to be trying to reassure himself that currently no one in his household was ill, and that women were less likely to fall sick from the contagion. It may have been considered that women were less likely to catch the sweating sickness generally, but this did not protect Anne who did, in fact, fall seriously ill. In another letter which must have followed the previous one, Henry VIII wrote:

> There came to me suddenly in the night the most afflicting news that could have arrived. On three accounts I lament it. The first, to hear of the illness of my mistress, whom I esteem more than all the world, and whose health I desire as I do my own, so that I would gladly bear half your illness to make you well … I should hope, by [the chief physician] and his means, to obtain one of my chief joys on earth – that is the care of my mistress – yet for want of him I send you my second, and hope that he will make you well.[34]

Henry VIII was devasted by Anne's illness and greatly feared losing her, as well as his chance for a son by her. Henry was notoriously scared of illness, so the fact that he claimed he would 'gladly bear' half of Anne's illness to make her well just proved how devoted he was to her. Henry's chief physician was otherwise engaged at the time, so the king sent his second physician to treat Anne. It is difficult to imagine the pressure that physician must have felt, knowing how much she meant to the king. To Henry's great relief, Anne survived. It is something that is a great what-if of the Tudor period – had Anne Boleyn died of the sweating sickness in 1528, what would Henry VIII have done? Would he have persisted with the annulment case and found another woman to marry? Probably.

Although Thomas, George, and Anne Boleyn all survived the sweating sickness despite all falling ill, Anne's brother-in-law, William Carey, was not so lucky. He died on 22 June 1528, leaving behind a wife and two young children. The French ambassador du Bellay wrote that 'The King keeps moving about for fear of the plague. Many of his people have died of it in three or four hours. Of those you know there are only Poowits [Sir Fras. Poyntz], Carey and Cotton (Compton) dead'.[35] By 21 July 1528, du Bellay reported that 'the danger in this country begins to diminish hereabouts, and to increase elsewhere. In Kent it is very great. Mademoiselle de Boulan (Boleyn) and her father have sweated, but have got over it'.[36] He also commented that 'I think 100,000 wills have been made off-hand, for those who were dying became quite foolish the moment they fell ill'.[37] Mary Boleyn was probably aged around 29 or 30, and she had been married to William Carey for eight years. Their children, Catherine and Henry Carey, would only have been aged around 4 and 2 when their father died, although their birth dates are not certain. In December 1538, Henry VIII assigned Mary an annuity of £100 which had once been paid to her husband.[38] Mary would remain widowed for six years before remarrying to Sir William Stafford in 1534. This second marriage angered Mary's parents and sister, who by this time was queen. Stafford was not considered a good enough husband for Mary, and she was banished from court. She would not return to court life and would settle in the country until her death in 1543.

While Anne Boleyn was lying ill at Hever Castle, her family home in Kent, Henry VIII was spending time with Katherine of Aragon and Princess Mary at Hunsdon House. Anne appears to have told Henry of her fears that the king would abandon her and return to his wife and daughter, forsaking her. Henry wrote to attempt to allay Anne's fears, asking her not to be 'uneasy' at his absence, and that he wished her 'in my arms, that I might a little dispel your unreasonable thoughts'.[39] Perhaps Anne was being unreasonable, but she knew how fickle the king could be. She had the example of her sister, Mary, to inform her opinion. Anne must have been feeling an immense amount of pressure to please the king, but also afraid of losing him. Being the cast-off of a king could have ruined her. Anne was back at court in August 1528, but it was a short visit, as she was sent back to Hever the following month due to the expected arrival of a papal legate to try the annulment case in England.

The love letters that Henry VIII sent to Anne Boleyn in the mid to late 1520s demonstrate that the king was certainly desperate to have Anne, and this may well have developed into a love for her as well as an obsession. Although, it is difficult to read true feelings from a distance of 500 years, and it is possible that even people at the time were unsure what the real sentiments between the couple were. John Guy and Julia Fox describe the letters as 'the most extraordinary series of seventeen letters that perhaps any king has ever written' and 'that Henry wrote them at all is astonishing' as he found writing tedious.[40] Eric Ives writes that 'charity demands that we recognise the genuineness of the king's passion; from a person who hated writing as much as Henry did, such letters are in themselves a remarkable testimony'.[41] We certainly do not have anything similar surviving for any other king, but then Henry VIII's situation was almost unique in English history. Yes, other kings since have been divorced and remarried, but not with the amount of upheaval that happened in England in the 1520s and 1530s which changed the fabric of the country. And these love letters are a testament to the passion that fuelled it. For Henry, 'Anne was worth the discomfort of picking up a pen himself'.[42] Sometimes it is small things, like a dislike for writing, which can give a real sense of a situation. Anne was 'like no other woman Henry had ever met' and 'she drove the king into a wild and uncontrollable lust for her'.[43] What we often hear in works about Anne Boleyn is that the king was obsessed with her, or in lust for her, but there seems to be less talk of love.

Did Henry VIII love Anne Boleyn, and did she love him? The question is certainly open to debate. Personally, it seems that they did love each other. It is possible that Henry did fall in love with Anne fairly early on in their relationship, attracted by her intelligence and wit, and that she could match him in so many ways. He certainly lusted after her and seemed obsessed by her, but that could have developed into a love and respect for her as the annulment case dragged on. It seems to be Anne's feelings which are generally more in doubt. Was the appeal for her a crown and to think of her children ascending to the throne in the future? Anne was intelligent enough to understand that becoming queen would not be easy and replacing such a popular and respected woman as Katherine of Aragon would provoke some adverse reactions. She must have believed that the difficulties and risk was worth it. No one in 1527 could have foreseen that Anne would end on the scaffold because there was no precedent for it, so she probably never believed her life would be endangered through marrying the king. Henry VIII was an attractive and handsome man in his youth, and he would have been in his mid-30s at the time that he and Anne began their relationship. Anne may have been attracted to the king for his looks as well as his power and the position he could give her. The pair worked well together during the annulment case, but feelings may have begun to change once they were married as Anne failed to adapt to the changed expectations of her new role, and the failure to produce a son must have weighed heavily on both of them. Their relationship of sunshine and storms may have become more storms than bright weather.

John Guy and Julia Fox sum up Henry VIII's feelings towards Anne Boleyn expressed in the series of love letters, thus:

> To none of his other wives nor, as far as anyone knows, to any of his handful of mistresses, did Henry surrender himself so completely. His raw emotion, his fears that his feelings are not reciprocated, his constant need for reassurance and support are naively, almost endearingly visible. His was the sort of love which is heady and obsessional. He holds nothing back. His longing for Anne in her absence is sometimes even sad, yet occasionally he gives a dark hint of the other Henry who needs to get his own way without question or objection, a man who looks for, and demands, obedience and makes his impatience menacingly clear.[44]

Henry appears open and almost vulnerable in the letters, demonstrating how much power he appeared to give Anne over him at this time. Perhaps this is why so many of the king's actions during his relationship with Anne are attributed to her, including his treatment of Princess Mary and Katherine of Aragon, and the executions of Thomas More and Bishop John Fisher. But as Guy and Fox astutely state, there were signs of the control that Henry VIII needed to exert within the letters. His tone when Anne is away from him is a mix of devoted servant and commanding king, and the command seems to come through more in the letters which are thought to be later in the series, perhaps as the king felt more sure of Anne's commitment to him. This part of Henry would shape his marriage to Anne and would play a huge part in her eventual downfall when she failed to adjust from the dominant role of mistress to the more submissive role of wife and mother.

Something which historians have debated over regarding Henry and Anne's relationship is exactly who was holding off from sexual relations. It is often assumed that it was Anne who was holding Henry at arm's length, refusing to yield to him without marriage and a crown. However, G. W. Bernard argues that 'the early love letters offer no support for the conventional view that Anne refused Henry's advances until he had actually made her his lawful wife and queen', and that 'what is abundantly clear from the succeeding letters is that any notion that it was Anne who held Henry's advances back for six years is nonsense'.[45] Nonsense is perhaps too strong a word, as it is plausible and possible that Anne held Henry off, not wanting to share the fate of her sister, Mary, for yielding too easily and then being discarded. However, it is also possible that it was Henry who held off sexually to make sure that any child he conceived with Anne would be legitimate. It can be argued, looking at the love letters, that 'it is clear … that Henry was the aggressor. Anne left his first letters unanswered. She rebuffed him, even leaving court and retreating to Hever'.[46] Henry places himself as the supplicant, appealing to Anne, almost begging her to even answer him. It does appear that Henry wanted more than Anne was willing to give. It is just as plausible, however, that it was a joint decision between the pair of them to abstain once they had committed to each other and to a marriage, to protect Anne's reputation, as well as ensure the legitimacy of any children born from their relationship. This does not have to be one or the other. As can be seen with the annulment case, Henry and Anne were working towards a joint goal, so it seems logical that the decision to abstain from sexual relations was also a joint one, formed once Anne accepted Henry's proposal of marriage. Bernard also suggests that 'it may well be that once Anne had responded favourably to his advances, Henry and Anne slept together for a time'.[47] Bernard's reasoning for this was Henry VIII requesting a dispensation to marry someone he had already had intercourse with. This does not necessarily mean, however, that Henry and Anne had already consummated their relationship at the time the dispensation was actually granted (which it was, but on the understanding that it could only be used if Henry and Katherine's marriage was annulled), but perhaps Henry was covering for the eventuality that he and Anne would slightly anticipate their wedding, as indeed they would do at the end of 1532. There is no evidence that Henry VIII and Anne Boleyn had sexual relations prior to the trip to Calais in 1532 in anticipation of their upcoming wedding.

As the sweating sickness abated from England in 1528, the Pope sent a representative to England to act in his stead and hold a trial of the royal marriage. This was Cardinal Lorenzo Campeggio. He would carry a commission from Pope Clement VII to try the marriage and make a decision on its legitimacy. The king wanted the legate to believe that his arguments for an annulment came solely from the pricking of his own conscience over the validity of the marriage, and not from his affections for, and desire to marry, Anne Boleyn so 'his sweetheart was sent home, and he played man and wife with Katherine'.[48] This must have been a hugely worrying time for Anne, with her future hanging in the balance, and Henry playing happy families with his wife. We know that Anne worried that Henry would return to Katherine and forsake her. These fears must have resurfaced during this period. Henry VIII did continue to write to Anne and keep her updated on how things progressed, in one letter reporting that:

> The legate whom we most desire arrived at Paris on Sunday or Monday last past, so that I trust by next Monday to hear of his arrival at Calais, and then I trust within awhile after to enjoy that which I have so longed for, to God's pleasure, and both our comforts.[49]

Henry wanted Anne to know that progress was being made towards their own marriage. But it was at a slower pace than either of them wanted or envisaged. By 1529, the pair had likely been betrothed for two years and could reasonably have expected to have married already and started to produce children. A step closer to an annulment was still a step closer to them being together. It was a form of reassurance to Anne that the king was still committed to their relationship, no matter the difficulties or barriers put in their way. It also demonstrates that Anne was an active political player in the 'Great Matter', being kept up to date on developments and discussing what was going on with the king to form their strategy. Anne was 'at the forefront of the debates and "strategies and stratagems" that would resolve the king's "Great Matter", proving herself to be an astute political player'.[50] Henry's reference to 'God's pleasure' in his letter moreover implies that he believed that his annulment and subsequent remarriage were what God wanted for him, to give him a son to continue the succession, which he knew could not have with Katherine of Aragon any longer. Anne Boleyn was the solution to his problems and his fears.

This legatine trial in 1529 was a major step forward in the 'Great Matter' even though it would not provide Henry with the outcome and the certainty that he craved in order to move on to a new marriage with Anne Boleyn. In the annulment case, Henry VIII 'adopted a scatter-fire approach to his task of seeking an annulment, attacking a vast array of targets, hoping that at least one shot might reach its mark'.[51] He was disorganised in many ways, not focusing on a single argument, but marshalling every possible argument, some of which did not work together and may in fact have jeopardised the validity of his case. Henry really hoped that this public trial would be the tactic to work, to confirm the scruples of his conscience and prove his own right. He wanted the Pope (or his representative) to tell Katherine of Aragon that she was wrong, and in a public manner which could leave no doubt as to the validity of his new marriage and their offspring. But an annulment would not be so easy to gain, and an agreement to marry did not easily turn into a marriage.

Chapter 5

Divorce Versus Annulment

Had Henry VIII always intended to gain an annulment as if the marriage had never existed? Or had he initially wanted a divorce, to separate from Katherine of Aragon but leave the legitimacy of their daughter intact? It seems that, by the time official wheels were put in motion, it was an annulment that the king wanted, 'not in the modern sense a divorce'.[1] Perhaps he had considered the notion of a divorce and leaving Princess Mary's legitimacy intact, but it seems unlikely. Henry came to believe that his marriage to Katherine was null and void because of her first marriage to his brother, Prince Arthur. If this was his belief and his argument, then a divorce in the modern way of thinking made no sense. It needed to be a fresh start. An annulment would leave him with a more-or-less clean slate to start again with a new wife and, hopefully, legitimate sons. Henry does not seem to have even considered the idea that Katherine of Aragon and Princess Mary could stand against him. He seems to have assumed that they would obey his wishes.

There was a precedent of royal kings getting annulments. Louis XII of France, when he became king in 1498, annulled his marriage to his first wife, Jeanne de Valois. She later founded the Order of the Annunciation of the Blessed Virgin Mary. Perhaps this is where Henry VIII got the idea for Katherine of Aragon to allow the annulment and retreat to a nunnery. Henry may have believed that Katherine would see this as a respectable way to end the marriage and allow the king to remarry and have a son. But this is not how Katherine saw it. She would be queen right up until her dying day in her eyes, whatever Henry said. Henry's sister, Margaret, dowager Queen of Scotland, had also annulled her second marriage, thanks to the Pope. The English king himself had expressed outrage over his sister's attempt to get her marriage dissolved. Henry VIII may have assumed with these precedents and, in his eyes, his own strong arguments, that it would be easy to get his own annulment.

Henry VIII's 'Great Matter' was not about obtaining a divorce from Katherine of Aragon, but an annulment to say that the marriage had never been valid and was in fact null and void from the beginning. The king believed this was the case as he and Katherine had offended God by marrying, as they were within the forbidden degrees of affinity. Katherine's previous marriage to Prince Arthur made her Henry's sister-in-law. They did obtain a dispensation from the Pope at the time to allow their betrothal and subsequent marriage, but the king and his advisers believed they could argue that this was faulty, and that the Pope could not dispense from such an impediment. This impediment and invalidity was supposedly proven by the fact that Henry VIII and Katherine of Aragon had no surviving sons, only a single living daughter, Mary. Henry took childlessness to mean a lack of sons, interpreting things in a way which would most benefit him. Henry VIII's 'handling of the affair was often clumsy and even perverse' but an argument can in fact be made, even a 'strong defence', that his marriage to Katherine was invalid and that the Pope had no power to dispense it.[2] It has even been argued that the bull broke new ground and 'might not have been issued had all the facts been known'.[3] Henry did have a valid argument, but the timing and international situation was against him.

Henry VIII took his guidance over the validity of his marriage from the book of Leviticus in the Old Testament, which said that:

> And if a man shall take his brother's wife, it is an unclean thing: he hath uncovered his brother's nakedness; they shall be childless.[4]

Henry VIII did not count his daughter, Mary, as an heir as he believed that women could not rule, and he took children to mean heirs. With Empress Matilda being the only example of attempted female rule, Henry did not seriously contemplate the idea of a woman on the English throne – 'no second Matilda was wanted'.[5] It is easy to imagine that Henry VIII saw female rule as an open door to civil war. But it would be Henry VIII and Katherine of Aragon's daughter, Mary, as Mary I, who would become England's first crowned regnant queen.

However, things were not as straightforward as the king might have liked to believe with his Leviticus argument, as there is a conflicting passage in the book of Deuteronomy. Both sides of the annulment debate 'might be accused of playing fast-and-loose with their translations and implicit assumptions', taking what they wanted from them and discarding anything which did not work with their arguments.[6] The passage in Deuteronomy says that:

> If brethren dwell together, and one of them die, and have no child, the wife of the dead shall not marry without unto a stranger: her husband's brother shall go in unto her, and take her to him to wife, and perform the duty of an husband's brother unto her. [7]

This passage effectively says that, if a man died, his brother should marry the widow to honour his dead brother. This directly contradicts Leviticus, so it seems little wonder that the arguments in the annulment case were not straightforward. It could be argued that 'the contentious verse does not on close examination cover Henry's case at all'.[8] The part in question is 'if brethren dwell together' as it could be argued that Henry and Arthur did not live together, with Henry in and around London with his sisters, and Arthur at Ludlow in Wales. Henry could thus argue that the Deuteronomy passage did not apply in his case. However, it could be argued that the Catholic Church determined which biblical provisions it regarded as being binding on Catholics and which were vestiges of Jewish observances that did not apply to Christians – Henry VIII and his supporters argued that Catholics never considered themselves bound by the provisions in Deuteronomy.[9] This could be his way of explaining why the quote in Leviticus took precedence over Deuteronomy and why the passage in Deuteronomy could not be used against his arguments for an annulment from Katherine of Aragon.

It is often asserted that Henry VIII did not go into his annulment case with any real coherent argument, assuming that the Pope would grant his desire without question. Henry may have believed that the Pope would grant his annulment, but that does not mean that he did not carefully consider the arguments he would put forward and take advice. It can therefore be argued that Henry VIII's annulment case was in fact coherent. Virginia Murphy claims that the king 'consistently attacked his marriage on grounds which disputed the Pope's authority to dispense, asserting that his union contravened divine law and could in no circumstances be dispensed from' and that it was 'a policy personally directed by the king'.[10] Henry VIII was not going to let anyone else direct this case, which he saw as crucial to his own happiness and the security of the realm. He was involved in compiling arguments and in every stage of the process across the years from 1526 to 1533 when he married Anne, and beyond into the Reformation years. One suggestion which was put forward was the 'embarrassing offer of a retroactive dispensation convalidating the disputed marriage'.[11] This was not what Henry wanted, and it did not deal with the issue of whether the Pope could dispense the affinity between the king and Katherine, instead adding another debated dispensation into the already confusing issue.

One of the central issues of the annulment case was whether Katherine of Aragon's first marriage to Henry VIII's elder brother, Prince Arthur, was in fact consummated in 1501. The pair were only married for around six months, before Arthur's death at Ludlow Castle on 2 April 1502. This is more widely discussed in chapter 1. Katherine herself always asserted that her first marriage was not consummated, although the testimony of some of Arthur's gentlemen suggest that it was, although this testimony was only given at the Blackfriars trial in 1529, over twenty-five years after the event. J. F. Hadwin writes that 'the strict application of canonical procedures in the case would appear to favour a verdict that Arthur and Katherine had indeed consummated their union'.[12] There is a lot of debate over the subject, and how it applies to the Leviticus ruling in the Bible, but we will likely never know the truth. To maintain the Anglo-Spanish alliance, Katherine was then betrothed to Prince Henry after Arthur's death, though it would take many years to come to fruition and Katherine was left in limbo during this period.

Historian Patrick Williams has asserted that it was Charles V's triumphs in Italy in the mid-1520s that 'ultimately cost Henry VIII his chance of winning an annulment or divorce and led in turn to the dreadful bitterness of the fate' suffered by Katherine of Aragon.[13] Katherine would die in exile at Kimbolton Castle, unable to see her only child or the man she still believed was her husband, but proclaiming herself queen to the end. Katherine's fate in the 'Great Matter' was a 'major political concern' to many.[14] She was also very popular with the people, seemingly unlike her replacement, Anne Boleyn. If Katherine was set aside, there were concerns over a possible war between England and the Holy Roman Empire, of which Katherine's nephew,

Charles V, was the emperor, which could then affect the rest of Europe. The possibility of Henry VIII petitioning for an annulment of his marriage to Katherine could serve as a threat to the emperor and encouragement to France which was a 'useful diplomatic lever'.[15] It gave Henry VIII more power in European affairs. If the annulment was granted in England without the Pope, then the Catholic Church would suffer in England, and its authority called into question, as was happening in different parts of Europe, including within the Holy Roman Empire, particularly in territories which are now part of modern-day Germany. There were wide-ranging potential political, foreign, and religious consequences for what might at first seem to be a simple question over the validity of a royal marriage.

Cardinal Thomas Wolsey convened an ecclesiastical trial in secret, beginning on 17 May 1527, at his residence at Westminster, to hear the evidence for and against the annulment of Henry VIII's marriage to Katherine of Aragon. He may have first been made aware of the king's scruples sometime in 1526, although the exact timing of the king confiding in his chief minister is uncertain. This would make sense if Anne Boleyn committed to Henry around New Year 1527. Katherine did not attend this first trial, seemingly unaware of it until it had begun without her. It was interesting because Henry VIII was not portrayed as the petitioner for an annulment of his marriage, but as the accused or victim of a miscarriage of justice. He was accused of cohabiting with Katherine without a legal marriage, effectively living in sin with his dead brother's widow. Wolsey went to great lengths to conceal the hearing, but the Spanish ambassador knew about it by the following day. The ambassador, Inigo de Mendoza, wrote to Emperor Charles V on 18 May that he:

> Hears on reliable authority that the Legate, as the finishing stroke to all his iniquities, has been scheming to bring about the Queen's divorce. She is so full of apprehension on this account that she has not ventured to speak with him (Mendoça). It is added that the King is so bent on this divorce that he has secretly assembled certain bishops and lawyers that they may sign a declaration to the effect that his marriage with the Queen is null and void on account of her having been his brother's wife. It is therefore to be feared that either the Pope will be induced by some false statement to side against the Queen, or that the Cardinal, in virtue of his legatine powers, may

> take some step fatal to the said marriage. He (Mendoça) is perfectly aware, though the Queen herself has not ventured and does not venture to speak to him on the subject, that all her hope rests, after God on the Emperor.[16]

The fact that the Spanish ambassador knew about this 'secret' court the day after it happened suggests that Wolsey's attempts at secrecy were not successful. It also meant that Katherine was aware of what was going on basically from the start, and was determined to let her nephew know, grasping that he could hopefully protect her and influence the Pope against an annulment. It would reflect badly on him to see his aunt removed from her position as queen of England and his cousin, Mary, replaced in the line of succession. Mendoza suspected some form of foul play would happen to push the annulment through. It seems that, right from the beginning, Katherine was aware that she would not get a fair hearing in England. Even a preliminary secret trial was portraying Henry as a victim. This hearing would, however, fail to reach a conclusion on the validity of the royal marriage – Cardinal Wolsey's first failure on the path to his eventual fall, as he could not give the king what he wanted.

An English envoy, William Knight, was sent to the Pope with an annulment petition, reaching Rome in December 1527 and having a meeting with Pope Clement VII. A revised document was signed on 23 December 1527, but Knight failed to understand that this bull was not what he had been sent to acquire – the bull would allow Henry VIII to marry Anne Boleyn, but only if and when his marriage to Katherine of Aragon was declared null and void.[17] It is described as a 'conditional dispensation' as it depended on the first marriage being annulled before it could be used:

> Proposed bull of dispensation for Henry VIII., in case his marriage with Katharine, his brother's widow, be pronounced unlawful, to marry another, even if she have contracted marriage with another man, provided it be not consummated, and even if she be of the second degree of consanguinity, or of the first degree of affinity, *ex quocumque licito seu illicito coitu*; in order to prevent uncertainty in the succession, which in past times has been the occasion of war.[18]

This was a hugely important step for the king. The crux of the annulment case is included in the bull, that Katherine was Henry's brother's widow.

But the bull is also interesting because it sets out the degree of affinity in which Henry VIII and his planned second wife, Anne Boleyn, were related and why Henry VIII had sought the dispensation for the marriage – 'to prevent uncertainty in the succession' and to avert a future war. The Wars of the Roses were only just leaving living memory and how the uncertainty of the succession had caused violence and war, only ended by Henry VIII's own father, Henry VII. The bull suggests that a prior relationship of Anne Boleyn's was a concern to the king – to have contracted a marriage or formal betrothal with another man. There may also be a reference to Henry's prior relationship with Mary Boleyn '*ex quocumque licito seu illicito coitu*' meaning from licit or illicit intercourse. Henry wanted to make sure that every possibility was covered, even though he was currently contesting his marriage to Katherine of Aragon based on a faulty dispensation. He wanted to ensure that the same questions about the validity of a dispensation could not be levied against his marriage to Anne Boleyn and their heirs.

Pope Clement VII wrote to Cardinal Thomas Wolsey, Henry VIII's right-hand man, in July 1529 to say he had 'long foreseen the difficulties of gratifying the King and Wolsey, and cannot do so without manifest danger, and causing a scandal to Christendom'.[19] It would not be possible in the annulment case to satisfy everyone, and there was a possibility of some kind of war taking place as a result, hence the 'manifest danger'. Scandal would be the putting aside of a very popular queen with powerful backing, to replace her with someone who was considered unworthy by many to hold the title of queen, with next to no international or royal connections. As it turned out, the danger was in fact to Cardinal Wolsey, and to the religious harmony of England rather than a foreign war. Pope Clement did technically have the power to overturn the original dispensation for the marriage, but he had reservations about 'failing to give deference to a recent public ruling by a predecessor Pope'.[20] This would undermine the papal power to dispense against affinity and could call into question other dispensations issued across Europe, and thus potentially the legitimacy of heirs. It was a much wider issue than a question over one royal marriage. Once Henry VIII had coalesced his opinions on the annulment, and particularly on the invalidity of the dispensation for his marriage to Katherine of Aragon, these were 'reinforced at a critical point by the presence of Anne [Boleyn], whereafter vacillation was at an end' for Henry.[21] But, the Pope would not gratify the king or Anne Boleyn, and it would take time for him to issue the sentence which would satisfy Katherine of Aragon in her belief that her marriage was valid. A sentence that Henry VIII would ignore. In the meantime, there was a lot of confusion, upset, and frustration as the legatine court failed to reach a conclusion and things stalled. Katherine was being pushed aside and gradually isolated as Anne was treated more like a queen and moved into her place.

English emissaries in Rome in 1528 had written to Wolsey in England to say that 'Gardiner with Fox and Sir Gregory [Casale] have been with the Pope, telling him we had despatched our post to report his Holiness's good mind, and that we expected short expedition to the satisfaction of the King and Wolsey'.[22] There was pressure on the Pope to satisfy the English king in his desires, and the envoys from England were well aware of the king's desire for a speedy resolution. The longer matters dragged on unresolved, the greater the danger to Wolsey as well. Henry VIII was not a patient man. The emissaries were using whatever means necessary. The response detailed in the letter was that:

> His Holiness said it was a question of law, in which he must depend on the opinion of learned men whom he had consulted on the point. He had pressed them to come to a determination with speed whether the marriage should be declared nought, and the dispensation void. Gardiner hoped the Pope would accept the evidences of the King's book, and Wolsey's relation of the opinions of learned men in those parts ... He was sorry and ashamed that he had no learning in the law himself, and feared his most trusted councillors would oppose whatever was done without their advice, even if it were right. But if he could get any comfort of these men he would obtain their opinions in the King's favor, to be published hereafter.[23]

Gardiner, Foxe, and Casale's report suggested that the Pope was delaying as much as he could, saying that he had no real knowledge of the law and had to rely on others, who often disputed and disagreed with him, but that he had to listen to their advice. He was not taking any responsibility for the king's case himself but putting it onto others, which is a pattern we see throughout the 'Great Matter', with various people not wishing to take responsibility for decisions or actions. The early quote puts the king and Wolsey together as a pair, almost as if they were of equal importance in this matter. The king wanted the annulment resolved as soon as possible so that he could remarry, but Wolsey must have realised the danger that his career, and possibly his life, were in at this time if he failed to deliver what the king wanted. There was a lot riding on the Pope's decision. But the Pope was refusing to act for fear of offending one party or the other.

Just prior to the legatine court opening in 1529 at Blackfriars, a second dispensation, or brief, was produced, which had been found in the archives in Spain. It had been sent to the dying Isabella I of Castile in 1504, Katherine of Aragon's mother. The brief had been granted by Pope Julius II before Katherine of Aragon and Prince Arthur Tudor's marriage in 1501 and it complicated Henry VIII's case for an annulment. It has been argued that divorce proceedings were effectively halted when this brief came to light and surprised the English.[24] The English lawyers needed to re-evaluate and re-structure their arguments in light of this brief, as it made good many of the deficiencies in the original dispensation for Katherine and Arthur's marriage, which Henry VIII had based his arguments for an annulment on. The English wanted it declared a forgery. 'Immense efforts' were made in England to seize the brief, however they could, though it was in the possession of Katherine's nephew, Charles V, in Spain.[25] He would not let it out of his sight. The Spanish allowed the English ambassador to see and examine the document but would not give it into his possession, for fear it would be destroyed to strengthen Henry's case. The push to have the brief declared a forgery was because Henry VIII's argument for an annulment was based on the previous marriage of his wife to his brother. If it could be seen that the papacy had granted a dispensation and made good any defects in that original dispensation, then the king's argument was completely undermined. The Spanish refused to give up the brief, thinking, probably correctly, that it would be destroyed as soon as the English got their hands on it. Henry VIII did not want there to be any chance of his annulment not being granted, and the brief had complicated things. Historian Herbert Thurston said that palaeographic experts of the day (the 1930s was when his article was published) pronounced the brief 'unquestionably authentic'.[26]

The legatine court would either grant the king's annulment as he so desired or would revoke the case to Rome for a papal judgement.

Armed with this brief, Katherine of Aragon began a 'war of attrition', sending a message to her nephew, Charles V, asking the Pope to halt divorce proceedings, and appeared before Cardinal Campeggio and denied in the confessional that her marriage to Prince Arthur was ever consummated.[27] Katherine urged Campeggio to tell the whole world what she had divulged to him. The brief itself was 'substantially identical' with the original dispensation whose validity was undisputed. There is, however, one 'significant divergence' in the brief compared to the dispensation, as the brief takes the consummation of Katherine of Aragon and Prince Arthur's marriage for granted, whereas the dispensation itself leaves a little room for doubt with the simple word 'perhaps'.[28] If there was room for doubt in the dispensation, then it could be argued that it was not valid. However, the brief deals with this uncertainty and adds clarity. Henry VIII claimed that the marriage of himself to Katherine was invalid because the dispensation had been granted on the assumption that her previous marriage to Prince Arthur was not consummated and, had it been issued under these terms, there was 'serious ground to contest its validity'.[29] The brief covers the alternate viewpoint, though in some ways it seems too good to be true for Katherine of Aragon that the brief surfaced just when she needed it, and it manages to make good all of the deficiencies in the original. Why were the English not aware of this brief at the time? This is probably a question which was also asked in the late 1520s, though perhaps Henry VII had been aware of its existence, as it was he who negotiated the betrothal with Katherine's parents, Ferdinand and Isabella. Maybe any reference to it was lost by accident, or later suppressed on purpose, somewhere in the archives.

There were lots of letters written about the betrothal of Henry and Katherine between 1502 when Prince Arthur died and Henry VIII's accession in 1509. Some of these focused on the dispensation and the precise wording, especially considering consummation of the marriage of Katherine and Arthur. In a letter from King Ferdinand of Aragon in August 1503, considering the dispensation for the marriage of Henry and his daughter, Katherine, he said that:

> In the clause of the treaty which mentions the dispensation of the Pope, it is stated that the Princess Katharine consummated her marriage with Prince Arthur. The fact, however, is, that although they were wedded, Prince Arthur and the Princess Katharine never consummated the marriage. It is well known in England that the Princess is still a virgin. But as the English are much disposed to cavil, it has seemed to be more prudent to provide for the case as though the marriage had been consummated, and the dispensation of the Pope must be in perfect keeping with the said clause of the treaty. The right of succession depends on the undoubted legitimacy of the marriage.[30]

The Spanish monarchs wanted there to be no question over the legitimacy of the marriage, so although they believed that Katherine was still a virgin on Prince Arthur's death, they were covering the bases to make sure that the marriage could not be questioned later on, nor the legitimacy of any children born from it. As it happened, both the marriage and legitimacy of their daughter would be the source of a lot of scrutiny, questioning, imprisonment, and even executions. Henry VIII was determined to get his own way and did not care what obstacles were put in his way. He would annul his marriage to Katherine of Aragon and marry Anne Boleyn in hopes of producing a male heir.

At least three drafts of commissions survive which, it was hoped, the Pope could be persuaded to sign, which would become known as the decretal commission. This would not give Cardinals Wolsey and Campeggio the power to judge the case, as that was outlined in the official commission. What the decretal commission did was to set out the path to be followed, and the specific issues to be resolved before a decision could be reached on the annulment case. The official decretal commission was destroyed by Cardinal Lorenzo Campeggio, probably not long after he had shown it to Henry VIII, in accordance with probable instructions from the Pope. Pope Clement VII was being asked to commit 'an indefensible piece of legal trickery' when approached with the decretal commission.[31] But the decretal is also 'one of the most extraordinary legal documents ever drafted'.[32] The commission itself does not survive, as previously explained, but we have to assume it was similar to the surviving drafts. When the English envoys had taken these drafts to the Pope to try and persuade him to sign it, 'he did not commit himself to any step that was really irretrievable' but he did make an 'unwise and weak concession' which he said afterwards he would have 'chopped off one of his fingers to recall'.[33] Was this an admission that the Spanish Brief was a forgery? When Katherine of Aragon produced the brief from Spain, a new decretal commission needed to be issued as the brief was not mentioned in the original, which would again slow the process down, which frustrated Henry VIII and Anne Boleyn, as it would need to go back to Rome.[34] A new commission needed fresh papal approval.

The draft of a decretal commission which survives, declares that the Spanish Brief was a forgery with the final section declaring that examining the brief, including the letter, seal, and signature, as well as the writing itself, found many things which demonstrated its falsity. The Latin phrase used in the brief 'de falsitate redarguendum' means to refute on the grounds of falsehood while another phrase, 'pro falso et nullo reputandum ducentes', means to consider false or void.[35] The brief that Katherine of Aragon hoped would help her case had been declared false and void by the Pope she wanted to declare her marriage valid. It complicated her case, certainly, and may have helped Henry's although things were far from certain as to how the case would turn out. Katherine still had powerful support, and Henry was jumping between different arguments to try and figure out which one would get him what he wanted.

The crux of the case in the decretal commission appears to have depended on three things: whether the Anglo-Spanish alliance could have been maintained without the marriage of Henry VIII and Katherine of Aragon; whether Henry VIII did not really want the marriage in the first place; and whether named people died before the bull came into effect. If it could be found that the three points could be answered in the affirmative, then the dispensation granted by Pope Julius II allowing the marriage was to be pronounced null and void. If the dispensation was null and void, then the marriage of Henry VIII and Katherine of Aragon was also to be declared invalid.[36] The commission was therefore concerned with issues of fact and not the theological or canonical impediments. This is what Henry concerned himself with in the Leviticus versus Deuteronomy argument he put forward, over the implications of the marriage of Prince Arthur to Katherine. It would then throw into question the power of popes to dispense over issues such as affinity. It was accepted at the time that the Pope could dispense for marriage with a deceased wife's sister, or a deceased husband's brother, despite Henry VIII later trying to establish the opposite.[37] This perhaps weakened the king's arguments because it was an established precedent, and the two passages in Leviticus and Deuteronomy contradicted each other so even that was not clear. Henry VIII would use what he needed to in order to get his marriage to Katherine of Aragon annulled and allow him to remarry and produce a male heir.

The court to judge the legitimacy of the marriage of Henry VIII and Katherine of Aragon opened at Blackfriars in London on 31 May 1529. Cardinal Lorenzo Campeggio had arrived in England in October 1528, but his health problems and legal wrangling meant that the court did not open for seven months after his arrival. This was a 'unique event in English history – the reigning king and queen summoned to appear at a public trial concerning the legitimacy of their long marriage'.[38] Nothing like this had ever happened before, and it would not happen again. After the trial failed, Henry would never again put any of his marriages in the public eye in the same way. Katherine had already declared that she was petitioning for the case to be revoked to Rome, as she did not believe that she would receive a fair and impartial hearing in England.

Katherine only appeared in the court for the first day of regular proceedings, accompanied by one of her staunchest supporters who would die in her defence, John Fisher, Bishop of Rochester. When called to confirm her presence, Katherine instead stood up and walked over to where her husband was sitting, fell to her knees before him and gave a heartfelt speech. Katherine pleaded for the king to allow her to have 'justice and right' as a 'poor woman and a stranger born out of your dominion', that:

> I take God and all the world to witness that I have been to you a true, humble and obedient wife, ever conformable to your will and pleasure, that never said or did anything to the contrary thereof, being always well pleased and contented with all things wherein ye had any delight or dalliance, whether it were in little or much I never grudged in word or countenance or showed a visage or spark of discontentation. I loved all those whom ye loved only for your sake, whether I had cause or no; and whether they were my friends or

> my enemies. This twenty years I have been your true wife or more, and by me ye have had divers children, although it hath pleased God to call them out of this world, which hath been no default in me. And when ye had me at the first, I take God to be my judge, I was a true maid without touch of man; and whether it be true or no, I put it to your conscience.[39]

In ending her speech, Katherine asked to be allowed some time to see how her friends in Spain would advise her, then committed her cause to God. She got up and curtseyed to the king, then left the court. She would not return. Her refusal to return to the trial would have been 'legally sufficient' for judgement to be given in Henry's favour.[40] Katherine of Aragon had made her position very clear – she was the true wife and queen of Henry VIII, and no one would convince her otherwise. She had been a virgin when she came to his bed, hence her first marriage to Prince Arthur was unconsummated and invalid, meaning that the Leviticus prohibition did not apply in their case. She also mentions their many children, evidence they were not childless, though God had called the children away from them which was not her fault. Katherine alludes in her speech to the fact that the king had affairs and that she did not like or appreciate some of his advisors, probably hinting at Wolsey more than anyone else, but that she accepted them as his friends in her position as his wife to honour and obey him. Katherine directly comments on many of the things that Henry found as a fault in his first wife, and counteracts them, undermining the king's entire argument.

In order to try and settle the matter of the validity of the royal marriage, Cardinal Campeggio did initially intend to avoid the issue altogether. A suggestion was made that Katherine of Aragon could instead enter a religious community of her choosing and leave the king free to remarry. This would also leave their daughter's legitimacy intact. The Spanish ambassador reported that:

> … in order to do away with the scruples and other greater evils which the discord between her (the Queen) and her husband the King was likely to produce, were they to live together, and in order also to remove any difficulties as to the succession to the crown of England (uviese menos inconvenientes), he (the Pope) thought that the best expedient to be adopted was that she (the Queen) should profess in some religious community, and take vows of

> perpetual chastity. That since Her Highness had already reached the third and last period of natural life, and had spent the first two setting a good example [of virtue] to the world, she would thus put a seal to all the good actions of her life, and could besides prevent by such religious profession the many and incalculable evils likely to arise from such matrimonial discord.[41]

John Guy and Julia Fox argue that Campeggio knew that the potential legality of this solution was questionable without annulment proceedings taking place 'but it wasted time'.[42] Campeggio appeared to hope that the longer proceedings dragged on, the king would change his mind, or that the Pope himself would intervene. If Katherine herself could be persuaded to accept the annulment, then that could have simplified matters as Henry would have been free to remarry and had Katherine voluntarily stepped down from her marriage then it could not have offended her nephew, the emperor.

On 23 July 1529, the Blackfriars trial convened for the final time. Henry VIII expected to be given a final judgement on his annulment, which he believed would leave him free to finally marry Anne Boleyn. However, Cardinal Campeggio adjourned the trial without giving a verdict, claiming that the court in Rome was now in summer recess and that the matter needed the consultation of Pope Clement VII. Henry VIII must have been absolutely furious and frustrated, as must Anne Boleyn. Katherine of Aragon may have seen it as a vindication of her arguments. Though the matter was far from over. It may be that Cardinal Campeggio had received secret instructions from the Pope which countermanded the terms of the written commission. Campeggio may have seen his duty to actually be as obstructive as possible, to delay things and not allow the court at Blackfriars to reach a final judgement.[43] Perhaps the Pope hoped that, with the passage of time, and the failure of the court to reach a judgement, the king would abandon his annulment and return to Katherine. This would not happen. J. F. Hadwin argues that 'with a better presentation of his cause, an unbiased court might well have concluded that, on canonical principles and precedents, the union with Katherine should not have been permitted'.[44] However, the international situation and the power of Emperor Charles V, prevented this verdict at the 1529 trial.

When the Blackfriars trial failed to give Henry VIII the desperately desired annulment, he turned to another possible solution – seeking the opinions of theologians at universities across Europe. This idea is often attributed to Thomas Cromwell and Thomas Cranmer, but Jerry Rabow believes that the king was intelligent and well-educated, so it is at least possible that, regardless of his actual beliefs, it was Henry himself who initially posited the idea to use theological grounds to annul his marriage.[45] It may have been that it was Cromwell and Cranmer who put Henry's wishes into action, and so became the source of blame by those who disagreed.

Thomas Cranmer was tutoring two boys in Waltham in summer 1529. The king was staying at Waltham Abbey nearby and, by chance, Stephen Gardiner and Edward Foxe, who had already travelled to Rome to see the Pope and try and persuade him to grant the annulment for the king, were billeted at the house where Cranmer was living. Cranmer suggested to the pair that Europe's universities be canvassed to gather opinions about the annulment case.[46] It might not provide a certain answer, but it would show which way the wind was blowing in terms of support for or opposition to the king's ideas and beliefs. It could potentially add more weight to the arguments Henry VIII was making to the Pope or could provide a potential different avenue for the annulment, though at this point Henry was most likely not seriously thinking about breaking with the Roman Catholic Church. That was still another three years away.

After the marriage of Henry VIII and Anne Boleyn had been accomplished in 1533, and after the birth of Princess Elizabeth, the Imperial ambassador, Eustace Chapuys, wrote to Charles V to say that Katherine of Aragon,

> … has expressly begged me to supplicate you that, omitting all other devices, you would procure a brief decision of the principal business; and if this be done, the King will listen to reason and return to the right way, notwithstanding the bravado and obstinacy which he has hitherto shown, and that for this no war will be required. As to this last point, however great the credit of the Queen may be in England, I do not think there is any one who would pledge himself for it, considering the great obstinacy and blindness of the King, which increases every day.[47]

Even once the annulment had been declared by the English Church, Katherine still believed that, if the Pope declared in her favour, the king would return to her and leave Anne Boleyn in order to avoid war. Katherine seemed to understand how to manage and placate Henry early in their marriage, but once the 'Great Matter' happened and their wants diverged so greatly, Katherine failed to grasp that Henry wanted a son more than anything, and that she was in the way of that. Katherine believed that a woman could rule, where Henry could not accept that. Katherine was right, that a woman could rule, but it would be Elizabeth and not Mary who would be considered England's first successful female ruler.

Henry VIII's 'Great Matter' was an annulment case rather than a divorce – he wanted the marriage ended as if it had never been. Of the king's eventual six marriages, three would end like this, including his marriage to Anne Boleyn after just three years. Henry wanted an acknowledgement from the Pope, from European kings, and from his own people, as well as from Katherine herself and their daughter Mary, that the marriage had never been legal and valid. He saw Katherine as nothing more than the dowager Princess of Wales, widow of his brother Arthur, and his own daughter Mary as a bastard, unfit to be the heir to the English throne. Henry turned the lives of these women upside down, all in his quest to beget a male heir which he believed England needed to be secure. Henry VIII believed he was acting in the best interests of England in trying to obtain an annulment and remarry, but his annulment case changed the face of the country forever.

Chapter 6

The Fall of Thomas Wolsey

Henry VIII expected his chief minister, Cardinal Thomas Wolsey, to be able to obtain an annulment of his marriage to Katherine of Aragon fairly quickly and without too much fuss. Where there was a political reason, annulment or divorce could be granted, possibly by offering a 'bribe' to the Pope to state a technicality in the dispensation which made the marriage invalid.[1] However, in the 'Great Matter', the international situation worked against both Wolsey and Henry. Charles V, Katherine's nephew, was gaining control in Italy, and over the Pope which complicated matters. Wolsey had also made a powerful group of enemies during his rise to, and time in, power, including Charles Brandon, 1st Duke of Suffolk, and Thomas Howard, 3rd Duke of Norfolk. The latter also happened to be Anne Boleyn's maternal uncle, and the former was the king's brother-in-law. With these powerful forces arrayed against him, did Thomas Wolsey stand a chance of remaining in the king's favour?

Katherine of Aragon had powerful connections of her own. She was a part of the house of Trastámara, and a daughter of the Spanish monarchs Isabella I of Castile and León, and Ferdinand II of Aragon. Her nephew, Charles V, was the Holy Roman Emperor and thus the most powerful man in Europe. These connections meant that it would not be easy for Henry VIII to annul his marriage to Katherine, especially not when the Imperial forces sacked Rome in 1527, and Pope Clement VII effectively became a prisoner of the emperor. The Pope would not annul a marriage which would anger the emperor while he remained his prisoner. Charles V would not easily allow his aunt to be humiliated and put aside, especially if she did not want it. It could have been a very different situation had Katherine of Aragon agreed to the annulment and retreated to a religious community of her choice, as was once proposed to her by Wolsey and Cardinal Lorenzo Campeggio in 1529.

Thomas Wolsey is thought to have been born around 1472 or 1473 in Ipswich, Suffolk, and he attended Magdalen College, Oxford. After completing a degree in Theology, he was ordained as a priest and went on to become the Master of Magdalen College School, then dean of divinity, though he would soon be looking for another living. It has been suggested that the reason Wolsey needed to look for other employment was because he was ousted from Magdalen College after having spent the college's money on building works without authorisation.[2] We see from Wolsey's later development of Hampton Court Palace that he liked to spend money on building works and creating great palaces for himself to live in and entertain the king. It is an early insight into what mattered to him. He would become a rector at Limington in Somerset before the beginning of his court career. In 1507, Wolsey became chaplain to Henry VII. His court career would only take off from here, as he made himself indispensable to Henry VII and then his son, Henry VIII. Historian David Starkey describes Wolsey's personality as follows:

> … there was a tendency to act first and seek authority afterwards; an insatiable love of grand building; a brusqueness with his betters; and a flamboyance and self-indulgence, which can also be seen as a huge capacity for enjoyment. His most important trait, the sheer, overwhelming force of his personality, needed a larger field of action fully to appear.[3]

Starkey writes this about Wolsey's early life and career under Henry VII, but it is reflected in his later life and career under Henry VIII as well. Hampton Court Palace stands, though now much altered by Henry VIII and then by the Stuarts and Georgians, as a testament to Wolsey's building ambitions. He did appear to have a very forceful personality, could guide Henry VIII the way he wanted him to go, and rose quite quickly in the Roman Catholic Church, which is in part what led to his downfall.

Wolsey was good at reading Henry VIII. He understood that the king was 'intelligent and well educated, but he had a short concentration span and was easily bored'.[4] There were other things that Henry wanted to be doing, like hunting and jousting. His father had restricted these activities when he was Prince of Wales, so now Henry was king, he was taking advantage of being able to do whatever he wanted. Understanding the king was the key to knowing how to aid him and becoming indispensable to him. Wolsey knew this and did everything he could to ensure that he was the one that the king relied on. He made sure to read all documents that were sent to the king, via him, and then offer the king a list of options where a decision was required, weighting them towards his own preference or solution.[5] These actions that Wolsey took to lighten the load on the king meant that Henry was 'wonderly pleased' as he 'loved nothing worse than to be constrained to do any thing contrary to his royal will and pleasure'.[6] Wolsey intended to make himself indispensable to the king and he achieved it. He only fell from power when he failed to do what the king wanted. The annulment was one of the most important things the king ever asked of Wolsey, and he could not achieve it.

Here we will not examine the entirety of Henry VIII and Wolsey's relationship, but it is important to understand how the relationship between the pair progressed to where it was at the time of the annulment case, and why Wolsey had made enemies, particularly of the nobility. He had risen from common roots to a place at the centre of the English court and government, and many nobles, like Thomas Howard, 3rd Duke of Norfolk, Charles Brandon, 1st Duke of Suffolk, and Edward Stafford, 3rd Duke of Buckingham resented this. They believed that the nobility should be advising the king, not those of common stock, regardless of how intelligent, hard-working, and diligent they were. These types of prejudices would later also affect the career of Wolsey's protégé, Thomas Cromwell, through the 1530s up to his dramatic fall in 1540.

Thomas Wolsey had been created a cardinal by the Pope in 1515. When the cardinal's hat was received in England, Wolsey was 'brought to London with suche triumphe as though the greatest prince of Christendom had bene come into the realme', but that people 'almost hated hym and disdayned hym'.[7] Hall's Chronicle was not published until the late 1540s, but Hall was alive throughout Henry VIII's reign, so he may have heard talk over what people thought of Wolsey and his influence. It is possible that this was written with hindsight, knowing what happened to Wolsey, and that people did not actually dislike him so much at the beginning, though it is difficult to be sure. Courtiers and nobles certainly resented him by the end, believing that they should rightfully have the power that he had accumulated.

Henry VIII's book, *Assertio Septem Sacramentorum* (Defence of the Seven Sacraments), was published in summer 1521. This was the king's answer to Martin Luther and was a defence of the Roman Catholic Church and the position of the Pope. It now seems ironic, given how Henry would break with Rome, that he was so effusive in defence of the Pope but within a decade he would be considering dividing the English Church from the rest of Christendom. There has been a question over whether the king himself actually wrote it, or whether the author was actually Wolsey.[8] The book had over twenty editions and translations into Dutch, German, Italian, and French, in the sixteenth century alone and was presented to Pope Leo X in October 1521. The Pope, as a reward for Henry VIII's loyalty, awarded him the title of 'Defender of the Faith'. Historian Phil Roberts suggests that the Pope put the matter of a title to the cardinals, who gave various suggestions including 'Rex Fidelis' (King of the Faith) and 'Orthodoxus' (Right-Believing), which were then put to the king to choose the one he liked best.[9] Henry VIII was delighted with his new title, and likely Wolsey was pleased too, for his master.

With hindsight, Anne Boleyn is often seen as the root cause of Wolsey's fall from power in the late 1520s. Henry VIII wanted to make her his wife and queen and had asked Wolsey for an annulment of his marriage to his first wife, Katherine of Aragon, in order for this to happen, in hopes of producing a legitimate male heir. Whether the king's relationship with Anne or the idea of an annulment came first is unclear, though both came together in 1526 and 1527 as Anne committed to the king and Wolsey began investigations into the validity of the royal marriage. Anne Boleyn and Cardinal Wolsey had a history, if you believe Wolsey's gentleman usher, George Cavendish. Cavendish recounts that Wolsey had broken a betrothal between Anne and Henry Percy, heir to the Earl of Northumberland, due to the king's own interest in Anne, and that she bore a grudge against Wolsey as a result. Wolsey was furious that Percy and Anne had entered into an agreement or betrothal between themselves without permission because 'it flew in the face of his attempts to control noble marriages'.[10] There is no doubt that the amount of control the cardinal attempted to wield over their lives made the nobility resent him even more. Wolsey married Henry Percy off to Mary Talbot, daughter of the Earl of Shrewsbury, and the plan had been for Anne to marry James Butler, son of Piers Butler, and unite the claims to the earldom of Ormond, though this never came to pass. The implication of the end of the Percy relationship at Wolsey's hands, was that Anne Boleyn was waiting for her moment to bring Wolsey down.

Cavendish describes Anne Boleyn threatening the Cardinal in 1522 or 1523 when he was at the height of his power, as 'both unwise and childish, and Anne was neither'.[11] It is important to reiterate here that Anne could not have foreseen in the early 1520s that circumstances would evolve in such a way that Wolsey would be weakened and brought down before the end of the decade, or that she would be in a position to be able to carry out her earlier threat against him. Wolsey had seemed all-powerful. It has been suggested by Cavendish, that, with the end of her relationship with Percy, Anne bore a 'grudge … that in process of time burst out to the utter undoing of the cardinal'.[12] The likes of Thomas Howard, 3rd Duke of Norfolk, Thomas Boleyn, 1st Earl of Wiltshire and Ormond, and Charles Brandon, 1st Duke of Suffolk, also allegedly wanted to bring Wolsey down. They perceived 'the great affection that the king bare lovingly unto Mistress Anne Boleyn, fantasying in their heads that she should be for them a sufficient and an apt instrument to bring their malicious purpose to pass'.[13] The suggestion was that Anne was being used by the men around her in order to bring down Wolsey so that they could replace him and gain the power that they believed he had usurped. The account of George Cavendish describes how Anne spoke out against the cardinal to the king, asking 'what things hath he wrought within this realm to your great slander and dishonour' and 'is it not a marvellous thing to consider what debt and danger the cardinal hath brought you in with all your subjects?'.[14] Cavendish has Anne acting on the will of others, almost like they put words into her mouth, but Anne Boleyn had more agency than Cavendish gave her credit for. She likely would not have acted had she not wanted to, or if it had not been in her interests. Josephine Wilkinson argues that 'it is too simplistic to attribute Wolsey's downfall to the machinations of Anne Boleyn'.[15] This seems logical. Wolsey would not have fallen unless the king had desired it, no matter the influence of Anne Boleyn.

Probably sometime in 1526, Henry VIII told Cardinal Wolsey that he believed his marriage to Katherine of Aragon was invalid because she had previously been married to his brother, Arthur, and their sons had all died. Wolsey's response to the king's announcement was to secure the opinions and support of scholars and churchmen on the annulment case and the validity of the royal marriage. He convened a private trial and investigation at Westminster in 1527, which was adjourned in May that year without having reached a decision.[16] This was Wolsey's first failure. Henry VIII had hoped that the annulment could be settled with as little fuss as possible, that Katherine of Aragon would step aside, and that he could marry Anne Boleyn and begin producing heirs with her as soon as possible. This was not to be. It was necessary 'in the early stages at least, for Anne and Wolsey to become allies … it was, therefore, a marriage of convenience, although it was not to last'.[17] Anne needed Wolsey to obtain the divorce, and Wolsey understood that he needed to be in Anne's favour in order to maintain his own power and position. They needed each other. The 'alliance' lasted until it became clear that Wolsey would not be able to obtain the annulment.

At first, Henry VIII did not tell Wolsey that he intended to make Anne Boleyn his wife and queen. It was a huge shock to Wolsey once he found out, and 'Henry's duplicity and the fact that he had concealed the depth of his emotions from his first minister were dangerous signs that the king no longer trusted him'. It was also 'an insult to the cardinal's own intelligence network, which had failed to inform him about the true nature of their relationship'.[18] Henry had previously appeared to tell Wolsey everything, so to withhold something so significant, when Wolsey believed that the king would negotiate for a foreign bride once his annulment was declared, complicated things and must have made Wolsey feel vulnerable. For Wolsey at the outset of the annulment case, 'the idea that any daughter of Thomas Boleyn could become Queen of England was so remote and absurd that he dismissed it out for hand' and that he believed that stalling negotiations with Rome would mean that the king would tire of Anne and would agree instead to a French bride.[19] As time would prove, the king tired of Wolsey and all of the delays before he tired of Anne Boleyn.

During the early stages of the 'Great Matter' in 1527, Wolsey travelled to France to conclude a treaty with Francis I. He wrote several letters back to Henry VIII and in one of them he started by saying that he was 'not a little troubled at the message sent from the King by Master Wolman, as if Wolsey questioned the king's secret matter'.[20] Wolsey was already being undermined before he even had a chance to try and prove himself. His first secret hearing had failed to reach a conclusion but there was still hope that the Pope would settle the matter. In the same letter, Wolsey reported that Katherine of Aragon:

> … desired to have counsel as well of strangers as of English,—a device which never could have come into her head except it had been suggested; and therefore Wolsey suggested that the King should handle her gently, until it was shown what the Pope and Francis would do. Norfolk and Suffolk were present on the occasion. Begs the King will believe that in all things concerning the King's honor Wolsey will be constant, even if all others should fail.[21]

This is particularly interesting because Katherine of Aragon would assert the same request for council from Spain in her impassioned speech at the Blackfriars trial in 1529, but Wolsey believed that she could not have thought of it herself, so there must have been someone in the court who was giving advice to Katherine even at this early stage of proceedings. Handling her 'gently' is likely a nod to the support that she could muster in her defence, so not to give others the excuse to act on her behalf. It is not surprising that Norfolk and Suffolk were present as the foremost peers in the realm representing the king, but they were known to be Wolsey's enemies, not liking the amount of power he wielded. Wolsey realised that, if he failed, he would be open to attack from enemies such as these, and placed his trust in the king, that he 'will be constant'.

There are several surviving letters from Anne Boleyn to Cardinal Wolsey, which show that the pair were polite and realised that they needed to work together in a way to achieve the annulment. Anne knew that Henry was depending on Wolsey for his annulment, and Wolsey soon realised that Henry intended to make Anne his wife. The pair worked together from necessity, although it seems neither particularly liked the other. In one letter, Anne wrote to Wolsey that 'I do know the great pains and troubles that you have taken for me is never like to be recompensed on my part, but alonely in loving you next unto the king's grace above all creatures living'.[22] The letter seems almost overly effusive in praise of Wolsey, perhaps to emphasise the relationship between them for the king, who we know likely read the letter since he added his own postscript to it. Henry wrote that 'the writer of this letter would not cease, till she had caused me likewise to set my hand' and that 'notwithstanding, we trust, by your diligence and vigilancy (with the assistance of Almighty God), shortly to be eased out of that trouble'.[23] The fact that Anne was asking Henry to put his own hand to her letter suggests that the pair were very much working together, and that Anne wanted Wolsey to know about her influence over the king. Henry's own postscript has an undertone of threat with his comment that he hoped soon to be out of his trouble. The letter was likely written sometime in 1528 as they talk about the legate (Campeggio) being on his way to England.

Another letter written after both Wolsey and Anne had survived the sweating sickness in summer 1528, says that Anne was 'most bound of all creature, next to the king's grace, to love and serve your grace, of the which I beseech you never to doubt, that ever I shall vary from this thought, as long as any breath is in my body'.[24] This echoes the sentiments expressed in the previous letter, and implies that Anne, Henry, and Wolsey were tied together in this annulment case. Outwardly, Anne is expressing her faith in Wolsey that he will be able to make her queen. Like Henry VIII added in his postscript to the previous letter, Anne goes on to say that 'if it be God's pleasure, I pray him to send this matter shortly to a good end'.[25] It is a consistent message being sent to Wolsey from the pair who were desperate for the case to be resolved so that they could marry and start producing sons. It is likely that Wolsey was feeling the pressure, being reminded at every turn what was expected of him. In another letter, Anne promises Wolsey reward for his service if he achieves the annulment and makes her queen, promising that 'look what thing in this world I can imagine to do you pleasure in, you shall find me the gladdest woman in the world to do it'.[26] There still seems a confidence that Wolsey could achieve what Henry and Anne wanted at this time, and a pressure on him to deliver it. Wolsey must have feared what would happen to him if he failed.

An incident which really seemed to pit Anne Boleyn and Cardinal Thomas Wolsey against each other was the Abbess of Wilton affair. In April 1528, Cecily Willoughby, abbess of Wilton, died. Wilton was a large Benedictine house with aristocratic connections. The obvious successor would have been Cecily's second in command, Prioress Isabel Jordan.[27] However, also living at the priory at Wilton was a sister of William Carey, husband to Anne Boleyn's sister, Mary Boleyn. William Carey wanted to see his sister succeed Cecily Willoughby. Henry VIII approved the appointment, likely as a favour to Anne, but then Eleanor Carey's past was revealed. Henry wrote to Anne in one of his letters to say:

> As touching the matter of Wilton, my lord cardinal hath had the nuns before him, and examined them, Mr. Bell being present; which hath certified me that, for a truth, she has confessed herself (which we would have had abbess) to have had two children by two sundry priests; and further, since hath been kept by a servant of the Lord Broke that was, and that not long ago. Wherefore I would not, for all the gold in the world, clog your conscience nor mine to make her ruler of a house which is of so ungodly demeanour; nor, I trust, you would not that neither for brother and sister, I should so disdain mine honour or conscience … I have done that neither of them shall have it, but that some other good and well-disposed woman shall have it, whereby the house shall be the better reformed …[28]

Henry VIII decided that Anne's sister-in-law Eleanor Carey was not fit to have the leadership of a religious house due to her having two children by two priests. But he also declared that the second-in-command, Isabel Jordan, would not have the leadership either; Jordan appears to have been Wolsey's preferred candidate, because she 'is so old that for many years she could not be as she was named'.[29] Henry made a concession to Anne that, as he was not appointing her preferred candidate, he would not appoint Wolsey's preferred candidate either. However, Wolsey took matters into his own hands and 'slipped up' in nominating Isabel Jordan to the position against the king's wishes, which resulted in 'one of those rare and terrifying letters' in Henry's own hand and 'a display of grovelling submission' by Wolsey'.[30] In this incident we clearly see the influence that Anne Boleyn had in political and religious matters, even over Wolsey who had served the king faithfully.

Cardinal Lorenzo Campeggio arrived in England in September 1528, having travelled from Italy, where he had been appointed by Pope Clement VII to travel to England and make a judgement on the validity of the marriage of Henry VIII and Katherine of Aragon, alongside Cardinal Wolsey. In discussions once Campeggio had arrived in England, Wolsey sought to persuade Campeggio that any reconciliation between Henry and Katherine was not going to happen.[31] The Pope believed that the easiest way to resolve the problem was to reconcile the king and his wife, rather than to grant an annulment of the marriage. However, Henry was not willing to reconcile with Katherine of Aragon because she could not give him the son that he so desperately craved. She was past the point of childbearing. Although Campeggio arrived in England in September 1528, the Blackfriars trial did not begin until 31 May 1529 when the legatine court opened. There had been delay after delay with Campeggio having health problems, for example. In a letter written to Campeggio after he arrived in England regarding the wishes of Pope Clement VII, it was said that:

> His Holiness has always desired that it should be protracted, in order to find some means by which he could satisfy the King without proceeding to the sentence … his Holiness has ever shrunk from having to take a step which would offend the mind of that most serene King. But since you have not been able to prevent the commencement of the proceedings, his Holiness warns you that the process must be slow, and that no sentence must in any manner be pronounced. For this purpose, you will not lack a thousand means and pretexts, if upon no other point, at least upon the breve which has been produced.[32]

The commencement of the legatine court was a hugely important moment for Henry VIII, which he believed would determine the case for his marriage in his favour. Anne Boleyn certainly hoped that was true. This letter to Campeggio tells us that, even before the trial had opened, the decision would not go in Henry VIII's favour. Campeggio slowed things down as much as he could on the Pope's orders. Katherine of Aragon wanted the case recalled to Rome, believing that only the Pope could decide on the validity of a marriage. For Cardinal Thomas Wolsey, this was the case which would decide his own fate. There was a lot riding on it.

As we saw in the previous chapter, Katherine of Aragon made an impassioned speech on her knees before the king on the one day that she appeared in front of the court at Blackfriars, when she was accompanied by one of her advisers on the case, John Fisher, Bishop of Rochester. She proclaimed that she was the true wife and queen of Henry VIII and that she had 'loved all those whom ye loved only for your sake, whether I had cause or no; and whether they were my friends or enemies'.[33] By this time at the very least, Thomas Wolsey would have been one of those that Katherine of Aragon counted as an enemy. He was the one leading the case to have her marriage to the king annulled. Wolsey probably had more riding on the outcome than Katherine did, but they were on opposite sides. After weeks of legal wrangling, the Blackfriars court met for the final time on 23 July 1529 where Cardinal Campeggio adjourned the trial without giving a verdict. This left Cardinal Wolsey in a very difficult position with the king; his power and position, and his very life, hung in the balance.

It was the collapse of the legatine court at Blackfriars which signalled Wolsey's downfall – 'a new approach was needed. New blood, it seemed, was also wanted'.[34] Henry VIII was angry that his chief minister and trusted friend had been unable to procure for him what he so desperately wanted. When you failed Henry VIII, as we will see later with Anne Boleyn and Wolsey's own successor as chief minister, Thomas Cromwell, he turned his back on you, and it could be incredibly sudden and violent. Wolsey, who had always before delivered what the king wanted, had failed in the thing the king wanted most of all. Wolsey's fall was, however, more protracted than that of either Anne Boleyn or Thomas Cromwell, and it seemed for a time he could perhaps regain the power he had lost. It seems Henry 'bore very little animosity towards Wolsey as an individual and treated him quite kindly in his newly reduced state. The act of removing Wolsey from power was more political than personal'.[35] Wolsey had not just served Henry, they seemed to be closer than that, more like friends at different points in time. However, ultimately Wolsey was a servant of the king's and when he failed, he was removed from his powerful positions. Henry VIII needed someone who could achieve his desperate desire.

Factional politics emerged throughout the 1520s, particularly with the rise of the Boleyn family and the overarching problem of the 'Great Matter'.

The crisis which led to Wolsey's downfall, as previously suggested, was outside the control of anyone in England. The international situation was critical because Wolsey was unable to get an annulment for the king due to Charles V's influence over Pope Clement VII. The timings of events did not favour Henry VIII and Wolsey. The Treaty of Cambrai, finalised on 5 August 1529, was the final nail in Wolsey's coffin. This ended the last chance that the Pope would grant the annulment. Wolsey's whole career and his future had depended on his ability to meet the king's desire to get rid of Katherine of Aragon and marry Anne Boleyn, and he had failed. Wolsey's enemies grouped together to destroy him, working on 'Henry's temporary disillusionment with his minister, and the pressure, coupled with Anne's skilful management of her lover, was enough to break the trust of almost twenty years'.[36] When Wolsey had failed, his enemies could bring him down. Had Wolsey succeeded, it is very likely that he would have remained in favour and Henry would have continued to make use of his talents.

On 9 October 1529 Wolsey was indicted for praemunire, which was asserting foreign authority in England against the will of the monarch. In Wolsey's specific case, it was the authority of the Pope that was being asserted, and Henry VIII did not like it. He did not want anyone to be able to exercise power over him, even the head of the Church. Wolsey travelled north to his diocese in York as Henry VIII allowed him to keep his archbishopric, even though he had to resign the chancellorship and give up political power. He also had to give up his palaces of Hampton Court and York Place. Henry VIII would massively expand and develop both palaces, with York Place becoming Whitehall Palace. Wolsey was replaced as lord chancellor by Sir Thomas More, another man who had known Henry since he acceded to the throne in 1509. But the choice went beyond their connection. More had an 'international reputation as a man of extraordinary learning, but he was equally known for his piety and integrity'. Henry planned 'an intellectual and moral crusade' and he needed Thomas More.[37] More initially refused to accept the post, unhappy that he would be involved with the king's 'Great Matter' as part of that role, but the king would not take no for an answer. He knew that More's reputation would hold great sway in the opinions of those who might speak against him in his quest for an annulment.

Cardinal Wolsey travelled north into Yorkshire for the first time. Despite being Archbishop of York, he had never visited there, always being occupied at court and with state matters. While there, he plotted a way to regain power, by conspiring with the Pope, and Katherine of Aragon, and by extension Emperor Charles V, to put a stop to the annulment case, force Henry to take back Katherine as his wife, and restore Wolsey to political power. This backfired magnificently though, and Wolsey was accused of treason, for trying to force the king to act in a way that he did not want to and did not agree with. The so-called plotting came to light through members of Wolsey's household, particularly Agostino Agostini, who was in service to Wolsey at the time and in contact with both the French and Imperial ambassadors in England. If Agostini is believed, then evidence of Wolsey's plotting was actually circulating in government circles long before he was arrested.[38] This is suspicious because it implies that things were allowed to develop to the point where there was too much evidence for Wolsey to go free. This seems to have been a conspiracy of sorts against the cardinal by his enemies to bring him down.

Thomas Wolsey, Cardinal and Archbishop of York, was arrested at Cawood Castle in North Yorkshire on 4 November 1530 once his plans and machinations to regain power had come to light. Perhaps it was a calculated move on Anne Boleyn's part to send Henry Percy, 6th Earl of Northumberland, the man she had allegedly once hoped to marry, to affect Wolsey's arrest and removal to London for trial. There is little evidence of how involved Anne actually was in Wolsey's downfall, but this choice of Henry Percy does appear to show her hand in it. Wolsey left Cawood on 7 November to travel south to London to be tried for treason. He stayed at Pontefract Abbey that night having travelled around 14 miles. Wolsey then travelled to Doncaster and on to Sheffield, where he stayed at Sheffield Manor Lodge, a later residence of Mary, Queen of Scots during her imprisonment in England under Elizabeth I. Sheffield Manor was a residence of the Earl of Shrewsbury, where Wolsey was greeted by George Talbot, 4th Earl of Shrewsbury and his wife. Shrewsbury was also the father-in-law of Henry Percy, 6th Earl of Northumberland.

A letter written from Sir Thomas Vaux during this period to Anne de Montmorency, 1st Duke of Montmorency, in France, worried for the cardinal. It seemed that the king had turned completely against him. The letter said that:

> … as to the Cardinal, I fear he cannot do well. They say they have many important causes against him; and the King says he has intrigued against them, both in and out of his kingdom, and has told me where and how, and that one and perhaps more of his servants have discovered it and accused him. I am much grieved for his danger.[39]

We get a sense of the charges against Wolsey and how wide-ranging they were said to be. He was being accused of intrigues both in and out of the kingdom, alluding probably to his communications with the emperor and the Pope, as well as with Katherine of Aragon and the French and Imperial ambassadors. There is a further letter from Sir Francis Bryan to Henry VIII around the same time. He was also in France and had received a letter from the king explaining Wolsey's crimes. Bryan writes that he had received the letter:

> … stating the detestable practices and conspiracies set forth by Wolsey, at Rome and within your realm, against your dignity. After I had studied them well I visited the Grand Master, who inquired, what news from England? and I learned from him that news had been received from the ambassador in England,—that the Cardinal was in hold, but for what offence he knew not; that the King (Francis), however, thought he deserved imprisonment. I told him that I had been sent to prevent any untrue surmises.[40]

Bryan claims that when he told the French king and queen of Wolsey's arrest 'they judged you to be so just a prince that you would not have punished the Cardinal but for his heinous deserts'.[41] It's an interesting letter as to the international response to Wolsey's arrest, as he had been at the centre of so much of international politics throughout Henry VIII's reign so far. Bryan relates that Francis I said that he thought:

> … that so pompous and ambitious a heart, sprung out of so vile a stock, would once show forth the baseness of his nature, and most commonly against him that hath raised him from low degree to high dignity as ye have done; and

> said he thought by his outrageous misbehaviours he had well merited other a life worse than death, or else of all deaths the most cruel.[42]

One of the biggest slanders against Wolsey was that he came from 'so vile a stock', raised 'from low degree to high dignity', and it sounds as if the King of France almost resented having to deal with a man who was not even a nobleman in international diplomacy. It almost also comes across as a slur against Henry VIII who had dared to raise this commoner to a station beyond his position and deserving. Wolsey had been at the centre of arranging the Field of the Cloth of Gold summit in 1520, which was supposed to seal an everlasting peace between England and France, but which had failed within just a few short years as Henry allied himself with Charles V instead. Francis appeared to be advocating for the death penalty for Wolsey's crimes, perhaps hoping that the king would appoint more noble advisers in his place who would be more sympathetic towards France, like the Boleyn family.

A detailed letter survives from Eustace Chapuys, ambassador to Emperor Charles V, dated 27 November 1530, which details some of the rumours about Wolsey's arrest, though he admits it is largely conjecture and rumour, and the charges against him. He places Anne Boleyn firmly at the centre of events at this time:

> The cause of his arrest is a mere conjecture. A gentleman told me that a short time ago the King was complaining to his Council of something that was not done according to his liking and said in a rage that the Cardinal was a better man than any of them for managing matters; and repeating this twice, he left them. The Duke, the lady, and the father have not ceased since then to plot against the Cardinal; especially the lady, who does not cease to weep and regret her lost time and her honor, threatening the King that she would leave him,—in such sort that the King has had much trouble to appease her; and though the King prayed her most affectionately, even with tears in his eyes, that she would not speak of leaving him, nothing would satisfy her except the arrest of the Cardinal.[43]

It seems that, within a year of Wolsey being banished from court, the king almost wished for him back, for him to take on the cares and strains of government again and remove them from the king's own hands. In Chapuys' account at least, this panicked Anne Boleyn, her uncle the Duke of Norfolk, and father, Thomas Boleyn, who worried what would happen to them if Wolsey regained his power and influence. It seems without doubt that Wolsey would have used whatever means possible to remove Anne and her family from around the king in order to cement his own position. Anne seems to have used some kind of emotional manipulation on Henry, threatening to leave him, so that he would do whatever it took to make her stay, even executing the cardinal. Chapuys goes on to say that it was 'pretended' Wolsey had written to Rome to be reinstated, and to France for assistance, and that the cardinal's physician is in government hands, now living in the Duke of Norfolk's house and 'he is singing the tune as they wished him'.[44] The implication is that Wolsey's servants were turning against him, probably to protect themselves, and that the insinuations and charges may not actually have been true against him. Things were being manipulated to get the outcome that the king, and Anne Boleyn, wanted.

Wolsey's gentleman usher, George Cavendish, who was with Wolsey during his fall and the tumultuous months that followed up to his death, recounted that, after his arrest, Wolsey spoke to George Talbot, 4th Earl of Shrewsbury, while at Sheffield. Cavendish's account has Wolsey lamenting 'for I am well assured, my lord, that there is no man alive or dead that looketh in this face of mine, who is able to accuse me of any disloyalty toward the king. Oh! How much it grieveth me that the king should have any suspicious opinion of me, to think that I would be false or conspire any evil to his royal person'.[45] Wolsey stated his loyalty to the king right to the end, never admitting any offence against his sovereign. However, he did go on to say, according to Cavendish, that 'the enemy that never sleepeth, but studieth and continually imagineth, both sleeping and waking, my utter destruction, perceiving the contentation of my mind, doubted that their malicious and cruel dealings would at length grow to their shame and rebuke, goeth about therefore to prevent the same with shedding of my blood'.[46] Anne Boleyn was not named as part of this account of Wolsey's words, but Cavendish continually links Wolsey's fall and death to Anne throughout his entire account, from the earlier relationship between Anne and Henry Percy, where Anne 'bore a 'grudge … that in process of time burst out to the utter undoing of the cardinal'.[47] When Wolsey died, Cavendish considered that his death lay at Anne Boleyn's feet.

Wolsey fell ill while at Sheffield, though he left to continue his journey south on 25 November 1530. He reached as far as Leicester Abbey by the evening of 27 November where he appears to have collapsed. He remained in bed the following day, gradually weakening, and he died on the morning of 29 November 1530. Wolsey's death at Leicester meant that he avoided the fate that the king probably had in store for him – trial and execution at the Tower of London, as befitted as traitor. Wolsey deprived the king of this, failing yet again to give the king what he wanted in a final twist of fate. Wolsey was likely relieved to be spared this ignominious end. G. W. Bernard writes that 'the fashionable explanation for these events is to see Wolsey as the victim of faction'.[48] However, Bernard concludes that Eric Ives, David Starkey, and J. J. Scarisbrick among others were incorrect, and that 'the dismissal of a papal legate and cardinal, for breaking the law of praemunire, simply because he was legate and cardinal, in an atmosphere of anticlericalism, would signal clearly to the pope that Henry was serious in threatening to go it alone if the pope refused to assist him'.[49] Wolsey's fall, like that of Anne Boleyn later on, cannot necessarily be explained by a single thing. Faction, along with Anne Boleyn, may have contributed to Wolsey's fall as it did later to Anne's own fall, but Wolsey could not have fallen had the king not wished it. Faction alone is not enough to explain why the man, who had been second in the kingdom only to the king for fifteen years, was brought down. Henry VIII bears ultimate responsibility.

Cardinal Thomas Wolsey, Cardinal, Archbishop of York and former Lord Chancellor of England, was buried in Leicester Abbey on the morning of 1 December 1530 after a funeral mass. The abbey was torn down after the dissolution and Wolsey's burial place has now been lost. The site of the abbey sits in what is now Abbey Park in Leicester. An ignominious end some might say for a man who was once one of the most powerful men in England. But he was brought down because he could not give a king an annulment. Henry VIII would marry Anne Boleyn, although it would take a few more years to achieve it. The case for annulment would be engineered by a man Wolsey had in his own household and had served him faithfully for many years: Thomas Cromwell.

Chapter 7

A Second Marriage

Henry VIII and Anne Boleyn officially married at Whitehall Palace, probably on 24 or 25 January 1533. The suggestion is that they were married in the gatehouse with just a few attendants – Henry Norris, Thomas Heneage, and Anne Savage, later Lady Berkeley.[1] Nicholas Harpsfield, writing twenty years after the event, believed that the ceremony may have been officiated by Rowland Lee 'long ere there was any divorce made' but that the king told Lee he had a licence from the Pope to remarry.[2] However, there has been a suggestion made that Henry and Anne in fact married sometime in November 1532 in France. They had been visiting to gain the approval of Francis I of France for their marriage, though the exact ceremony that could have been conducted at this time is unclear. Perhaps this was a firm commitment ceremony that, once consummated, would make the union permanent and legal. Anne Boleyn was already pregnant by the time of the official wedding at Whitehall in January 1533, and it seems unlikely that she would have submitted completely to the king without some kind of firm commitment that she would be Henry's wife and queen. Anne had already held off giving herself to Henry for around seven years, so she would not have submitted after so long without a certainty. The marriage would last just 1,083 days from coronation to execution. The period was revolutionary, with new parliamentary acts passed to change the law, including the First Succession Act, the Act of Supremacy, and a new Treason Act.

From Henry VIII's point of view, his wedding to Anne Boleyn marked the beginning of his first marriage, though we consider Anne his second wife. Henry considered his first marriage to Katherine of Aragon to be null and void, and that he had in fact been a bachelor for the first twenty-four years of his reign, living in sin with his brother's widow. Katherine was now considered by Henry and the wider court to be the dowager Princess of Wales as the widow of Prince Arthur, and never queen. Her daughter, Princess

Mary, was made legally illegitimate and unable to inherit the crown. Henry would then change his mind again in 1536 and considered his third wedding to Jane Seymour to be the beginning of his first marriage, having annulled his marriages to both Katherine of Aragon and Anne Boleyn. But that was in the future. In January 1533, Henry VIII and Anne Boleyn were newly married, happy, and Anne was pregnant with what was believed to be a son. There was no reason to suspect that the couple would not have multiple children, and that this would be Henry's final marriage. A king who married six times and executed two of those six wives was unheard of at the time.

Archbishop Thomas Cranmer assembled a court at Dunstable Priory on 8 May 1533. Katherine of Aragon refused to attend the court, saying that she did not recognise its validity – she remained firm in the belief that only the Pope himself could decide on the status of her marriage as she had declared at the Blackfriars trial four years earlier. Cranmer, as a result of the court deliberations, declared that the marriage of Henry VIII and Anne Boleyn was 'good and consonant to the laws of God' and that the marriage of Henry to Katherine of Aragon was 'directly against the laws of God' and thus was null and void.[3] Seven years after the 'Great Matter' first came to the attention of people across Europe, a decision had been reached, but it was not a decision that everyone could accept. Katherine of Aragon would never accept her marriage was invalid, and she would maintain she was the rightful queen until her dying day. This divine conclusion from the foremost clergyman in England was what Henry VIII had been waiting for, and it meant that Anne Boleyn could be recognised and crowned as queen four months after their wedding.

Anne Boleyn was officially recognised as queen at Easter 1533 when she attended Mass in full regalia with her household on 12 April 1533. She was then crowned at Westminster Abbey on 1 June 1533 when she was around six months pregnant. The coronation was a 'dramatic statement that Henry VIII was 100 percent committed to his new queen and their child, whatever Catholic Europe or many of his subjects and nobility might think'.[4] Henry was determined to assert that Anne's child would be his heir and no other. Henry was resolved to outdo previous coronations, including his own, to prove that Anne Boleyn was the rightful and legitimate queen, and their unborn child the heir to the throne. The ceremonies and celebrations lasted for days and included travel by barge from Greenwich Palace to the Tower of London, the creation of Knights of the Bath during the stay at the Tower, and the traditional procession from the Tower to Westminster Palace. Then there was the coronation itself in Westminster Abbey, which was the pinnacle of the celebrations, followed by the coronation banquet in Westminster Hall. The strain this must have placed on a heavily pregnant Anne must have been incredible. It was the moment of her greatest triumph, but it would also have been exhausting. The royal apartments at the Tower of London had been specially refurbished for Anne's coronation, under the guiding hand of Thomas Cromwell. Henry VIII would accept nothing but the best for Anne Boleyn, whom he hoped was carrying his son and heir that he had been waiting twenty-four years for. The Imperial ambassador, Chapuys, however, described Anne Boleyn's coronation as a 'cold, poor, and most unpleasing sight'.[5] But Chapuys was a staunch supporter of Katherine of Aragon and Princess Mary. He was steadfastly against the annulment of Henry and Katherine's marriage and Henry's remarriage to Anne. He would never accept that Anne's daughter, Elizabeth, replaced Katherine's daughter, Mary, as heir. We cannot always take Chapuys' comments at face value, although his master, Charles V, would have expected to be given an accurate account, so we cannot dismiss his comments out of hand.

On 29 May 1533, Anne Boleyn travelled to the Tower of London from Greenwich, where she would stay for two days, as was traditional before a coronation. The procession from the Tower to Westminster then took place on 31 May, the day before the crowning itself. There were pageants and celebrations along the procession route, to demonstrate Anne's majesty and right to be queen. One such pageant, at Leadenhall, made a connection between Anne Boleyn and St Anne, said to be the mother of the Virgin Mary. This comparison, with Anne Boleyn already visibly pregnant, was symbolic of the hope of her producing the much-wanted son and heir. The falcon is used to represent Anne herself with the verse:

> Behold and see the Falcon White!
> How she beginneth her wings to spread,
> And for our comfort take her flight [...]
> For whose cause an Angel celestial

Descendeth, the Falcon white as swan,
To crown with a Diadem Imperial!
In her honour rejoice we all.
For it Cometh from God, and not of man.[6]

The suggestion is that Anne Boleyn's crowning and her quickness to conceive a child were the wish, will, and work of God; that Anne's new position was divinely ordained. Describing the falcon 'white as swan' is an ode to beauty, elegance, love, and fidelity, which swans are said to represent.[7] The colour white is indicative of purity and innocence and associated with new beginnings.[8] These are qualities which the culture of courtly love prized. Henry VIII adored the game of courtly love, so no doubt these nuances pleased him. He would have seen his marriage to Anne and her coronation as a new beginning for him and for England, with hopes of settling the succession once and for all. Eric Ives points out that the white falcon was also a demonstration of Anne's links to the Irish Butler family and the earls of Ormond, a title which Anne's father, Thomas Boleyn, had held since 1529 when he was granted it by Henry VIII.[9] The Boleyns and the Butlers had been disagreeing over the rightful holder of the title for many years and it was most likely Anne Boleyn's relationship with the king which settled the dispute in her father's favour.

With the coronation, Anne's position seemed unassailable – she had been anointed with the holy oil and imbued with divine acceptance, she had the love of the king, and a child in her belly which it was believed would be a son. Anne had already been created Marquess of Pembroke in her own right in September 1532, in preparation for her marriage and the visit to Calais. Anne Boleyn was at the most secure point of her relationship with the king. He could not easily put her aside now, and he would not while she was pregnant and hopeful of a son. If Anne gave birth to a boy as the result of her first pregnancy, the king would never cast her aside, and she would be safe, as would the succession. The groundwork was already being laid to change the succession. But the best-laid plans still need a dose of luck.

On 7 September 1533, Anne Boleyn gave birth to a daughter, Elizabeth, at Greenwich Palace, not the much longed-for son. It was a disappointment to both mother and father, but there was no reason to believe that sons would not follow. Anne carried easily to term and birthed a healthy child. The only problem was the sex. Henry VIII firmly believed that he needed a son to succeed him. It was why he had annulled his marriage to Katherine of Aragon in order to marry Anne. He could not have had any inkling that it would in fact be his daughter by Anne who would triumph and rule England for forty-five years. But it would also be her childless state and marriage to England that would end the Tudor dynasty in 1603. The chronicler Edward Hall wrote of Elizabeth's birth that:

> The seventh day of September, being Sunday, between three and four of the clock after noon, the Queen was delivered of a fair lady, which day the duke of Norfolk came home to the christening and for the Queen's good deliverance, Te Deum was sung in continently and great preparation was made for the christening.[10]

Tracy Borman's research into the relationship between Anne Boleyn and Elizabeth I is insightful. She suggests that the focus on Elizabeth's virginal state, or on the six wives, has meant that 'along the way, we have missed the most fascinating relationship of all: that between a mother and daughter who changed the course of British history'.[11] It is often assumed that, as Elizabeth was not yet 3 years old when her mother was executed, that Anne cannot have had much influence over her daughter's life. But there are signs, such as Elizabeth taking Anne's white falcon emblem as her own when she became queen in 1558, and an effigy of Anne Boleyn appearing in Elizabeth's coronation procession the following year. Borman has also discussed an act passed in 1559, at the beginning of Elizabeth's reign, known as *An Act whereby the Queen's Highness is restored in blood to the late Queen Anne Her Highness' Mother*. This meant that Elizabeth could be the legal heir of her mother once again, which had been denied to her after Anne's conviction. Elizabeth I did not revoke the annulment of her parents' marriage as she was 'too great a pragmatist' to do so, but she could restore the maternal bond.[12] The clues are often subtle, but they are there, to show an almost reverential and respectful relationship from Elizabeth towards Anne.

Princess Elizabeth was christened on 10 September 1533 in the Church of the Observant Friars at Greenwich, where Henry VIII had married

Katherine of Aragon in 1509 and where Elizabeth's half-sister, Princess Mary, had also been christened in 1516. Edward Hall described how, at the christening, the Duchess of Norfolk, Anne Boleyn's aunt, held Elizabeth, who was dressed in a mantle of purple velvet and a long train edged with ermine. As the ceremony ended in the church, the Garter King of Arms proclaimed, 'God of his infinite goodness, send prosperous life and long to the high and mighty Princess of England, Elizabeth!'.[13] At this point, Elizabeth was being treated as the rightful heir to the throne, in spite of her being a girl rather than the son Henry VIII desperately wanted. She was the heir presumptive until Anne birthed a son. Pushing for Elizabeth to be recognised as the rightful heir can almost be seen like a practice run for the son Henry believed Anne would deliver next, and this was bolstered by the First Succession Act which was passed in 1534.

Eustace Chapuys wrote to Emperor Charles V, Katherine of Aragon's nephew, on 15 September 1533 and reported that the child born to Anne Boleyn eight days earlier was to be named Elizabeth and not Mary after all.[14] There is no evidence that the child was ever going to be called Mary, aside from this letter from Chapuys. It is possible there were rumours at court, and that calling the new princess Mary would be replacing Henry's first daughter in absolutely every way, taking not just her position but her name. However, in the end, the child was named Elizabeth, quite possibly for both of her grandmothers – Henry VIII's mother, Elizabeth of York, and Anne Boleyn's mother, Elizabeth Boleyn née Howard. Chapuys also described how the christening, like Anne's coronation three months earlier, was 'very cold and disagreeable, both to the Court and to the city, and there has been no thought of having the bonfires and rejoicings usual in such cases'.[15] It was not unusual when a princess was born, rather than a prince, for jousts and other celebrations to be cancelled. It was the same after the birth of Princess Mary in 1516.[16] A girl was not as valued as a boy in terms of the succession, especially for Henry VIII, who believed that women could not and should not rule. When Elizabeth was born, the king must have been even more disappointed than he was at Mary's birth. Henry had torn the country apart for Anne Boleyn in expectation that she would give him a son, and, in his eyes, she had failed. But, she had fallen pregnant quickly and easily the first time and carried to term without problems, so there was hope.

Anne's pregnancy and childbirth history can be seen to begin to resemble Katherine of Aragon's, sadly. However, Anne had a much shorter period of marriage than Katherine to get pregnant. With hindsight, their pregnancy history is often compared, and Henry VIII must have been very aware of the similarities, with just a single living daughter from each woman. For Anne, John Dewhurst claims that a 'varying number of miscarriages has been postulated' but that the only pregnancies we can be sure about are those in 1533 which led to the birth of Elizabeth, and the miscarriage in January 1536.[17] Marie Louise Bruce proclaims that Anne during the first six months of 1534 'appears to have had one miscarriage after the other'.[18] This seems implausible in a six-month period, the most would likely be two, but these would have had to have been in the early stages, and there is little evidence for it.

There is evidence of a pregnancy in 1534, but it seemed to be ongoing, rather than a series of miscarriages. There is a comment on 28 January 1534 from Chapuys to Charles V that 'there is already a daughter, and Anne Boleyn is now pregnant and in condition to have more children'.[19] The wording suggests that he had only recently found out about the pregnancy, so it likely was in the early stages. In a letter to Lady Lisle on 27 April, George Taylor wrote that 'the King and Queen are merry and in good health. The Queen hath a goodly belly, praying our Lord to send us a prince'.[20] A 'goodly belly' suggests the pregnancy was visible at this time. In July, Anne's brother, George, Lord Rochford, was sent on embassy to France, and he was given instructions to defer a planned meeting between Henry VIII and Francis I, because Anne 'being so far gone with child, she could not cross the sea with the King, and she would be deprived of his Highness's presence when it was most necessary'.[21] This implies that she may have been entering the final stages of this pregnancy. There is a suggestion that Anne would suffer a miscarriage in the summer of 1534 and if these accounts are all from the same pregnancy, which seems likely, it would have been a nearly full-term baby, for Chapuys to have reported it in January. A 'goodly belly' in April suggests that Anne had started to show, and 'being so far gone' with child that she feared Henry would miss the birth if he was away, suggests that her confinement may have been imminent. There is no evidence that survives of a confinement being prepared, however. There is also no record of when or how the pregnancy ended, or whether it was a boy or a girl. If it was a boy, then there was proof after Elizabeth's birth that Anne could in fact conceive a son. Next she needed to prove to the king that she could conceive and carry a son to term.

However, Henry's eye was wandering away from the woman he had been obsessed with for so many years. Anne Boleyn had power as a mistress when she could withhold sexual intercourse from the king but, once married, that power ebbed away, especially when she did not birth a male heir. Had she produced a son, she likely would have retained influence. In a letter dated 27 September 1534, after the miscarriage which must have resulted from the comments discussed above, Chapuys reported that:

> Since the King began to doubt whether his lady was *enceinte* or not, he has renewed and increased the love he formerly had for a very beautiful damsel of the Court; and because the said lady wished to drive her away, the King has been very angry, telling his said lady that she had good reason to be content with what he had done for her, which he would not do now if the thing were to begin, and that she should consider from what she had come, and several other things. To which it is not well to attach too much importance, considering the changeable character of the said King and the craft of the said lady, who knows well how to manage him.[22]

It is difficult to imagine that Anne had hidden a miscarriage or stillbirth from the king if it was as visible as reports suggest – 'so far gone with child' – that a trip to France had been cancelled. Perhaps Anne had believed she was again pregnant after the 1534 miscarriage, hence Chapuys' comment about the king doubting Anne was 'enceinte'. But we see that the king had started to look at other women. Whether this relationship went beyond looks, gifts, and talking is unknown, or even who the woman was. Suggestions have been made that it may have been Anne's cousin, either Mary or Margaret Shelton, or even that it could have been the king showing an early interest in Jane Seymour, who would later replace Anne on the throne. Chapuys' account also demonstrates evidence of some kind of regret on the part of the king for his marriage to Anne, that she had yet to produce a son despite him pulling England apart to marry her. Blame was often placed on the woman for a failure to conceive, or the lack of a son. It was not understood in the sixteenth century that it was in fact the sperm which decided the sex of a child.

When it became clear that Henry VIII's eye was wandering away from Anne Boleyn, other ladies at court and ambitious courtiers realised that they did not just have to be a king's mistress if he asked them, but that they could also aspire to be queen. Anne Boleyn had set a dangerous precedent. Margaret Shelton (also known as 'Madge') was the daughter of Thomas Boleyn's sister, Anne, who had married Sir John Shelton. Lady Anne Shelton was appointed as governess to Princess Elizabeth when her household was set up at Hatfield House. Philippa Jones states that Madge Shelton 'was certainly the kind of lady whom Henry found attractive – possibly fair, and quite possibly quieter and more subservient than her forceful cousin'.[23] There is a suggestion that possibly the Howards or Boleyns put Madge Shelton in Henry VIII's path, either to weaken Anne Boleyn's authority, or in hopes of replacing her as queen as they hoped Margaret Shelton could be better managed so that they could hold onto power.[24] Kelly Hart believes that it was not Margaret Shelton who was the king's mistress, but actually her sister, Mary Shelton. Hart describes the confusion coming from how a 'y' was written, making it look like a 'g', making it 'Marg' for Margaret rather than Mary.[25] Amy Licence states that it is unclear which Shelton sister was meant in the reports.[26] We also cannot be sure as to the state of the relationship. It could have been a sexual relationship, although we have no conclusive evidence for this, or it could have been a courtly love relationship without a sexual element. It is important not to express this relationship as fact without the evidence to back it up.

There is even a train of thought that Anne herself may have placed one of her Shelton cousins in the path of the king, believing that it was better to keep it within the family, since she was possibly pregnant again and it would be better for the king's mistress to be someone of her trusted circle who would not speak against her. Hart, however, does not believe that Anne Boleyn was involved in her Shelton cousin becoming the king's mistress as not all Boleyn and Howard relatives supported Anne as queen.[27] Margaret and Mary Shelton's mother, Lady Anne Shelton, was one of the ladies in 1536 who was in the Tower of London with Anne Boleyn during her imprisonment, reporting her words back to Thomas Cromwell via William

Kingston. This does not necessarily mean that the Sheltons did not support Anne as queen, as they were given control over the household of Anne's daughter, Elizabeth. Their actions in May 1536 could be seen as trying to protect their family and their survival. Chapuys reported on 25 February 1535 that 'the young lady who was lately in the king's favour is so no longer. There has succeeded to her place a cousin of the concubine, daughter of the present governess of the princess'.[28] This suggests that the woman discussed in 1534 was not one of the Shelton sisters but another lady. We have no evidence of the king's interest in Jane Seymour until early 1536, so it may be an unknown court lady who the king showed an interest in, in 1534.

This does not mean, however, that Henry and Anne's marriage was already doomed at this time. Henry and Anne's relationship was always one of sunshine and showers, and there were almost violent arguments and passionate reconciliations. What this comment does demonstrate is that Henry would not put up with Anne arguing with him as his wife. That was acceptable from a mistress who had the power in the relationship, but not from a wife, queen, and mother. Chapuys recognised the changeable nature of Henry and Anne's relationship in his comments in the letter from September 1534 and that there may be nothing in the remarks the king made, adding to his reliability as a narrator of these events.

There has been a suggestion that Anne Boleyn had a further possible miscarriage or stillbirth in 1535, although it is difficult to find any contemporary evidence for it. There is one comment made in a letter from William Kingston to Lord Lisle in June that year which says that 'the King and Queen are well, and her Grace has a fair belly as I have seen'.[29] But this seems to be a lone comment with no corroboration. It is possible that this can be explained by pseudocyesis, otherwise known as a phantom or a false pregnancy. There is often a visible swelling of the abdomen despite there being no pregnancy. This could also possibly explain Chapuys' earlier comment about Henry doubting whether Anne was *enceinte*. This can occur in women desperate to prove their fertility or produce specifically a son in Anne's case. It stems from anxiety or stress.

We know for certain that Anne then miscarried a son in January 1536, which will be discussed further in chapter 10. With hindsight of Anne Boleyn's eventual fate, this is seen as 'never was fortune more cruel' as

Anne 'had miscarried of her saviour'.[30] She would not conceive again. So, Anne had one live child, a daughter, and then at least two, possibly three, miscarriage or stillbirths. Anne was only married to the king for just over three years, so four pregnancies is still a lot in this time period. Had she lived for longer and continued in her marriage, there is no way to know whether this pattern would have continued, or whether Anne could indeed have produced more living children. There has been a suggestion that the miscarriages and stillbirths suffered by both Katherine of Aragon and Anne Boleyn may have in fact been down to Henry VIII. The theory is that perhaps Henry was Kell positive – 'a Kell positive father frequently causes negative reproductive outcomes for his reproductive partner after the first Kell negative pregnancy' which is what was experienced by both of Henry's first two wives.[31] The majority of people are Kell negative, with only a few being Kell positive. If a mother is Kell negative and a father is Kell positive, then there is a 50/50 chance of a baby being Kell positive. The first pregnancy typically carries to term, unless there are other problems, but a small amount of blood from the infant transfers to the mother who will develop anti-Kell antibodies, which will then attack any future Kell-positive foetus which is conceived.[32] This means that any future pregnancy has a higher risk of ending in miscarriage or stillbirth. If Henry was Kell positive, because it is much rarer, it is unlikely that his partner would also have been Kell positive, producing the reproductive problems. This could help to explain why so many of Katherine of Aragon's pregnancies ended in miscarriage or stillbirth, and why Anne Boleyn seemed to be having similar problems as well. But we will never know if this was the reason. It would be ironic and very sad if it was Henry, who was so desperate for a son, but it was he who was stopping those pregnancies going to term. It would have been interesting had Jane Seymour survived the birth of Prince Edward to see if she produced any further children with the king.

While Anne tried to conceive and produce a son, Princess Elizabeth was growing up well, and she was having visits from both of her parents during her early years, as it was reported in April 1534 that 'the King and Queen were at Eltham, and saw my lady Princess, as goodly a child as hath been sent, and her grace is much in the King's favour as goodly child should be'.[33] Anne Boleyn was also lavishing gifts on her only child, Elizabeth, spending

1. Arthur Tudor, Prince of Wales, eldest son of Henry VII and Elizabeth of York, older brother of Henry VIII. He was the first husband of Katherine of Aragon, and their short marriage would come under intense scrutiny during the annulment case.

2. Henry VIII was the second son of Henry VII and Elizabeth of York and originally was not intended to inherit the throne until the death of his older brother, Arthur. The annulment of his marriage to Katherine of Aragon and marriage to Anne Boleyn would change England forever.

3. Katherine of Aragon was the first wife of Henry VIII having previously been married to his older brother, Arthur. This image is from around the time that Henry VIII was considering an annulment as Katherine had failed to give him a living son.

4. Cardinal Thomas Wolsey was the man who Henry VIII believed would get him his annulment. Wolsey dramatically fell from power after the Blackfriars trial in 1529 when the case was adjourned to Rome to await a papal verdict.

5. Henry Fitzroy, Duke of Richmond and Somerset, was Henry VIII's only acknowledged illegitimate child, by his mistress Bessie Blount. He was born just after Katherine of Aragon's final pregnancy ended in sadness and disappointment.

6. The Priory of St Lawrence at Blackmore was where Henry VIII's mistress, Bessie Blount, gave birth to his son, Henry Fitzroy. It was at a distance from the court but still close enough that Henry could get there should he wish to.

7. Mary Boleyn, sister of Anne Boleyn, was Henry VIII's mistress, though the exact timing and length of the affair is unclear. Her two children, Catherine and Henry Carey, are rumoured to be the children of Henry VIII, though there is no firm evidence to support this.

8. A romanticised image of Katherine of Aragon pleading with Henry VIII at the Blackfriars trial which, Henry believed, would decide on the validity of their marriage. Katherine's speech was impassioned, and the case would be recalled to Rome without a verdict being given.

9. Catherine Carey Knollys, pictured during the reign of Elizabeth I. She was the daughter of Mary Boleyn and rumoured daughter of Henry VIII from her mother's affair with the king, though legally she was the child of William Carey, Mary's first husband.

10. Anne Boleyn would become Henry VIII's second wife. She was the catalyst for the annulment case and the Break with Rome as Henry was so desperate to marry her and for her to give him a son. She would fail and would be executed in 1536.

11. Hever Castle in Kent, the childhood home of Anne Boleyn. This is likely the place where Anne received Henry VIII's love letters to her when she was away from court, and replied to him, though her replies are now lost.

12. Thomas Cromwell was the man who would help Henry VIII to achieve his annulment and allow him to marry Anne Boleyn. Cromwell had been in Cardinal Wolsey's household but rose to power after his old mentor's fall. Cromwell would follow Anne Boleyn to the block in 1540.

13. John Fisher, Bishop of Rochester, was executed in 1535 for refusing to accept Henry VIII's second marriage to Anne Boleyn, or his new position as Head of the Church in England. He was made a saint 400 years after his death and is immortalised in stone in Rochester Cathedral.

14. The burial place of Katherine of Aragon in Peterborough Cathedral. Katherine died alone in exile at Kimbolton in January 1536. She continued to assert to the end that she was the true queen, and that Henry VIII was her husband.

15. The site of the scaffold on Tower Hill. This was where Anne Boleyn's 'lovers' were executed in May 1536 – George Boleyn, Henry Norris, Francis Weston, William Brereton, and Mark Smeaton.

16. An engraving of the execution of Anne Boleyn on 19 May 1536. She was beheaded by a French swordsman rather than an English axe, and all because, essentially, she failed to give the king a son, and he wanted to replace her.

17. The White Tower is the oldest part of the Tower of London and would have been a sight that Anne Boleyn, Thomas More, and John Fisher knew well. The royal apartments where Anne stayed prior to her coronation and execution no longer survive.

18. The tomb marker for Anne Boleyn in the Chapel of St Peter ad Vincula within the Tower of London. The markers were laid under Queen Victoria after excavations in the chapel. It is unlikely that the remains of those buried here are actually under the markers, however.

19. Jane Seymour, Henry VIII's third wife, who followed Anne Boleyn on the English throne. She would succeed where both Katherine of Aragon and Anne Boleyn failed and provide Henry VIII with a son in the future Edward VI.

20. The tomb of Henry Fitzroy, Duke of Richmond and Somerset, Henry VIII's illegitimate son. He died just months after Anne Boleyn in July 1536, leaving Henry with no son at all, until Prince Edward was born in 1537. He is buried in St Michael's Church at Framlingham.

21. An engraving of the Whitehall Mural, originally completed in the late 1530s. The original was destroyed in a fire in 1698. It shows Henry VII and Elizabeth of York at the back with Henry VIII and Jane Seymour in front as the founders and continuators of the Tudor dynasty.

22. An image of the Tudor succession from the reign of Elizabeth I. Mary I and her husband Philip II of Spain are to the left, Henry VIII with young Prince Edward in the middle, and Elizabeth I to the right but also the front.

23. An engraving of Henry VIII with his fool Will Somers, and then his three children – Edward VI, Mary I, and Elizabeth I, from the early nineteenth century.

24. Edward VI, the longed-for son of Henry VIII by his third wife Jane Seymour. Jane would die within weeks of Edward's birth, and Edward himself would die aged just 15 in 1553, after six years on the throne.

25. Mary I, daughter of Henry VIII and Katherine of Aragon. She was declared illegitimate in 1533 when Henry married Anne Boleyn. She became queen in 1553 on the death of her half-brother, Edward, and was succeeded by her half-sister, Elizabeth, in 1558.

26. Elizabeth I, daughter of Henry VIII and Anne Boleyn. She grew up under the cloud of her mother's fate and her own declared illegitimacy. But she would be triumphant, succeeding to the throne in 1558 and ruling England for 44 years.

around £40 a month on clothes and accessories for herself and her daughter. The total annual bill for Elizabeth's household was around £2,000 – much higher than that of her half-sister, Princess Mary when she was still in favour.[34] The £40 a month on clothes and accessories equates to around £17,600 today, and the £2,000 annual bill for Elizabeth's household is approximately £882,500 today. Perhaps Anne Boleyn purposefully made sure that Elizabeth had a larger and more luxurious household than Mary ever had, in order to emphasise that Elizabeth was the rightful and legitimate child and heir of Henry VIII, and not Mary. Anne wanted to outdo Katherine of Aragon in every way in order to emphasise her status as the rightful and true queen.

But it is important to focus on more than just the pressure of producing an heir for Anne Boleyn's marriage to Henry VIII. This period in the early to mid-1530s was a time of great change in England. We see the rise of Thomas Cromwell along with his role in the Reformation and how it ties to the 'Great Matter' (see chapter 8). There were also massive religious and political changes. The First Succession Act and Act of Supremacy were introduced in 1534, along with a new Treason Act. These were all intended to enshrine in law Anne Boleyn as queen, and her children with the king as heirs, as well as the king's position as Head of the Church in England. Princess Mary was debased to Lady Mary, and Princess Elizabeth declared the true heir to the throne. There were two queens in England – Anne Boleyn at the centre of the English court in London, and Katherine of Aragon in exile at Buckden Palace until 1534, and then at Kimbolton Castle in Cambridgeshire until her death in January 1536. It is often said that the marriage of Henry VIII and Anne Boleyn was in decline from the birth of Elizabeth in September 1533, but this is not true. It was a relationship of sunshine and storms, it always had been, with tempestuous arguments and passionate reconciliations. But their relationship weathered it all, until 1536. Women at the time lost children due to miscarriage or stillbirth, it was not unusual, so even Anne's first miscarriage in 1534 would not have been too much of a blow; a disappointment for sure, but there was no reason to suspect it would become a pattern, like Katherine of Aragon's pregnancies tragically did.

Anne Boleyn as queen was determined to have a household beyond reproach, 'to be attending on her, ladies of great honour, and yet of greater choice for reputation of virtue undoubted witnesses of her spousal integrity'.[35] Ladies of honour would enhance Anne's own honour and prestige as queen. This was written with hindsight, which probably explains the reference to 'spousal integrity', given the later accusations against Anne. It is a point that is important to make, though. Anne would have been surrounded by her ladies day and night as queen, and was rarely, if ever, alone. She could not have committed adultery without the connivance of at least one of her ladies. This is played out years later in the case of Henry VIII's fifth wife, Katherine Howard. Katherine was accused of adultery in 1541, and she was executed in 1542 alongside Jane Boleyn, Viscountess Rochford, Anne Boleyn's sister-in-law, who was accused of facilitating Katherine's meetings with her supposed lover. None of Anne's ladies were ever arrested or accused of complicity, so how was she supposed to have committed adultery? This remains a contentious point and is seen as evidence of Anne's innocence in the crimes of which she was accused in 1536.

Anne surrounded herself with many of her Boleyn relatives, including her sister-in-law, Jane Boleyn. On 13 October 1534, Chapuys reported to Charles V that Anne Boleyn had conspired with her sister-in-law, Jane Boleyn, to get rid of a woman from the court who the king was showing interest in:

> Of late days lord Rochford's wife has been banished the Court because she had conspired with the Concubine to procure the withdrawal from Court of the young lady whom this king has been accustomed to serve … whose influence increases daily, while that of the Concubine diminishes, which has already abated a good deal of her insolence.[36]

Anne Boleyn was used to having Henry VIII's full attention and did not seem to deal well with it when the king's eye wandered away from her. Anne was determined to maintain her hold over the king, so seems to have plotted with her sister-in-law to get rid of the woman she perceived the king was paying attention to. We are not told what the scheme was, but Jane Boleyn was eventually received back at court having been banished by the king in the aftermath of the incident. There is no evidence of any bad feeling between Anne and Jane on her return, but it does demonstrate Jane Boleyn's loyalty to the Boleyns.[37] This is important to note as Jane is often vilified as an enemy of the Boleyns, informing on her husband and sister-in-law, for which there is no evidence. She was a Boleyn, and the downfall of Anne and George hugely affected her own position. Anne's sister, Mary Boleyn, was also at court until her second, secret, marriage in 1534 to William Stafford.

George Wyatt declared that 'neither also were [Anne's] virtues only enclosed in her own breast or shut up in her own person'.[38] This suggests that Anne tried her best to share good fortune, giving alms to the poor, promoting the reform of religious institutions, and wanting to set up educational institutions with the proceeds of the dissolutions of the monasteries. Anne wanted to set a good example to others, and she did:

> … those works in the sight of God, which she caused her maids and those about her daily to work in shirts and smocks for the poor. But not staying here her eye for charity, her hand of bounty passed through the whole land, each place felt that heavenly flame burning in her, all times will remember it, no place leaving for vain flames, no times for idle thoughts.[39]

Often when considering popular perceptions, it is Katherine of Aragon who is portrayed as sewing shirts and giving charity to the poor. It is probably an exaggeration to say that Anne's hand of bounty 'passed through the whole land' as the court was largely based around London, and Henry and Anne never travelled north on progress. In his whole reign, Henry never travelled further north than York, where he went in 1541 with his fifth wife, Katherine Howard. The north also remained stubbornly Catholic. The Reformation spread more strongly in the south, in the areas surrounding London so, in that respect, viewing Anne as a reformer, the north was likely against her and for Katherine. The idea of Anne burning with a 'heavenly flame' suggests some kind of divine intervention, like it was Anne's destiny and God's plan for Anne to be queen, to promote the reformed religion, conduct charitable work, and produce a great future monarch.

The First Succession Act was passed soon after the birth of Princess Elizabeth, in 1534, in order to cement Anne Boleyn's position as queen, and the rights of her children as heirs to the throne. Their first child was a daughter, but Henry VIII was confident that sons would follow. The act starts by asking the king to 'foresee and provide for the perfect surety of both you, and of your most lawful succession and heirs', referencing a time of 'great divisions' where 'several titles pretended to the imperial crown'.[40] The king did not need reminding that the succession needed to be resolved. He was the most anxious of all for it to be settled and settled as he desired it. The wording evokes a sense almost of fear, that England could return to a time of infighting like the Wars of the Roses, still in living memory for some. It was not as clear in 1534 as it is today that the wars were over. The Tudors feared they could be overthrown like so many before. This is likely a deliberate evocation of the Wars of the Roses in order to instil a fear of a repeat in the people, so that they would support the changes Henry VIII was making.

The act says that the marriage of Henry VIII and Katherine of Aragon is 'absolutely declared, deemed, and adjudged to be against the laws of Almighty God, and also, accepted, reputed, and taken of no value or effect, but utterly void and annulled'.[41] The assumption is, therefore, that any issue born of the marriage is illegitimate. An argument could be made, however, that from a marriage entered into in good faith, the issue could still be considered legitimate. However, Henry VIII and Anne Boleyn did not want Katherine of Aragon's daughter to sit above their own children. The act then goes on to specify that:

> The lawful matrimony had and solemnised between your highness and your most dear and entirely beloved wife Queen Anne, shall be established, and taken for undoubtful, true, sincere and perfect ever hereafter, according to the just judgment of the said Thomas, archbishop of Canterbury, metropolitan and primate of all this realm, whose grounds of judgment have been confirmed, as well by the whole clergy of this realm in both the Convocations, and by both the universities hereof.[42]

The legitimacy of the marriage had been declared by Thomas Cranmer, Archbishop of Canterbury, at Dunstable in May 1533. It would be he who, within just a few short years, would then annul Henry and Anne's marriage as well. But the legitimisation of the marriage had been backed by the clergy, and the universities, so it had both ecclesiastical and theological backing from clerics and intellectuals, though not from the Pope.

There is an interesting line in the First Succession Act which states that papal dispensations for marriages within the forbidden degrees of affinity 'of right ought not to be granted, admitted, nor allowed; for no man … has power to dispense with God's laws'.[43] Henry VIII and Katherine of Aragon, as previously discussed, were related within the forbidden degrees of affinity as brother and sister-in-law. But Henry VIII and Anne Boleyn were also within the forbidden degrees of affinity due to Henry's previous relationship with Anne's older sister, Mary. The king passed an act designed to protect Anne and her offspring, but within it may have been a get-out clause to annul his marriage to Anne, whether consciously or not.

Henry VIII may have had a declaration made by the Archbishop of Canterbury that his marriage to Katherine of Aragon was null and void and his marriage to Anne Boleyn was legal and valid, but the Pope finally made his judgement on 22 March 1534 that Henry VIII's marriage to Katherine was legal and valid, and his marriage to Anne was null and void. The judgement read:

> … that the said matrimony always hath stood, and still doth stand, firm and canonical … and that the aforesaid Henry king of England is and shall be bound and obstrict to the matrimonial society and cohabitation with the said lady Katherine his lawful wife and queen, to bold end maintain her with such love and princely honour, as becometh a loving husband, and his kingly honour, to do.[44]

England and the Papacy were now set squarely against one another, with little chance of a reconciliation. Had the Pope declared in Henry's favour, he may have been willing to try and reconcile, though it still seems unlikely as Henry did not like having to answer to anyone else. But the judgement did give Katherine of Aragon a lifeline to cling to. In the eyes of the Catholic Church, she was in the right, and all of her actions over the preceding eight years had been right. It also enshrined in Katherine's eyes the legitimacy of her daughter, Mary. Katherine possibly believed that this judgement from the Pope would mean that she would be restored. But it was not to be. Henry was enshrining his rights as Head of the Church and Anne Boleyn's position as queen, in law and making it treason to dispute it.

Passed around the same time as the First Succession Act, the Treason Act of 1534 tries to dishonour all those with 'cankered and traitorous hearts' who might make 'shameful slanders, perils, or imminent danger or dangers' against Henry VIII, Anne Boleyn, or their children and heirs.[45] It also has a much wider reach than issues surrounding the succession, tackling head-on the religious changes which allowed the marriage of Henry and Anne to go ahead, stating that it would be treason to call Henry VIII 'heretic, schismatic, tyrant, infidel, or usurper of the crown'.[46] There were effectively punishments for heresy being enacted as part of the treason laws. The two were being considered as one and the same. In Henry VIII's eyes, if you disagreed with him on religion, then you wanted to deprive him and his heirs of his throne. The two were too intertwined to differentiate.

The 1534 Treason Act expanded the existing definition of treason, meaning that there were more things which could be adjudged to be treason, and which were harder to disprove. By the 1351 Treason Act, treason was defined as actions or deeds, including:

> Compassing the Death of the King, Queen, or their eldest Son; violating the Queen, or the King's eldest Daughter unmarried, or his eldest Son's Wife; levying War; adhering to the King's Enemies; killing the Chancellor, Treasurer, or Judges in Execution of their Duty.[47]

However, when Henry VIII introduced his new Treason Act in 1534, the definition expanded to include words and thoughts, as well as deeds. It was a new, dangerous time in English history as the new act declared:

> That if any person or persons ... do maliciously wish, will or desire, by words or writing, or by craft imagine, invent, practise, or attempt any bodily harm to be done or committed to the king's most royal person, the queen's, or their heirs apparent, or to deprive them or any of them of their dignity, title, or name of their royal estates.[48]

This was revolutionary. Never had words or thoughts been treason before and it heralded a dangerous period in England where men very close to the king would suffer for their beliefs and where, some believe, they were manipulated into condemning themselves. It had come about because of Henry VIII's marriage to Anne Boleyn and the steps he had to take to make it happen, and then to enshrine Anne as queen and their children as heirs in law.

Chapter 8

Thomas Cromwell and the English Reformation

Thomas Cromwell rose from the ashes of Thomas Wolsey's fall across the minefield that was Henry VIII's annulment case. When Cardinal Thomas Wolsey fell from power in 1529 and died the following year, there was a new rising star at court. Thomas Cromwell had begun his career at the English court in the service of Wolsey and would remain dedicated to him and his memory, even as he moved into the king's service. However, the pair had very different and contrasting religious views. Thomas Wolsey was a staunch traditionalist Catholic, whereas Thomas Cromwell favoured more radical religious reform and even evangelicalism. Cromwell's biographer, Diarmaid MacCulloch, describes how Cromwell 'shaped a great revolution in his own country's affairs, which has in turn shaped much of the modern world'.[1] Cromwell was one of the most influential figures in the English Reformation and at the English court throughout the 1530s, up to his fall and execution in 1540. During these years, there was lots of new legislation pushed through parliament to legalise the Break with Rome and change the succession to the throne multiple times. Cromwell was at the heart of these changes which influenced the development of England for decades to follow.

Wolsey was a man of the Church, whereas Cromwell held secular beliefs, though he had a lot of involvement with religious matters. Henry VIII would make him Vicegerent in Spirituals, effectively as his deputy in the Royal Supremacy. Cromwell and Wolsey are often compared, as Cromwell replaced Wolsey as the king's adviser, having learned the ropes in his household. One of the notable differences between Thomas Wolsey and Thomas Cromwell is that 'Wolsey loved pomp and circumstances; Cromwell was unusually indifferent to the outward show of power', though Cromwell was also 'more aware of its realities'.[2] Wolsey liked to display his power ostentatiously, whereas Cromwell did not. Perhaps Cromwell realised that Wolsey's ostentatiousness had worked against him in the end and made the nobility jealous of his wealth as well as his power which worked to bring him down. Wolsey did not realise the power that Henry would take onto himself as a result of the 'Great Matter' whereas Cromwell saw what was possible and how it would change English politics forever. Whether he intended the radical measures that Henry VIII would take to resolve the annulment case is up for debate, but he certainly took advantage when they happened to cement and exploit his own power, even when it meant the fall and destruction of his mentor, Wolsey.

It is interesting to note, from recent discoveries made by Dr Owen Emmerson, Kate McCaffrey, and Alison Palmer, that Katherine of Aragon, Anne Boleyn, and Thomas Cromwell, all owned a copy of the same printing of a Book of Hours from 1527. Katherine, Anne, and Cromwell would be intricately linked by events but also divided. This book offers an insight into the connection between them. A Book of Hours was traditionally a Catholic text filled with prayers for different times of the day, usually split into eight devotional cycles, based on the 'rigid daily lives' of monastic communities.[3] The date is also important to remember here. In 1527, the lives of all three of these figures were about to be changed forever, with Anne and Cromwell on the rise, and Katherine's star on the wane. All three would be inextricably connected in the events which followed. McCaffrey's research into these Books of Hours has come up with several theories as to how the books came into Katherine, Anne, and Cromwell's ownership. One theory is that they requested them on hearing that the printer, Germain Hardouyn, was producing them. Each one is slightly differently illustrated, possibly on individual request. The three obviously shared an appreciation for well-made, personalised devotional texts, and these were made for a wealthy English clientele.[4] Thomas Cromwell was a rising star at the English court, and he made the best use of the position he found himself in. Cromwell's own copy of this Book of Hours is the book that sits on the table in front of him in the famous portrait by Holbein, with its gilt and jewelled decoration on the cover.

Thomas Cromwell was born the son of a Putney blacksmith. He travelled a lot in his youth on the continent, spending time in Italy and Antwerp among other places, though little is known of his actual movements. Dr Owen Emmerson describes Thomas Cromwell spending time with the Frescobaldi family where he learned business, banking, and trade.[5] Caroline Angus concurs, with Cromwell coming to the Frescobaldi household after the Battle of Garigliano, north of Naples, in 1503. Cromwell may have been begging on the streets after the battle, struggling to make ends meet, but he was taken in and spent nearly a decade with the family, where he benefitted from their knowledge and training.[6] Antwerp may well have been where Cromwell first came into contact with ideas of religious reform as merchants came and went from various different places and a mix of religions, cultures, and beliefs all came together at this centre of trade.

It is unclear exactly when Thomas Cromwell returned to England, though it is likely to be sometime between 1510 and 1515. The year 1513 seems probable for his return as Cromwell is registered in a Court of Chancery case in 1514.[7] In around 1524, Thomas Cromwell entered the household of Cardinal Thomas Wolsey. With his skills in banking and business, he was no doubt a huge asset to Wolsey in building his wealth and managing investments, as well as providing legal advice. The previous year, in 1523, Cromwell had become a Member of Parliament (MP), likely for Bath, and opposed the raising of a subsidy for the French campaign, arguing that such a war was not affordable.[8] Thomas Cromwell, it seems, had quite a moral compass to protect the people he served as an MP. He also helped Wolsey to dissolve several monasteries to found his Cardinal College at Oxford in 1529. Chapuys later reported in 1535 that 'the cardinal of York, seeing his vigilance and diligence, his ability and promptitude, both in evil and good, took him into his service, and employed him principally in demolishing five or six good monasteries'.[9] Chapuys also recognised Cromwell's qualities which could be of use to both Wolsey and, later, Henry VIII.

When Cardinal Wolsey fell from power in 1529 and died the following year in disgrace, Cromwell made his way into the king's service. From here, he became involved more deeply in the king's 'Great Matter', quite possibly encouraging the king to break with Rome and begin dissolving the monasteries on a bigger scale. Cromwell was not a knight or a gentleman and many of the established nobility resented his influence, as they had Wolsey's too, and were jealous of Cromwell's close relationship with the king.[10] This seems very likely. Many within the nobility believed that only they had the titles, wealth, and proper position to advise and influence the king, and resented that those from lower backgrounds, like Wolsey and Cromwell, had the king's ear and, in fact, were more powerful than themselves in terms of influencing Henry VIII. It was something which would contribute to Cromwell's own fall in 1540.

Cromwell's influence is nowhere more pronounced than in the Reformation Parliament, which opened in 1529 and would remain in session until 1536. This was a period which would see some of the biggest changes of the Tudor period and cemented the Break with Rome in law. The parliament attacked clerical abuses, such as the ones which Wolsey was said to have been party to, like the massive building works he completed, and other ostentations, his mistress and illegitimate children, and his abuse of power. It also attacked bishops holding multiple dioceses, which Wolsey was also guilty of. Initially, the Church was being reformed from within, rather than setting up a new Church of England. The Submission of the Clergy in 1532 was where the English clergy gave up their right to form Church laws without the king's consent, giving the monarch more power over the Church than any had previously had:

> The Clergy shall not make any Constitutions except in Convocation with the King's Assent, &c. On Penalty of Fine and Imprisonment.[11]

Henry VIII wanted complete control over the Church as well as the State, and any laws and decisions that were made in his kingdom. It is during the 'Great Matter' and these massive changes to Church and State that we really see Henry VIII's tyranny come to the fore. There were hints before, such as in the execution of Edward Stafford, 3rd Duke of Buckingham, in 1521, but the tantalising prospect of ever-increasing power was too much for the king to hide it anymore. Cromwell helped the king to achieve what he desired, over and above his annulment, which was total power and authority over the Church and State. There then followed the Act of Restraint in Appeals in 1533 which forbade appeals to the Pope from England on both religious and secular matters. This meant that the king would be the final authority on all such matters, which included his own annulment case. The act forbade Katherine of Aragon appealing to Rome against any decision on her marriage made in England. Cromwell was the architect of this law, which provided the means for the annulment to be declared in England.

It is difficult to imagine the English Reformation without Thomas Cromwell. He was at the centre of the barrage of legislation, which was passed, including the Act of Restraint in Appeals of 1533, the Act of Supremacy and the First Succession Act of 1534. He also had a hand in the new Treason Act of 1534, making it treason to question the king's title as Supreme Head of the Church in England. Cromwell's legal knowledge would have been invaluable to the king to get these acts drafted and passed in parliament.

It is often said that Thomas Cromwell and Anne Boleyn were allies due to their shared religious beliefs, and we see this a lot in popular culture. But what evidence is there for this close relationship or alliance between the two in reality? Very little, actually. They may have worked together as a matter of course at various points when their aims aligned, but there is no evidence of a concerted partnership or alliance. It seemed to be almost too easy for Cromwell to turn against Anne in 1536 and, with the king's permission and likely encouragement, plot her downfall and execution, along with ending the lives of five men. In 1534, Chapuys reported to Emperor Charles V in relation to the positions of Katherine of Aragon and Princess Mary that Cromwell 'said he would do all he could to make things better, but I think he will not dare say a word for fear of the concubine'.[12] Anne still had huge influence and Cromwell dared not do anything to upset for fear of his own position and even his life in 1534. Chapuys reported the following year in 1535 that Cromwell now 'stands above every one but the Lady, and every one considers he has more credit with his master than Wolsey had'.[13] It is quite possibly one of the greatest compliments Chapuys could have paid Cromwell, as Wolsey was close to the king for well over a decade, but he was still second to Anne Boleyn, which demonstrates how much influence she still had over the king as late as 1535.

Eric Ives wrote that 'although [Cromwell] would eventually grow to become a cuckoo in the Boleyn nest, until then there is nothing to suggest that Anne ever saw the secretary as anything other than her loyal dependent, and to all outward appearances he remained "her man"'.[14] Anne and Cromwell worked together for as long as it was necessary, and perhaps it did appear to people at court that Cromwell was Anne's man, but Cromwell was focused on serving his king and on self-preservation, far more than loyalty to Anne Boleyn. Caroline Angus notes that 'for as long as Anne Boleyn sat at King Henry's side, Cromwell could never be titled like his peers'.[15] This again suggests that Cromwell and Anne were not so much allies as two people who worked together when necessary to achieve a common aim. Cromwell was not rewarded as Anne's allies were during the period of her rise and queenship, implying that they were not as close as some accounts would have us believe. Diarmaid MacCulloch says that, given Cromwell and Anne's 'shared enthusiasm for evangelical reform in religion' it has been 'natural to assume over the centuries' that the pair were allies. However, 'Cromwell shows no sign of being Anne's enthusiastic partisan'.[16] A lack of evidence of hostility between Cromwell and Anne in surviving letters and documents is 'not surprising' as 'clashes were kept carefully out of sight until the final crisis of 1536'.[17] It was in the interests of Protestant writers like John Foxe to smooth over the relationship between Cromwell and Anne in their narratives to promote the English Reformation, as their work was propaganda to promote a particular point of view. Just as there is no real evidence of a rift between Thomas Cromwell and Anne Boleyn prior to 1536, there is no evidence of a real alliance either. They certainly disagreed over how money from the dissolution of the monasteries should be spent, and they had different views on foreign policy – Anne favoured a treaty with France and Francis I, likely dating from her time there in the 1510s, while Cromwell favoured the Holy Roman Empire and Charles V.

The main thing that Thomas Cromwell and Anne Boleyn disagreed upon was their religious beliefs and how money from the dissolution of the monasteries should be spent. Sir George Wyatt, Anne Boleyn's first biographer and grandson of the man Anne was said to have had a relationship with, Sir Thomas Wyatt, wrote about how she 'had procured to her chaplains, men of great learning and no less honest conversing'.[18] Anne Boleyn wanted to promote those who she felt shared her beliefs and would assist her in reforming the Church, getting rid of abuses, and promoting education. Cromwell also wanted religious reform but may have wanted to go further than Anne. The two certainly disagreed on how the proceeds from the dissolution of the monasteries were to be spent. Cromwell wanted to pour the money into the royal treasury for the king and make him rich. Anne, however, had a more altruistic plan in mind and wanted the wealth of the monasteries to be redirected into educational and charitable causes, to help the people, rather than enrich the king. Anne wanted to direct the wealth of the monasteries to 'better uses' like colleges, which Wolsey had done in his foundation of Cardinal College at Oxford. Cromwell, however, saw the dissolution as a way of 'confiscating ecclesiastical land and thereby solving the king's deep-rooted financial problem' to make Henry VIII the richest prince in Christendom, which had the king's 'enthusiastic concurrence'.[19] It is quite possibly this disagreement about the diversion of funds from the dissolution of the monasteries which led Cromwell to the realisation that it was he or Anne— both of them could not survive at the English court.

The relationship between Thomas Cromwell and his master, Henry VIII, seemed to be one of respect in many ways. Henry respected how Cromwell could achieve what he wished, and he had multiple qualities which made him useful to the king; 'he speaks well in his own language, and tolerably in Latin, French, and Italian; is hospitable, liberal both with his property and with gracious words, magnificent in his household and in building'.[20] Cromwell's language skills would certainly have come in useful in diplomacy and dealing with ambassadors. What may surprise people are the words describing Cromwell as 'hospitable' and 'liberal' with words and property. Cromwell is so often painted as a villain that it is often difficult to conflate the, sometimes ruthless, side with this more genial and gentle side which he also had. This is perhaps evidenced most in his treatment of young men who he took into his household, including his nephew, Richard Cromwell, and Rafe Sadler.

But Cromwell was not so magnanimous to everyone who crossed his path. He had a ruthless streak. The two most notable executions of the 'Great Matter' were those of Sir Thomas More, and John Fisher, Bishop of Rochester, both of which took place within weeks of each other in the summer of 1535. However, these were preceded by other deaths as 'the members of the London Charterhouse and other Carthusian monks became the king's and Cromwell's first target'.[21] Joanne Paul describes how Cromwell sent his servant, John Rastell, to question the monks over the king's supremacy but this proved futile. On 28 April 1535 Cromwell had three Carthusian monks brought to Westminster Hall to face their judges, but their defence was that their refusal of the oath was not malicious.[22] The 1534 Treason Act states that a person or persons would be judged guilty of treason if they:

> … do maliciously wish, will or desire, by words or writing, or by craft imagine, invent, practise, or attempt any bodily harm to be done or committed to the king's most royal person, the queen's, or their heirs apparent, or to deprive them or any of them of their dignity, title, or name of their royal estates, or slanderously and maliciously publish and pronounce, by express writing or words, that the king our sovereign lord should be heretic, schismatic, tyrant, infidel or usurper of the crown …[23]

The monks claimed that they had not acted maliciously, so their words were not in fact treason under the act. This did not work, and they were condemned to death. The Carthusian monks were hanged by the neck until they were almost dead, cut down, and then their entrails were pulled out of their bodies in front of their eyes before they were beheaded and their bodies cut into quarters. It was an awful death, perhaps considered worse by the people because they were religious men.

Both Thomas More and John Fisher had also refused to take the Oath of Supremacy, rejecting Henry VIII's new status as Head of the Church in England. They also both had scruples over accepting the annulment of Henry's marriage to Katherine of Aragon, and his subsequent remarriage to Anne Boleyn, and the rights of the king's children with Anne to succeed to the throne, which was also included in the oath. Fisher and More had been imprisoned in the Tower of London for over a year prior to their executions, as the wheels of parliament moved, introducing the 1534 Treason Act which made it treason to deny in words the king's supremacy or the validity of his marriage and legitimacy of his offspring. The people most commonly blamed for these executions, aside from the king, are Anne Boleyn and Thomas Cromwell. How far either of them is really to blame is a matter of conjecture. Neither More nor Fisher, however, could have been executed without the king's authority. John Fisher, Bishop of Rochester, was beheaded on 22 June 1535. Sir Thomas More followed him to the scaffold on 6 July 1535. It appears that Cromwell may have done his best to save More, at the very least. More was willing to swear part of the oath, but not all of it, and it was the king who insisted on an all-or-nothing approach to the oath.[24] G. R. Elton claims that More was convicted on the perjured evidence of Sir Richard Rich who tricked More into speaking treason and denying the king as Head of the Church in England during his imprisonment.[25] It is difficult to deny that Cromwell was involved, as the king would have directed him to act, but his culpability in creating the case against them from the start seems in doubt. The king was driving actions; Cromwell was responding to his needs as a loyal servant.

Prior to the executions, the Italian Bishop of Faenza wrote that 'the Admiral, though he takes Fisher's case much to heart, has great fears for his life, especially as the Pope says in the brief that he created him a cardinal to make use of him in the Council'.[26] The suggestion here is that the Pope's own actions condemned Fisher, as he intended to use Fisher to promote the papal primacy in England, and Henry VIII had no intention of allowing this to happen. By making Fisher a cardinal during his imprisonment, Pope Paul III demonstrated his own power over the Church, and the king used his actions to make an example of Fisher, to show that the protection of the Church did not give protection under English law. When Thomas More was 'examined whether he would accept the King as Supreme Head in Earth of the Church of England, pursuant to the statute, [he] refused to give a direct answer, saying "I will not meddle with any such matters, for I am fully determined to serve God, and to think upon His Passion and my passage out of this world"'.[27] The account continues to say that:

> Afterwards, 12 May 27 Hen. VIII., the said Sir Thomas, knowing that one John Fissher, clk., was then detained in the Tower for divers misprisions, and that the said Fissher had refused to accept the King as above, wrote divers letters to him, which he transmitted by one Geo. Golde, declaring his agreement with Fisher, and intimating the silence which he, More, had observed when interrogated. In these letters he wrote as follows:—'The Act of Parliament is like a sword with two-edges, for if a man answer one way it will confound his soul, and if he answer the other way it will confound his body'.[28]

More and Fisher seemed to be of one mind regarding the supremacy and their willingness to die for what they believed in. More's final sentence is saying that if he accepts the Royal Supremacy, his soul would be damned, but if he rejected it, his body would be destroyed. As with the Carthusian monks, 'the entire trial hung on the word "maliciously"' and 'on balance, little evidence had been presented to impute malice to Thomas More's word, regardless of precisely how and in what context he had expressed them'.[29] The evidence against More is now thought to be weak.

A key piece of evidence against Thomas More was the testimony of Solicitor General, Richard Rich, who had visited More in the Tower on 12 June 1535. They began discussing hypotheticals, such as if parliament declared Richard Rich was king, would More accept it? More said yes since it was decreed by Act of Parliament. A more controversial discussion ensued in which More said:

> he would put a higher case:—'Suppose it should be enacted by Parliament that God should not be God, and that opposing the Act should be treason; and if it were asked of you, Ric. Ryche, whether you would say that God was not God according to the statute, and if you were to say so, would you not offend?' To which Ryche answered More, 'Certainly, because it is impossible that God should not be God. But because your case is so high, I will put a medium one. You know that our lord the King is constituted Supreme Head on Earth of the Church of England; and why ought not you, Master More, to affirm and accept him so, just as you would in the preceding case, in which you admit that you would be bound to accept me as King?' To which More, persevering in his treasons, answered that the cases were not similar; because a King can be made by Parliament, and deprived by Parliament, to which Act every subject being at the Parliament may give his assent; but as to the primacy, a subject cannot be bound, because he cannot give his consent to that in Parliament.[30]

More places the papal primacy above the power of any parliament. This is what the king objected to. He saw his own power over the Church in England as being above that of the Pope, but More and Fisher placed it the other way around. More was condemned for treason and sentenced to a traitor's execution at Tyburn. Joanne Paul, in her brilliant biography of Thomas More, says that 'More did not see himself as his opponents did – a lone voice pitted against a thundering majority ... he counted himself one of a far vaster majority, extending across time and space, whose size and scope made the king and parliament – and even all the oath-taking subjects of England – look like a feeble spark before a roaring inferno'.[31] More believed that the people of England in fact believed as he did and that he was voicing the thoughts of the majority, rather than the lone voice he appeared to be. Many of the people of England may have believed the same as More, but they took the oath regardless, likely fearful of the deadly repercussions of not doing so. Cromwell's role in the trial is not necessarily obvious, but he was behind the 1534 Treason Act under which More was condemned, and he may have been behind Rich's testimony, although it is uncertain. Caroline Angus writes that 'while Fisher did not weigh on Cromwell's conscience, More clearly did'.[32] Perhaps Cromwell's thought was that, if the king could kill a loyal servant like Thomas More, after having caused the downfall of Thomas Wolsey, what was to stop him killing Cromwell, or anyone else?

International opinion was largely outraged at the deaths of John Fisher and Thomas More. The Bishop of Faenza wrote of Bishop Fisher on the scaffold that:

> ... from age and suffering he was more like a shadow than a man, he spoke to the people boldly, telling them to be loving and obedient to their King, who was good by nature, but had been deceived in this matter; that he was led to death for wishing to preserve the honour of God and the Holy See; at which he did not grieve, but was content, for it was the will of God. Hears now from the English ambassador that he only said, that being of flesh, which naturally feared death, and knowing that Peter three times denied Christ through fear of death, and having always had the mind to die, if necessary, for the love of Christ and his Holy Church, now that he was come to it, he begged all present to pray to God to grant constancy and firmness to his fragile flesh to suffer cheerfully his approaching punishment.[33]

Fisher seems to have made clear that the reason for his execution was that he could not accept the king as Head of the Church in England, that he wished to 'preserve the honour of God and the Holy See'. As to fearing death, even if one makes up their mind to die for a cause, it will still be frightening, not knowing how fast or otherwise it might be, especially when it is at the hands of someone else. Fisher's motives seem clear and obvious in his intent to die for his faith. The same letter from the Bishop of Faenza goes on to speak of Thomas More, who 'is thought to be already executed, or, at least, condemned to death with perhaps thirty other virtuous persons, religious and secular; so that we now see clearly that the tragedy will go far, and that there is no hope of good from the King'.[34] The blame is laid firmly at the king's feet, as much as Cromwell may have been actively involved as the king's agent. Henry VIII was clearly in charge of events and pushing them through in order to cement his supremacy over the Church.

On 5 July 1535, the day before his execution, Thomas More wrote to his daughter, Margaret Roper, asking for blessings on his family and stating that 'tomorrow is St. Thomas Even, and the Utas of St. Peter, and therefore he longs to go to God; it were a day very meet and convenient for him'.[35] Like Fisher, More seems ready to embrace death and expects to be welcomed into Heaven. After a year in the Tower of London, he probably sees his execution as the inevitable conclusion of not being able to agree to what the king wished. One account of More's end says that, once he was condemned and returning to the Tower to await execution:

> … one of his daughters, named Margaret, pushed through the archers and guards, and held him in her embrace some time without being able to speak. Afterwards More, asking leave of the archers, bade her have patience, for it was God's will, and she had long known the secret of his heart. After going 10 or 12 steps she returned and embraced him again, to which he said nothing, except to bid her pray to God for his soul; and this without tears or change of colour. On the Tuesday following he was beheaded in the open space in front of the Tower. A little before his death he asked those present to pray to God for him and he would do the same for them [in the other world]. He then besought them earnestly to pray to God to give the King good counsel, protesting that he died his faithful servant, but God's first. Such was the miserable end of More, who was formerly in great reputation, and much loved by the King, his master, and regarded by all as a good man, even to his death.[36]

More is presented as a family man, principled and following his conscience. He accepts his fate and his death. The idea of exhorting people to pray for 'good counsel' for the king suggests that More possibly believed that the king was being led astray by his councillors, men like Cromwell, on the issue of religion, and he hoped that the king would return to his conservative and papal allegiance. More believed that he remained the king's servant, but his first allegiance would always be to his own beliefs and his own conscience. Thomas More and John Fisher were both canonised by Pope Pius XI in 1935, 400 years after their deaths.

It is worth saying that we do not see Cromwell gaining many honours under Anne Boleyn's queenship. His star rises after her death when he becomes Lord Privy Seal in July 1536, an office previously held by Thomas Boleyn, Earl of Wiltshire and Ormond, the father of Anne Boleyn, who was deprived of the office after his daughter's execution. Cromwell is eventually elevated to the peerage and created Earl of Essex in April 1540, along with being granted the office of Lord Great Chamberlain. Unfortunately, Cromwell did not get to enjoy this privilege for long as he was arrested on 10 June 1540 and taken to the Tower of London. He was sentenced by an Act of Attainder, ironically something Cromwell himself had popularised the use of in England. He was accused of forcing radical religion on the king, protecting Protestants accused of heresy, corrupt practices, and acting for personal gain. He was 'brought down by the flailing tail of a severely wounded Catholic establishment'.[37] An Act of Attainder meant that Cromwell was condemned to death in parliament without a trial and no chance to defend himself in open court. Cromwell had allowed Anne Boleyn a trial, so that royal justice could be seen to be done, but it was denied to him. Thomas Cromwell was publicly beheaded on Tower Hill on 28 July 1540, the very same day that Henry VIII married his fifth wife, Katherine Howard, at Oatlands Palace. The exact circumstances of his execution are debated. Some say that it was a botched beheading and that it took several strikes to sever his head from his body. Others say that it was a clean death. It is the botched beheading that is often shown in popular culture to create drama. So ended the life of Thomas Cromwell, the man who managed to obtain Henry VIII his first annulment of his marriage to Katherine of Aragon in order to marry Anne Boleyn and then oversaw and planned the downfall of Anne.

Cromwell is often said to be a radical in religion, but how true was this? He certainly wanted religious change in England and promoted the dissolution of the monasteries and the Royal Supremacy rather than the primacy of the Pope. What about other evangelical, Lutheran, or Calvinist beliefs? Creating an English vernacular Bible 'would be Cromwell's greatest achievement'.[38] Cromwell did also establish close links with evangelicals. Diarmaid MacCulloch asserts that Cromwell 'was essentially a rationalist and this was why he sympathised with the challenge emanating from Germany and the centres of humanist thought' and that 'he understood that the ecclesiastical establishment was totally incapable of reforming itself'.[39] John Schofield says that 'there need be no doubt about Cromwell's Lutheran faith', although we do not know when it first 'kindled in his heart' it is likely to have been late 1530 or 1531.[40] Tracy Borman writes that, throughout the annulment case, 'both Cranmer and Cromwell increasingly absorbed the evangelical ideas that were sweeping across Europe' and this was 'due to genuine piety as well as political pragmatism'.[41] These new religious ideas helped to make progress on the king's annulment case after the fall of Cardinal Wolsey, but Cranmer and Cromwell took them to heart. As Schofield says, 'this was a risky time to be nourishing evangelical beliefs', but that Cromwell did not take the safe option and instead 'embraced the new learning first and set about trying to commend it to Henry afterwards'.[42] This was a dangerous path to be treading, but Cromwell seems to have planted some of these new ideas into Henry's head, probably along with the influence of Anne Boleyn who was also eager for the annulment to be achieved without too much more delay.

Thomas Cromwell is a man often vilified in popular culture, such as Showtime's *The Tudors*. But you can also see a different, kinder, and more sympathetic view of him in Hilary Mantel's *Wolf Hall*. How far any of these adaptations are accurate is unclear, but Cromwell was neither wholly good nor bad. As most people are, he was shades of grey. His kindness towards the likes of Rafe Sadler who he looked after and trained up, as well as his nephew, Richard, who he took into his household, shows a very caring side to him, in sharp contrast to the man who we know planned and implemented the violent and shocking death of Anne Boleyn. Cromwell had a key role in the 'Great Matter' and in the Henrician Reformation, which would then be taken further by Henry's son and heir, Edward VI. Perhaps Cromwell would have approved of the more Protestant and reforming beliefs and actions that

Edward initiated, like the Book of Common Prayer. He certainly seemed to be more radical in his religious beliefs than Anne Boleyn was. Cromwell understood that his power lay in people, notably in the king himself, but also 'in his control of the personnel of the inner apartments of the court, and of the Privy Chamber in particular'.[43] Cromwell wanted to control who had access to the king and could influence him in terms of policy and religion, but he did not go as far as Wolsey had intended in the 1526 Eltham Ordinances, having people removed from the Privy Chamber. Wolsey's actions caused problems with courtiers and alienated them. However, we do see Cromwell taking down people who might speak against him during Anne Boleyn's fall, whether on purpose or not. It does seem likely to have been a deliberate decision on Cromwell's part, to remove Anne as the king desired, and to take down some of his own enemies at the same time.

The English Reformation was, of course, a much longer period than that of Thomas Cromwell's time in power. But Cromwell's interlude was crucial as he took the steps needed to complete the king's annulment in England and to break with Rome to achieve it. Joseph Ban describes how Cromwell 'brought important parties together, here the king and parliament, and assisted each in doing its important task' and that 'Cromwell was clearly the agent of the king' as he 'performed an important function as a broker'.[44] Thomas Cromwell set up the idea of reform which would later be carried on by Edward VI. Henry VIII himself was not as reformist or evangelical as Cromwell would have wished, though Edward certainly made up for it. It was Thomas Cromwell's foundations that allowed Edward VI and his protectors, Edward Seymour and John Dudley, to continue down the road of Reformation, and which led to Edward nominating Lady Jane Grey as his Protestant successor rather than his Catholic half-sister, Mary I. In the end, though, it would not be Protestant Jane who would triumph, but Catholic Mary.

Cromwell's power was less personal than Wolsey's, and he 'showed himself a supreme master of the bloody game of faction politics' during the 'Great Matter'.[45] Faction is often cited as a reason for the downfall of many, including Wolsey, Cromwell, and Anne Boleyn. Faction was stronger than Cromwell's own personal power and the king's reliance on him. Cromwell cemented his power during this period because he could do what the king asked of him. He achieved an annulment where Cardinal Wolsey could not, and it was likely, at least in part, a result of his influence on Henry VIII that the Henrician Reformation took off in England, paving the way for further reformist changes in religion in the reigns of Edward VI and Elizabeth I. Thomas Cromwell rose from the ashes of Thomas Wolsey's fall at the right moment, when the king needed someone more radical to achieve his own aims. Cromwell became that man for the king, helping Anne Boleyn to the throne in hope that she would provide the king with a son, and then removing her when she failed in her primary objective. It was Cromwell who planned and engineered events, but it was Henry VIII who was the driving force. Cromwell could not and would not have acted without the king's permission and authority.

Caroline Angus describes Cromwell as 'a charming, ruthless, and scrupulous man' who 'became the right man, at the right place, at the right time to upset an entire country' and pull England into 'the light of renaissance and reformation'.[46] To be both charming and ruthless is a combination that perhaps helped Cromwell to achieve the king's desires. He could cultivate positive relationships, while acting to ensure that what needed to be done was done. Historian Tracy Borman makes a great insight into Cromwell's character which may be unexpected, as he is often portrayed as a hard-nosed and ruthless man, the king's 'fixer'. However, Borman describes Cromwell thus:

> Cromwell was a man of great personal charisma, as well as ability, and had such a sharp wit that even his enemies could not help laughing at his humorous asides. He was also a man of voracious intellect, and since returning from the Continent he had built up a library so impressive that even the likes of Edmund Bonner, Wolsey's former chaplain and future Bishop of London, sought to borrow from it. Far from being cowed by authority, Cromwell had a natural irreverence and was not afraid to poke fun at or criticise even the highest-ranking members of the court.[47]

Borman's description highlights Cromwell more as a person than a politician or loyal statesman to the king. He had a sense of humour and could make people laugh. Though one has to wonder how far the nobility, like the conservative Duke of Norfolk, laughed along with Cromwell. Another description has Cromwell as 'one of England's greatest statesmen – the architect of the Reformation and the Tudor Revolution in Government'.[48] Cromwell's time in power in England, combined with Henry VIII's ruthlessness and determination, changed the face of the country forever. Cromwell did what the king wanted, was loyal to him, and helped those in need in his family and household. Thomas Cromwell was not a bad man or a villain but acted according to his own conscience.

Thomas Cromwell's period in power and his role in the beginnings of the English Reformation were crucial to the development of the English State as a whole. To achieve Henry VIII's annulment of his marriage to Katherine of Aragon, his remarriage to Anne Boleyn, changes to the succession, and the Break with Rome and dissolution of the monasteries required diligence, commitment, hard work, and a hard-nosed approach. Cromwell embodied these qualities and pushed on to begin the Reformation which would shape the remainder of the Tudor century, including the mid-Tudor crisis as religion changed with each successive monarch, finally settling into something resembling the Church of England today during the reign of Elizabeth I. Cromwell really is a fascinating figure in Tudor history, and one who shaped the England that was to come.

Chapter 9

Princess Mary and the Rivalry

The relationship between Queen Anne Boleyn, and Princess, or Lady, Mary, the daughter of Katherine of Aragon, was never going to be smooth. Anne had replaced Katherine on the throne against the wishes of many of the English people, as well as against the wishes of Katherine and Mary themselves. Princess Elizabeth had replaced Mary in the line of succession, also against the wishes of many people in England. Mary consistently refused to recognise that the marriage of her parents was invalid, and that she herself was illegitimate, no matter how much pressure was put on her. It was only after Anne's death that Mary finally capitulated when she realised that Anne's execution would not soften her father's attitude towards her. Mary had always believed that Anne Boleyn was at fault for her father's poor treatment of her and it was only after Anne's death when she was not immediately restored to his favour, that she realised Anne may have been the catalyst, but Henry was the cause. That was a pivotal moment for Mary, and she would never forgive herself for signing the document Henry VIII requested of her. When she became queen in 1553, reversing her own capitulation and restoring her parents' marriage would be almost the first thing she did.

Katherine of Aragon had been sent away from court in July 1531 to live in exile, in preparation for Henry and Anne's marriage. It would still be another year and a half before they could marry, but Anne was increasingly treated as queen, despite not being married to the king yet. Henry did not say goodbye to his first wife, instead he rode out hunting with Anne, leaving Katherine at Windsor Castle with Princess Mary, and never returned. Katherine and Mary were then separated and forbidden to communicate, even by letter, from May 1533, just as Anne was about to be crowned, as the king feared that the pair would be more powerful together. This fear came from the potential support of Charles V and the might of Spain, and the idea that Katherine and Mary could raise a large following in England, and foment an uprising against him. Whether this was paranoia on Henry's part is unclear. Katherine certainly had the guts to do it, and possibly the popularity to pull it off, but would she have raised an army against a man she knew was the rightful king and she firmly believed was her husband, as well as her daughter's father? It does not quite seem plausible, though you can never judge what people will do when they are desperate.

Eustace Chapuys, the Imperial ambassador to England from 1529 (an important year as we have seen) was a staunch supporter of both Katherine of Aragon and her daughter, Princess Mary. He believed that they were the true queen and princess, not Anne Boleyn and Princess Elizabeth. His embassy came at a complex time, as the Blackfriars trial had just concluded in 1529 when he took up his post, without judgement being given, much to Henry VIII's disappointment and chagrin. Katherine was being gradually sidelined as Anne Boleyn was treated more and more like a queen. Just after Katherine of Aragon's death in 1536, Chapuys wrote that Mary 'did not care about the offers made to her on her part and would rather die a hundred times than change her opinion or do anything against her honour and conscience'.[1] This echoes sentiments we know Katherine expressed during her lifetime about the validity of her marriage. Mary's opinions would form early on in the annulment case, and she would not waver from support for her mother until her eventual capitulation after Katherine's death and Anne Boleyn's execution in 1536. Mary was very devoted to her mother and even the death of that lady and queen would not change Mary's opinion while Anne Boleyn lived. Her capitulation would only come once her mother's supplanter and successor was dead, and when she realised that it was her father's decision and his actions.

Mary had quite possibly believed that Anne Boleyn was at the root of her father's poor treatment of her and she appears to have expected there to be an immediate upturn in her fortunes once Anne was dead. However, Henry would not relent so easily, which demonstrates that it was the king's own decision on his treatment of his daughter, perhaps influenced in part by Anne when he showed signs of weakening towards her. During Mary's reign, the Venetian ambassador recorded that during her father's reign:

> … seeing herself, with the same impiety, disinherited and declared a bastard, instead of legitimate, and only daughter, and heiress of the kingdom, as she was. But yet worse treatment awaited her, for with very great indignity she had to serve as her mistress (*come a patrona*) a public strumpet (*una publica meretrice*), her father's concubine, that famous Anne Boleyn, whom she saw not only succeed to her mother's place, but also, during that mother's lifetime, raised to the crown of England.[2]

The blame for Mary's poor treatment is very much placed on Anne Boleyn in this letter as she was forced to serve her. However, Mary did not serve Anne directly, but her daughter, Elizabeth. It seems unlikely that Anne would want to have Mary at court around her father, where she might be able to regain his affections. This same letter talks about Mary's hatred for Elizabeth, who was legally the heir in 1557 by the terms of their father's will, and the 1544 Act of Succession. Mary struggled with the idea that Elizabeth would succeed her as queen, refusing to name her. Her fear and disquiet stemmed from her difficult relationship with Anne Boleyn. What 'disquiets [Mary] most of all is to see the eyes and hearts of the nation already fixed on this lady (*sopra costei*) as successor to the Crown' and how difficult it was 'to see the illegitimate child of a criminal who was punished as a public strumpet, on the point of inheriting the throne with better fortune than herself, whose descent is rightful, legitimate, and regal'.[3] The stain of illegitimacy was still following Elizabeth more than twenty years after her mother's execution on the eve of her own accession to the throne, not helped by the fact that Mary had her parents' marriage declared valid, automatically meaning that Henry VIII's marriage to Anne Boleyn was invalid, because the two overlapped. But, more than a year before Mary's death, focus was shifting to Elizabeth as the heir, much as Catholic eyes had been focused on Mary before Edward VI's death. Mary tried to resist the ghost of Anne Boleyn and her treatment of her still in her mind.

There is a suggestion in a letter from Chapuys in 1536, that Mary could say that she was 'strongly desirous of entering religion', whether true or not.[4] Perhaps it was hoped that this show of piety and devotion would soften her father towards her or could protect her life if Henry or Anne decided to act against her. A suggestion had been made for Mary's mother, Katherine of

Aragon, to do the same during the annulment case, and enter a nunnery. It seems that Mary found much comfort in her religion and beliefs during particularly tumultuous periods in her life. Mary was still part of international negotiations as pertained to her marriage. In 1535, the Bishop of Troyes asked Henry VIII to fulfil the old treaty for Princess Mary to marry the French dauphin. Henry would not accept or permit the marriage to go ahead. Mary would once have been an asset in whatever marriage was arranged for her, but unless she accepted the annulment of her parents' marriage and her own illegitimacy, 'she would be a loose cannon and could not be allowed to leave England'.[5] It was possible that, had Mary been allowed to marry the dauphin, there would have been a French invasion of England on Mary's behalf, which must also have occurred to Henry VIII. The proposal for a French marriage for Mary must have worried and upset Anne Boleyn, who had wanted a French marriage for her own daughter, Elizabeth, but it never happened.

In 1531, as previously explained, Katherine of Aragon was left at Windsor Castle as Henry VIII left with Anne Boleyn to go hunting. The king said nothing to Katherine, not even a goodbye, and he would not see her again. Princess Mary was then sent to Richmond, and mother and daughter would not meet again either. There is a letter from Eustace Chapuys, dated 27 September 1534, in the *Letters and Papers of Henry VIII*, which says that:

> The Princess has been very ill. Having been obliged to remove and follow the Bastard when a little indisposed, it increased her illness, but she is better. It has been a great comfort to her that the King her father sent her his physician, and permitted the Queen also to visit her, and the apothecary from whom she has received all her medicines for four years.[6]

This suggests quite clearly that Katherine of Aragon was permitted to visit her daughter when Anne Boleyn was on the throne. Chapuys always called Katherine queen and never referred to Anne as queen in his letters, so it is clear who he is referring to. However, it is not quite so clear cut in truth because the same letter in the *Calendar of State Papers: Spain* has a slightly different translation:

> The Princess has lately been very ill, owing to her having been obliged, whilst in delicate health, to move from where she was, and follow the bastard. In consequence of the fatigues of the journey, and of the many annoyances to which she is daily subjected, her illness increased considerably, though, thanks be to God, she has since recovered, and is now well. The King sent his own physician to visit her, and permitted that her mother's, and the apothecary who has been her medical adviser for the last three years, should also be in attendance; which permission has considerably helped to her recovery.[7]

The letter in the Spanish State Papers is dated four days earlier than the one in the *Letters and Papers*, which may account for the time between when the letter was written and sent, and when it was delivered. But the biggest, and crucial, difference between the letters is that, where the *Letters and Papers* translation has Katherine of Aragon visiting Mary, the Spanish State Papers has Katherine of Aragon's physician visiting Mary, rather than Katherine herself. This makes more sense. It is difficult to believe that Henry VIII would allow Katherine herself to visit her daughter when Anne Boleyn was on the throne, though Anne had just lost a child so perhaps Henry was feeling vulnerable at this time. It is more likely that the Spanish State Papers version is correct and that Henry allowed Katherine's physician to visit Mary, to give her a little comfort and likely some news of her mother, rather than allowing the two women to meet in person.

This separation was devastating for both of them, particularly as the years passed. Henry VIII believed that the pair were more powerful together, so determined to keep them separate, perhaps hoping that Mary would give way to his wishes if separated from her strong and stubborn mother. When Henry married Anne Boleyn in 1533, Katherine was told that she was no longer to be referred to as Queen of England, but as Princess Dowager of Wales, her title as the widow of Henry's elder brother, Prince Arthur, who had died thirty-one years earlier in 1502. Princess Mary was no longer to be afforded the title of princess, but to be referred to instead as Lady Mary, as the illegitimate daughter of the king. Mary's title of princess would be taken by Anne Boleyn's daughter, Elizabeth. Neither Katherine nor Mary was willing to accept their demotion and their treatment at the hands of Henry VIII became 'increasingly severe'.[8] Mary's health suffered as a result, and she would be afflicted with health problems throughout her life, as can be seen in the letter previously discussed where multiple physicians were sent to help Mary. With all of these changes, 'religion, personal desires and politics became hopelessly confused with one another'.[9] This statement can be applied to England and to Mary herself. Everything would become tied up for Mary in the events of the late 1520s and early to mid-1530s which would affect the rest of her life.

When the 'Great Matter' was really in its infancy, perhaps Mary believed, as Katherine possibly did, that Henry VIII would soon tire of this new woman and return to her mother and to herself. Historian Melita Thomas suggests that 'the public behaviour of Henry toward Katherine may also have lulled Mary into believing all would turn out well'.[10] Mary was not always at court, spending a lot of time at other royal palaces like Richmond and Eltham with her tutors. It might thus have been easier for her parents to put on a show around her and make everything seem like it was okay. Katherine of Aragon undoubtedly loved her daughter and would have wanted to shield her for as long as possible from what was happening. During the Blackfriars trial in 1529, Mary would only have been 13 years old and though she likely would have heard rumours of what was happening, it seems unlikely that she was told everything. She instinctively, however, sided with her mother over her father, choosing to believe her parents' marriage was lawful and she was legitimate, the rightful heir to the English throne. Though anyone might have taken the same stance over their own legitimacy, particularly when it could lose them a throne.

Some historians believe that Anne Boleyn 'utterly loathed Mary and everything she stood for'.[11] Perhaps Anne did come to loath Mary, but it seems likely that fear was at the heart of Anne's feelings towards Mary from early on in their relationship. Mary was 'intelligent, gifted, not unattractive and of a winning disposition, popularity made her adherence more important and her opposition more dangerous'.[12] If Mary gave in to her father and acknowledged Anne Boleyn as queen, the people might be more willing to accept it as well, but if Mary refused, the people had a figurehead for their own dissatisfaction with the situation. It has been said that Anne had 'feelings of insecurity' over Katherine of Aragon, and 'feelings of inferiority' when she compared her own daughter's position in the world with Mary's.[13]

Anne knew for many years that Henry VIII intended to annul his marriage to Katherine of Aragon and replace Princess Mary in the succession with her own children, and that this was generally unpopular with the people. But Anne also must have realised that, if she failed to produce a son and birthed only daughters, as she would, that Mary would inevitably stand as a rival to her own daughter. Mary set herself up in her mother's image as the symbol of the Roman Catholic faith, whereas Anne Boleyn was a reformer. It would become a religious stand-off as well as a political one. Mary would not forget Anne Boleyn, even after she was dead, seeing Anne's daughter, Elizabeth, as a threat to her own reign in the 1550s, the same as Anne had been to Katherine of Aragon nearly thirty years earlier.

In December 1533, after the birth of Princess Elizabeth in the September, Eustace Chapuys wrote to his master, Charles V, that 'the King, who, for a month past, ought to have made or sent me an answer for what reason he claimed to deprive the Princess of her title, legitimacy, and primogeniture' had sent Anne Boleyn's uncle, Thomas Howard, 3rd Duke of Norfolk, and Thomas Cromwell to find out what he wished to say on the matter.[14] Chapuys then explained his arguments to them over Mary's position:

> … that the King could not allege illegitimacy, or deprive the Princess of her title, they replied that my arguments might be true and well founded in civil law, which had no force here, but that the laws of this kingdom were quite otherwise. But on showing them that I rested my argument only upon the decision of the canon law, which in a spiritual matter no prince's decree could prejudice, they knew not what to reply, except that they would report it to the King, and afterwards declare to me his intention.[15]

The suggestion in Chapuys' letter is that the councillors were not actually sure what would happen to Mary and what her position would be. But Chapuys put forward arguments which the councillors reasoned did not apply in England any longer as she had changed her laws. Though it also seems that Norfolk and even Cromwell could not fully counter Chapuys' arguments, hence they would report to the king and await his response. Perhaps Chapuys had argued that Mary could not be declared illegitimate because, whatever the alleged impediments to her parents' marriage, it was conceived in good faith and therefore Mary's legitimacy stood firm.[16] Or perhaps he asserted that only the Pope could dissolve a marriage, and he had not yet passed judgement on the marriage of Henry VIII and Katherine of Aragon. That judgement would come, and it would be in Katherine and Mary's favour.

Mary's position was not uncertain for long. Within weeks of Elizabeth's birth, while Mary was at Beaulieu, John Hussey, 1st Baron Hussey of Sleaford, Mary's chamberlain, was sent by the council to tell Mary and her household that her high estate and title of princess was to be diminished. The king may have assumed that Mary would obey, as a daughter's first obedience was supposed to be to her father, but she refused. Mary told Hussey she was the king's lawful daughter and that, without a direct command from the king, she would not accept any alteration to her status, and her servants backed her up.[17] Hussey's own wife was one of Mary's attendants and would soon be imprisoned for continuing to call Mary 'princess'. Hussey had been sent with a verbal command, but no written instructions from the king, which is what Mary was demanding. Perhaps she was not willing to believe her father would do this to her and needed to see the evidence in front of her.

Mary's household was dissolved on 11 December 1533, and she was sent to join Elizabeth's household at Hatfield House in Hertfordshire, to attend on the princess. Elizabeth's household had only arrived at Hatfield the day before Mary was told her own household was to be dissolved. This suggests that it was a deliberate decision made almost from the moment that Elizabeth was born, to combine the households of the two daughters of the king rather than maintain separate establishments for them. Whose idea it was for Mary to serve Elizabeth is unclear. Eustace Chapuys wrote to Charles V a few days after these events to relay them, referring to Mary as 'Princess' and Elizabeth as 'bastard':

> … the said bastard was taken three days ago to a house 17 miles from here; and although there was a shorter and better road, yet for greater solemnity, and to insinuate to the people that she is the true Princess, she was taken through this town with the company which I wrote in my last; and next day the duke of Norfolk went to the Princess to tell her that her father desired her to go to the Court and service of the said bastard, whom he named

> Princess. The Princess answered that the title belonged to herself, and to no other; making many very wise remonstrances, that what had been proposed to her was strange and dishonorable. To which the Duke could not reply. After much talk, he said he had not come there to dispute, but to accomplish the King's will …[18]

Mary saw that she had no choice. The king had commanded it, and the Duke of Norfolk was not one to disobey orders, and neither was Mary, except when it came to her conscience. She could not logically refuse to move house when ordered to by her king and father, but she could not be made to declare her own illegitimacy which would have such a huge influence on her own conscience. Mary retreated to her chamber for a short time, as Chapuys said to make 'a protestation which I had sent her, in order that, if compelled by force or fraud to renounce her rights or enter a nunnery, it might not be to her prejudice'.[19] Mary was protecting her soul and her rights as best she could in the trying circumstances she found herself in. In this same letter, Chapuys reports that Margaret Pole, Countess of Salisbury, a cousin to the king and Mary's governess, asked if she could continue to serve Mary at her own expense,

> … But it was out of the question that this would be accepted; for in that case they would have no power over the Princess, whom it is to be feared they mean to kill, either with grief or otherwise, or make her renounce her right, or marry basely, or make her stain her honor, to have grounds for disinheriting her.[20]

Henry VIII wanted Mary 'like Katherine, to be separated from those she trusted to encourage her submission'.[21] The idea that Mary would be killed seems to come from Chapuys' assertion of the hatred Anne Boleyn had for her stepdaughter, and her fear that Mary would triumph over her own children by the king. If Mary could not be killed, then she could be dishonoured, so that she was not seen as good enough to be the heir to the throne. Chapuys goes on to say that the king 'is bewitched by this cursed woman in such a manner that he dares neither say nor do except as she commands him'.[22] The very definite implication here is that Anne Boleyn is at the root of all the trouble for Mary and Katherine of Aragon, and that Anne wanted the pair out of the way so as not to threaten her or her children.

It has been said that Anne Boleyn believed it would be either her or Mary, and that Anne's daughter, Elizabeth, could not thrive while Mary lived. In June 1534, Chapuys reported that:

> I am informed by a person of good faith that the King's concubine had said more than once, and with great assurance, that when the King has crossed the sea, and she remains gouvernante, as she will be, she will use her authority and put the said Princess to death, either by hunger or otherwise. On Rochford, her brother, telling her that this would anger the King, she said she did not care even if she were burned alive for it after. The Princess quite expects this, and thinking that she could not better gain Paradise than by such a death, shows no concern (*na fait cas du monde*), trusting only in God, whom she has always served well and does still better now.[23]

It is likely that Anne did not really mean to carry out her threat, if it really was made, with it again stemming from fear over the vulnerability of her position and Mary's popularity. Had Anne had Mary killed, the king would likely never have forgiven her as he still seemed to love Mary despite everything, and the English people may have rebelled, given the popularity of Mary and her mother. Mary's 'obstinacy was an insult, a denial of Anne's own identity and integrity' and her language was 'violent and threatening, but this sprang not from malevolence but from self-defence'.[24] Anne Boleyn wanted to do everything she could to protect Elizabeth, and Mary was an obstacle to Elizabeth's position and security. Mary and Elizabeth would continue to be pitted against each other later in their lives, as Katherine and Anne had in the 1520s and 1530s. They would be the first two regnant crowned queens of England, though it would not be an easy path for either of them to get there. Mary came into conflict with her half-brother, Edward VI, over religion, and Elizabeth would do the same with Mary when the latter succeeded Edward as queen.

Mary does appear to have kept up small acts of defiance during Anne Boleyn's reign as queen. Shortly after Mary arrived in Elizabeth's household, Chapuys wrote once again to his master Charles V to say:

> When the Princess, who was taken off with only two attendants, had arrived where the bastard was, the Duke asked her whether she would not go and pay her respects to the Princess. She replied that she knew no other Princess in England except herself, and that the daughter of Madame de Penebrok had no such title; and that it was true that since the King her father acknowledged her to be his, she might call her 'sister', as she called the duke of Richmond 'brother'. On her removing, the Duke asked her what word he should carry to the King; to which she replied, Nothing else, except that his daughter, the Princess, begged his blessing; and when he said that he would not carry such a message, she told him curtly he might leave it; and after protesting several times that what she did at the King's command should not be to her prejudice, she retired to weep in her chamber, as she does continually. Though the said Duke treated her very roughly, the King reproached him for not having accomplished his charge; that he went about it too softly; and he was resolved to take steps to abate the stubbornness and pride of the Princess.[25]

Mary's refusal to recognise Elizabeth as princess emphasised her views on her own position and the validity of her parents' marriage. The Duke of Richmond was Henry Fitzroy, Henry VIII's illegitimate son by Bessie Blount, born in 1519. Mary called him brother as they shared a father, though he was not a prince. Mary was offering to acknowledge that she and Elizabeth shared a father, but not her position as a princess and heir to the throne. The Duke of Norfolk refused to carry any message to the king that might anger him, even just that his daughter Mary requested his blessing. Henry was focused on Anne Boleyn and the possibility that she would give him a son. He did not want to be reminded of his former wife and eldest daughter. Chapuys reports at the end that Henry VIII was angry even without the message of his daughter requesting his blessing being delivered. It seems that he resolved to bring Mary to obedience, as she was echoing the stubbornness and pride of her mother in the matter of the validity of Henry and Katherine of Aragon's marriage.

In this same letter describing how Mary arrived in Elizabeth's household, Chapuys reports on how the king's commissioners were dealing with Katherine of Aragon who was in exile at Buckden Palace in Cambridgeshire, having moved there from Ampthill in Bedfordshire in summer 1533. Chapuys writes that the men were:

> ... commissioned to bring the Queen by force to a house surrounded with deep water and marshes, which is, as she is informed, the most unhealthy and pestilential house in England; and she, seeing the evident danger of it, refused to go except by force.[26]

Katherine may well have seen this as an attempt to try and force her illness and death by moving her to a house which was so unhealthy. This house was Somersham House in Cambridgeshire. Both Katherine and Mary were being tested in order to try and break their spirits, but neither would give in – 'with the tenacity worthy of any Tudor, [Mary] determined to be as difficult as possible'.[27] There was not much she could do in the grand scheme of things, but she could be difficult in Elizabeth's household and make things awkward.

Mary is said to have eaten large breakfasts so that she would not have to eat dinner in the great hall, where she would be seated in an inferior position to her half-sister, Elizabeth, and then pleaded sickness to have supper brought to her room. Lady Anne Shelton, Anne Boleyn's aunt, who presided over the household at Hatfield, would be reprimanded over the years of Anne's queenship, for showing Mary too much respect and kindness.[28] When Anne heard, for instance, that Mary was being allowed to eat in her chamber and was continuing to use the title of princess, she sent word to Lady Anne Shelton 'who has charge of the Princess [Elizabeth], telling her not to allow her to use that title, and if she did otherwise, she must box her ears as a cursed bastard'.[29] Chapuys reported lots of things that Anne Boleyn is supposed to have said against Mary, though where he heard it is never said. It was likely passed on to him from those at the royal court who continued, even secretly, to support Katherine of Aragon and Mary. In one letter, Chapuys reported that the French ambassador told him that the king 'had not spoken to the Princess on account of her obstinacy, which came from her Spanish blood, and when the ambassador remarked that she had been very well brought up, the tears came into his eyes, and he could not refrain from praising her'. Chapuys then went on to say that 'Anne is aware of the King's affection for the Princess and does not cease to plot against her. A gentleman told me yesterday that the earl of Northumberland told him that he knew for certain that she had determined to poison the Princess'.[30] Accusations of poison would dog Anne, from John Fisher, Bishop of Rochester, to Henry Fitzroy, to Princess Mary and Katherine of Aragon.

It seems that Anne Boleyn did attempt to reconcile with Mary at several points during her queenship, however. She must have realised that having Mary on her side and recognising her as queen would weaken her enemies. But Mary would not give in, and it made Anne angry and a little reckless. Chapuys records one such attempt by Anne and Mary's reaction to it:

> When the King's 'amye' went lately to visit her daughter, she urgently solicited the Princess to visit her and honor her as queen, saying that it would be a means of reconciliation with the King, and she herself (*ladite amitie*) would intercede with him for her, and she should be as well or better treated than ever. The Princess replied that she knew no queen in England except her mother, and if the said 'amye' (whom she called madame Anne de Bolans) would do her that favor with her father she would be much obliged. The Lady repeated her remonstrances and offers, and in the end threatened her, but could not move the Princess. The other was very indignant, and intended to bring down the pride of this unbridled Spanish blood, as she said. She will do the worst she can.[31]

Anne's terms for reconciling Mary to her father was that Mary recognise her as queen. Mary would never renounce her mother while Anne was alive, so she would not conform. The 'abasement which Henry [VIII] exacted scarred [Mary] for life'.[32] But Anne's downfall and execution meant that Mary was never forced, at least, to recognise her as queen.

Thomas Howard, 3rd Duke of Norfolk, Anne Boleyn's uncle, is claimed to have said, after his niece Anne Boleyn's fall and execution, that Mary was 'so unnatural' to oppose the will of the king, who was trying to get her to submit and admit that the marriage of Henry VIII to her mother, Katherine of Aragon, was null and void and that she was illegitimate. He said that, if Mary were his daughter, he 'would beat her and knock her head so violently against the wall that they would make it as soft as baked apples'.[33] This comment gives a sense of the type of pressure that was being piled on Mary through the years. At this point, Mary had expected to be returned to royal favour after the execution of Anne Boleyn, yet she was still being pressured to submit. This must have been devastating to realise that it was in actual fact her father behind the treatment of her, and not her stepmother. This is what Mary was facing from 1533 onwards as Anne Boleyn sought to cement her own position and that of her daughter.

In a letter dated 10 February 1536, after Katherine of Aragon's death and Anne Boleyn's final miscarriage, Eustace Chapuys wrote that it was rumoured that the king 'means to increase [Mary's] train and exalt her position' and hoped it was so, 'that no scorpion lurks under the honey'.[34] It was too early to think of Mary's restoration in February 1536, though Chapuys reports that he got his information from Cromwell. In the event, Mary would only be received back into her father's good graces after Anne Boleyn's execution in 1536, and only once she signed a paper accepting that her parents' marriage was null and void, and that she was illegitimate. She also had to accept the 1534 Act of Supremacy and Henry VIII's position as Supreme Head of the Church in England. Mary would never forgive herself for this capitulation. In the same letter of February 1536, Chapuys reported to Charles V that he suggested to Mary that 'if she be reduced to extremity' when pressed to take the oath, 'to offer that if the King her father have a son she will condescend to his will'.[35] This was a very sensible approach to take. While Henry VIII did not have a son, Princess Mary still had some vestige of power as the eldest daughter, and many still considered her the king's only legitimate heir. If Anne Boleyn produced a son after Katherine of Aragon's death, it could easily be argued that the son was in fact legitimate. In that case, Mary agreeing to take the oath and submitting to her father might well preserve her life.

Chapuys reported that Henry VIII had wanted the news of Katherine of Aragon's death on 7 January 1536 to be kept from her daughter, Mary, 'intending to go or send some good personage to console her', but that 'her *gouvernante* told her the news four days after the Queen's death, before which time I had already written a consolatory letter for her, and had sent it to one of her ladies to present to her, which letter gave her great consolation'.[36] This news must have been a huge blow to Mary as her mother had been such a source of comfort and strength for her, and she may have realised that more pressure would now be brought to bear on her to accept the annulment of her parents' marriage and her father's position as Head of the Church in England. The question of who Henry VIII would have chosen to break the news to his daughter is an interesting one. Would it have been someone who could put pressure on Mary when vulnerable to get her to agree to the annulment? Or would he have been merciful and chosen someone who had been close to Katherine? We do not know. Chapuys went on to say that Mary wrote to him more after the death of her mother, perhaps hoping to draw strength from him. Chapuys seemed proud when he said that 'certainly she shows great sense and incomparable virtue and patience to bear so becomingly the death of such a mother to whom she bore as much love as any daughter ever did to her mother, who was her chief refuge in her troubles'.[37] Chapuys did love Mary in his way, almost as a daughter; he respected her stance and her fortitude and strength in the face of adversity.

After Katherine died, the Imperial ambassador reported that Mary wanted to 'know particulars of her mother's illness and death'.[38] Perhaps she was worried that there was some kind of foul play, or poison, which was suggested at the time. When Anne Boleyn was accused and condemned of adultery, one of the charges related to her giving gifts to the men with whom she was accused. Eustace Chapuys reported that 'she had received and given to Norris certain medals, which might be interpreted to mean that she had poisoned the late Queen and intrigued to do the same to the Princess'.[39] The inference that Chapuys draws from these gifts is that they were some kind of payment for the poisoning of Katherine of Aragon and Princess Mary; that Katherine's poisoning was successful, and that Mary was under threat of suffering the same death.

With Anne Boleyn's arrest on 2 May 1536, there was a hope among some at court and in the wider population that Princess Elizabeth would be made illegitimate, which they believed would mean the restoration of Princess Mary to the succession. However, one did not mean the other. Both Mary and Elizabeth were in fact made illegitimate, which was reinforced by the Second Succession Act 1536. When Henry VIII was talking to Jane Seymour about their marriage in 1536, Chapuys reported:

> I hear that, even before the arrest of the Concubine, the King, speaking with Mistress Jane Semel of their future marriage, the latter suggested that the Princess should be replaced in her former position; and the King told her she was a fool, and ought to solicit the advancement of the children they

> would have between them, and not any others. She replied that in asking for the restoration of the Princess she conceived she was seeking the rest and tranquillity of the King, herself, her future children, and the whole realm; for, without that, neither your Majesty nor this people would ever be content. Will endeavour by all means to make her continue in this vein.[40]

Chapuys was not as convinced that Mary would immediately be restored to favour, as others of her supporters appeared to be. He expressed his 'fear as regards her' that when the king was asked by parliament to restore her rights, that he would require her to yield and admit to the invalidity of her parents' marriage and the king's supremacy over the English Church. Chapuys admits 'she will not easily yield, although I should advise her to acquiesce in everything as far as she can without prejudice to her conscience and her own rights'.[41] Jane Seymour was a religious conservative, as was Princess Mary, as Katherine of Aragon had been. But Jane's attention to Mary seems to go beyond that. Jane had served Katherine before transferring to Anne Boleyn's service, and her sympathies remained with Katherine, and her daughter. It was during Jane's reign that Mary was brought back into her father's arms and court, though it was not without huge sacrifice on Mary's part. With Henry VIII's execution of a crowned and anointed queen, there was a new understanding of what he was capable of. If he could do that to a wife who failed to live up to her promise of providing a son, there was nothing to stop him doing the same to a daughter who failed to admit that he was right and she was wrong, especially when his decisions were enshrined in English law.

Historian Beverley A. Murphy claims that Thomas Cromwell was the 'principal architect' of Mary's return to her father's good graces after Anne Boleyn's execution.[42] Mary responded to a letter from Cromwell when the king was trying to persuade her to submit to him and admit to the invalidity of her parents' marriage and her own illegitimacy. Mary starts her letter by saying 'I do thank you with all of my heart, for the great pain and suit you have had for me, for the which I think myself very much bound to you'.[43] Cromwell had drafted a submission for Mary to sign as her letters up to that point had not given enough ground on the issues which mattered to the king. Nothing would be enough except her total submission. On 22 June 1536, just over a month after the execution of Anne Boleyn, Mary Tudor signed the formal statement required of her, acknowledging the invalidity of her mother's marriage, her own illegitimacy, and her father's headship over the Church in England. The submission begins with the following:

> The confession of me, the lady Mary, made upon certain points and articles under written, in the which, as I do now plainly and with all mine heart confess and declare mine inward sentence, belief, and judgment, with a due conformity of obedience to the laws of the realm; so minding for ever to persist and continue in this determination, without change, alteration, or variance, I do most humbly beseech the King's Highness, my father, whom I have obstinately and inobediently offended in the denial of the same heretofore, to forgive mine offences therein, and to take me to his most gracious mercy.[44]

Mary feared for her own life, and this was the only way to save it. Had she refused at this juncture, the king may well have proceeded against her for treason. Mary had no other choice. But 'in one stroke she had been compelled to betray the memory of her mother and the Catholic faith of her childhood' and 'it was in this moment of total and agonising submission that the seeds of Mary's future defiance were sown'.[45] Mary would never forgive herself and would spend her reign as queen trying to right everything that she believed had gone wrong in her life as a result of the 'Great Matter'.

Mary's own reign in the 1550s would focus on restoring Roman Catholicism to England, and she would also revoke the annulment of her parents' marriage. The latter happened in her very first parliament which closed before Christmas 1553. Within seven months of Mary succeeding to the throne, she had legitimised herself and reinforced the illegitimacy of her half-sister, Elizabeth.[46] After all, if Mary was legitimate, then Elizabeth could not be, as their mothers' marriages to Henry VIII overlapped. When she became queen, Mary tried to turn back the clock, and not just on religion. Mary reversed the treason laws, the acts of supremacy and succession, and the annulment of her parents' marriage. She tried to take England back to her happy childhood. But things could not be reversed so easily.

There was a rivalry between Anne Boleyn and Princess or Lady Mary. But Anne was executed, and Mary restored to her father's favour, though only after huge emotional duress for her. Mary would become queen, as would Anne's daughter, Elizabeth, but Mary has earned the 'Bloody Mary' reputation, not entirely deserved, while Elizabeth is seen as a shining light, Gloriana. Elizabeth's reign was not perfect, and Mary's was not all doom and gloom either. Anne and Mary's rivalry in the early 1530s doubtless had an effect on the relationship between Mary and Elizabeth in later years, but did either woman really triumph? Both were crowned and anointed queens, but neither ended their lives particularly happily, both having had huge ups and downs throughout. 1536 would not have a happy start for Mary, though things would be very different by the close of the year.

Chapter 10

The Year of Three Queens

The year 1536 was an interesting and decisive moment in Tudor history. It was tumultuous. There were three queens in England in this one year. Katherine of Aragon just lived into 1536, dying at Kimbolton Castle in Cambridgeshire on 7 January, but she left a long shadow which would indirectly affect the fate of her successor, Anne Boleyn. The first half of 1536 was centred around Anne Boleyn, who was executed at the Tower of London on 19 May. The second half of 1536 was the time of Jane Seymour, who married Henry VIII just eleven days after the death of her predecessor, on 30 May. It would be Jane who would be the 'successful' wife, providing Henry with the son and heir he so desperately craved and claimed he needed. Jane died in the process, before Henry could tire of her.

But let us start at the dawn of 1536 and how things stood between Henry VIII's first three queens. Katherine of Aragon was seriously unwell, and dying, at Kimbolton Castle, having been exiled from the English court since 1531, and forbidden any contact with her daughter, Mary, who was 20 years old. The Imperial ambassador, Eustace Chapuys, had requested permission to visit her, having heard how unwell she was. Katherine's old friend and former lady-in-waiting, Maria de Salinas, Baroness Willoughby de Eresby, would also find her way to Kimbolton to visit Katherine before her death. Maria had travelled to England from Spain with Katherine in 1501 when Katherine married Prince Arthur. Anne Boleyn was queen of England and had been for two and a half years. She had a single living daughter, Elizabeth, aged 2, and had suffered at least one, possibly two, miscarriages or stillbirths. She was, however, pregnant again and hoped for a son. The woman who would become Henry VIII's third wife, Jane Seymour, was in service to Anne Boleyn, and soon the first mention of her in connection to the king came in a letter from Chapuys. It is possibly around this time that Henry began to pay court to her.

Henry VIII's first wife, Katherine of Aragon, died on 7 January 1536 at Kimbolton Castle in Cambridgeshire. She had received visits from Chapuys, as well as Maria de Salinas. Chapuys had gained official permission to visit, while Maria gained entry to Kimbolton by subterfuge. Both were staunch supporters of Katherine during the annulment case and, having not seen her for several years, managed to visit as she was dying, knowing it would be their last chance. Henry VIII had forbidden Katherine to have visitors without his approval. Maria arrived at Kimbolton on New Year's Day 1536. As Katherine of Aragon's gaoler, Sir Edmund Bedingfield would write to Cromwell, 'my lady Willoghby came to us upon New [Year's Day], about six of the clock at night … she being ill a[t ease by] reason of a fall from her horse'.[1] Maria claimed she had fallen from her horse in the vicinity of Kimbolton and Bedingfield demanded to see her papers allowing her permission to see Katherine. The letter is damaged, but Maria, Lady Willoughby, did not have permission to see Katherine. Nevertheless, she gained access, and Bedingfield goes on to say that, from the visits of both Maria and Chapuys, Katherine 'hath somewhat taken comfort upon the coming of these folks, and somewhat falleth to more rest in the night, but he fears it will be a long continual sickness or she recover'.[2] The visits seemed to temporarily make Katherine feel better and she settled.

Chapuys arrived at Kimbolton the day after Maria, on 2 January 1536, and Bedingfield was present for their initial meeting, recording that Chapuys 'saluted her in Spanish, which I do not understand, but Mr. Vaghan, who was present, can declare to your Mastership the effect of their communication'. Chapuys visited Katherine a further two times over the following two days, but only him, his steward, and the doctor were present, 'and her old trusty women, who, I think, do not understand Spanish'.[3] Chapuys himself wrote an account of his visit to Charles V, stating that the king had sent a friend of Cromwell to accompany him, probably to report back on what was said. He reported that Katherine said that his visit was 'a thing that she had very ardently desired, thinking that my coming would be salutary for her, and, at all events, if it pleased God to take her, it would be a consolation to her to die under ray guidance (*entre mes braz*) and not unprepared, like a beast'.[4] Katherine obviously knew that she was dying at this time and wanted a chance to thank those who had supported her and her daughter, like the Imperial ambassador and Maria de Salinas. She had been abandoned and left alone, but not forgotten. As much as these visits cheered Katherine, she would not get better and would die just five days after Chapuys's final visit to her.

The last will of Katherine of Aragon is very traditionally Catholic, despite the fact that the man she was determined to remain her husband had broken with the Roman Catholic Church. She asks to be 'buried in a convent of Observant Friars; that 500 masses be said for her soul; that some personage go to our Lady of Walsingham on pilgrimage and distribute 20 nobles on the way'.[5] Katherine did not have many goods to distribute but, to her beloved daughter, Mary, she left 'the collar of gold which I brought out of Spain', along with gifts of money to her ladies and other servants.[6] Katherine would not be buried in a convent of the Observant Friars, but in the north transept of Peterborough Abbey (now Peterborough Cathedral) on 29 January 1536. The shrine at Walsingham would not long outlast Katherine, being destroyed in 1538. Thomas Cromwell, Henry VIII's right-hand man, was determined to make the best of Katherine's death, writing to Stephen Gardiner and John Wallop, the English ambassadors in France, that 'considering the death of the Lady Dowager, and that as the Emperor has now no occasion of quarrel, he will seek the friendship of Henry'.[7] Katherine's death had removed the greatest obstacle to friendship between England and Spain so Cromwell wanted to warn the ambassadors in France that there may be a chance of orders for them as a result of the death. With Henry's treatment of Katherine when she was alive, there had been a fear that Emperor Charles V would make war on Henry for his aunt's honour. But that fear was now removed.

There is a letter which survives, which purports to be the final letter Katherine of Aragon wrote to Henry VIII from her deathbed. There have been questions asked as to whether this letter is genuine or a later creation, as it does not appear in the state papers or other official documents. Polydore Vergil quotes it thus:

> My most dear lord, king and husband, The hour of my death now drawing on, the tender love I owe you forceth me, my case being such, to commend myself to you, and to put you in remembrance with a few words of the health and safeguard of your soul which you ought to prefer before all worldly

> matters, and before the care and pampering of your body, for the which you have cast me into many calamities and yourself into many troubles. For my part, I pardon you everything, and I wish to devoutly pray God that He will pardon you also. For the rest, I commend unto you our daughter Mary, beseeching you to be a good father unto her, as I have heretofore desired. I entreat you also, on behalf of my maids, to give them marriage portions, which is not much, they being but three. For all my other servants I solicit the wages due them, and a year more, lest they be unprovided for. Lastly, I make this vow, that mine eyes desire you above all things.[8]

The letter certainly demonstrates Katherine's devotion to Henry VIII and her assertion that she is his rightful wife and queen, and will remain so until her death. It also shows her devotion to her Catholic faith, and her care for her husband's soul, as well as her hopes that the king will reconcile with their daughter and be a father to her. The letter requests the payments should be made to her ladies and servants which are also highlighted in Katherine's will. Amy Licence says that it is 'by no means certain' that this is a genuine letter and acknowledges that some historians describe it as a forgery or even part of a later dramatic work.[9] Giles Tremlett describes the letter as 'almost certainly fictitious' but that it is not unreasonable to suggest that it may in fact have reflected something of what was in Katherine's mind as she lay dying.[10] The letter seems to reflect Katherine's stubborn, steadfast, and pious mindset, as well as her care for her daughter and those who served her loyally. It could have been written by Katherine of Aragon, but that does not necessarily mean that it was.

There was also a suggestion, when an autopsy was carried out on Katherine of Aragon's body after her death, that she may have been poisoned. The Imperial ambassador, Chapuys, wrote to Charles V that the man who conducted the autopsy 'had found the body and all the internal organs as sound as possible except the heart, which was quite black and hideous … and also some black round thing which clung closely to the outside of the heart'.[11] Katherine's own physician was not allowed to attend the autopsy, 'presumably' in case he claimed to have seen evidence of poison.[12] The king would not have wanted to fan the flames of rumour and make people more sympathetic towards Katherine than they already were, and for he and

Anne Boleyn to be blamed. Amy Licence points out that the actual cause of Katherine's illness cannot be established with any certainty and so 'we cannot rule out poison administered over a period of time'.[13] This would explain the long illness and the slow deterioration as well as the discoloured heart, if that report is true. However, there are also other explanations. Giles Tremlett claims that a 'secondary melanotic sarcoma was almost certainly to blame'.[14] A sarcoma is a type of cancer that can appear anywhere in the body, due to its origins in the connective tissue. John Guy and Julia Fox describe Katherine's final illness as 'what may well have been stomach cancer'.[15] The consensus from most historians today seems to be that Katherine of Aragon died from some kind of cancer which explains her long final illness, and not poison.

Katherine of Aragon's death actually made Anne Boleyn's position more precarious, rather than strengthening it. While Katherine was alive, Henry VIII would have been expected to return to her had he abandoned Anne, but this would have involved Henry admitting he was wrong. The king could not and would not admit that he was wrong. Katherine's death freed Henry to get rid of Anne and, at the same time, not have to admit that his first marriage was valid. He could remarry without any problems, since most of Europe did not recognise his marriage to Anne Boleyn as valid anyway. Chapuys reported that 'notwithstanding the joy shown by the concubine at the news of the good Queen's death, for which she had given a handsome present to the messenger, she had frequently wept, fearing that they might do with her as with the good Queen'.[16] It appears as if Anne understood the vulnerability of her position; that although she was now the only queen of England, the king could easily put her aside. She was not popular with the people, had no real international support, and was losing the king's love. Outwardly, Anne showed joy at Katherine of Aragon's death as would be expected of her, but her fear still showed through. Patrick Williams reports that, on learning of Katherine of Aragon's death, Henry VIII dressed himself in 'celebratory yellow' and danced and feasted to rejoice in the death of the woman he once loved.[17] John Guy and Julia Fox have pointed out that 'the fact is sometimes questioned' that Henry and Anne Boleyn both wore yellow the day after Katherine's death.[18] There is no real contemporary evidence that it happened, though it is largely taken as fact today. It has been said that yellow was the colour of mourning in Spain, but Alison Weir has disputed this, saying that it is a 'misconception', and that Anne's choice to wear yellow was 'no less than a calculated insult to the memory of the woman she had supplanted'.[19] Perhaps if Henry VIII's eye had not alighted on Anne Boleyn at a time when his mind was contemplating an annulment, Anne and Katherine of Aragon might have got on quite well as they were both intelligent and pious women, but the years of competition and Anne's ambitious nature meant that Anne may well have celebrated Katherine's death.

A letter written by Eustace Chapuys to his master Charles V on 10 February 1536 is useful to examine in more detail at this point. It gives a good insight into how the situation stood between the first three wives of Henry VIII at the beginning of 1536. Chapuys began his letter with the funeral of his beloved Queen Katherine of Aragon, describing how her place of burial in Peterborough Cathedral, where she was laid to rest on 29 January, is 'far removed from the high altar, and much less honourable than that of certain bishops'.[20] He recognised that Katherine was seen as Princess Dowager of Wales as the widow of Prince Arthur, at the time of her death by Henry VIII and his government, rather than queen as the wife of Henry himself. He claims that even if she was a 'simple baroness' they could not have given her 'a less honourable place', but espouses the hope that they will 'repair the fault' by making a monument to her in a more 'suitable' place.[21] Katherine of Aragon would be joined sixty years later by another disgraced queen, Mary, Queen of Scots, who was originally buried at Peterborough Cathedral, before being moved to Westminster Abbey by her son, James VI of Scotland, when he became James I of England. The political situation was contentious as the English parliament declared Henry and Katherine's marriage invalid, and there was a different queen on the throne. As Princess Dowager of Wales, Katherine was still Henry's sister-in-law so perhaps Chapuys' hope of a monument was not too far-fetched.

Chapuys, goes on to report in his letter of 10 February that, on the day of Katherine of Aragon's funeral on 29 January, her successor as queen, Anne Boleyn:

> ... had an abortion which seemed to be a male child which she had not borne 3½ months, at which the King has shown great distress. The said concubine

> wished to lay the blame on the duke of Norfolk, whom she hates, saying he frightened her by bringing the news of the fall the King had six days before. But it is well known that is not the cause, for it was told her in a way that she should not be alarmed or attach much importance to it. Some think it was owing to her own incapacity to bear children, others to a fear that the King would treat her like the late Queen, especially considering the treatment shown to a lady of the Court, named Mistress Semel, to whom, as many say, he has lately made great presents.[22]

The timing of the miscarriage that Anne suffered in January 1536 is often seen as critical. It has been suggested that it was Katherine of Aragon punishing Anne from beyond the grave, or a kind of retrospective justice on Anne's treatment of Katherine and her daughter, Mary. It was really bad timing for Anne. Despite Chapuys' assertion that the foetus Anne miscarried was around three and a half months gestation, John Dewhurst argues that the foetus was actually around seven months gestation, and that Anne had conceived around June 1535.[23] Had this been the case there would have been comments from ambassadors and courtiers about Anne's pregnancy much earlier, including the quickening, and we do not see anything in the sources, so it is fairly safe to disregard this claim. Although Katherine's death meant that Anne Boleyn was now the only queen in England, ironically, it was Katherine's death which actually destabilised Anne and her last chance of a son died soon after. She would not fall pregnant again. Henry VIII could now get rid of Anne without being expected to take Katherine back as his wife. He could discard Anne and remarry without repercussions. It was historian J. E. Neale who said that 'never was fortune more cruel', as Anne 'had miscarried of her saviour'.[24] Even with Katherine's death, had Anne produced a son she would have likely been safe from Henry's wrath. He would not have risked disowning a son, even from a woman he had perhaps fallen out of love with, and whom he had risked tearing apart his country for.

George Wyatt reported that in the run-up to Anne's miscarriage 'the time was taken to steal the king's affection from her, when most of all she was to have been cherished' and that 'unkindness grew, and she was brought a bed before her time with much peril of her life, and of a male child dead born, to her greater and most extreme grief'.[25] The Bishop of Faenza, Rodolfo

Pio da Carpi, wrote in a letter that he believed Anne Boleyn had faked being pregnant at this time, referring to her as 'that woman', claiming that she could not carry a child and to 'keep up the deceit' she would not allow anyone to attend her except her sister.[26] There is, however, no evidence of Anne's sister, Mary Boleyn, returning to court after her secret marriage to William Stafford in 1534. Dr Pedro Ortiz, writing from Rome back to his masters in Spain, also claimed that Anne Boleyn 'pretended the miscarriage of a son' so that the king would not leave her, seeing that she could conceive sons.[27] Anne did not just need to conceive a son, but to birth a live son. This could not have happened from a fake pregnancy and would soon have been discovered. There are plenty of conspiracies around Anne, but it does seem likely that she was in fact pregnant and did miscarry a son.

Charles Wriothesley describes Anne Boleyn as miscarrying 'three daies before Candlemas' which would place it on 30 January 1536, and she was thought to be 'but fiftene weekes gonne with chield'.[28] As Natalie Grueninger points out, this discrepancy in dates 'may point to Anne having suffered a long miscarriage', likely that she began experiencing the early symptoms of a miscarriage not long after the king's fall from his horse, which happened on 24 January.[29] It is often said that this fall was during a tournament but there is no record of a tournament on this day, so it is likely that the king was practicing running at the ring in the tiltyard. As Henry was talking about having been denied male children in a letter Chapuys wrote on 29 January, even if it was not common news at court, Henry must have known that Anne had or was miscarrying the child in her belly. This is compounded by the fact that Anne blamed the miscarriage on her fright at hearing of the king's fall, suggesting that the miscarriage began shortly afterwards.[30] Grueninger's reasoning is compelling and not something that seems to have been posited before, but makes complete sense. It seems more than likely that Anne Boleyn's final miscarriage was a long one, which must have compounded her distress.

After Anne Boleyn's final miscarriage, Chapuys heard about a comment that the king made, via Gertrude Blount, Marchioness of Exeter, a supporter of Katherine of Aragon. He does not seem willing to take the comment at face value, which is sensible. The marchioness reported that:

> … this King had said to some one in great confidence, and as it were in confession, that he had made this marriage, seduced by witchcraft, and for this reason he considered it null; and that this was evident because God did not permit them to have any male issue, and that he believed that he might take another wife.[31]

This is the first possible suggestion we have of witchcraft relating to Anne Boleyn, though there is no evidence that Anne Boleyn was ever accused of or indicted for witchcraft. The fact that it is not reported whom the king was speaking to means that it lacks veracity. It is also important to consider that the Marchioness of Exeter was a staunch supporter of Katherine of Aragon and Princess Mary, and an enemy of Anne Boleyn, so we need to consider bias. She may have been reporting something that did not actually happen, or twisting words that the king had said in order to paint Anne in a more negative light and persuade the Imperial ambassador that the king was looking to replace Anne. This report came, and the letter was written, at the end of January 1536, meaning Anne still had another three months of freedom before her arrest. If Henry had decided at this point to replace Anne, would he have acted sooner? There is no real evidence at this point that the king had taken, or would take, any action to replace his queen.

This letter in February 1536 is the first mention we have of Jane Seymour, 'Mistress Semel', with regards to a relationship with the king. Chapuys records that Jane was given 'great presents'.[32] We do not know what these presents were, but it does seem to be how Henry's relationships began. We see the same at the beginning of his relationship with Anne Boleyn, and later with his fifth and sixth wives, Katherine Howard and Katherine Parr, as well – giving them gifts to try and woo them. After mentioning Jane Seymour, Chapuys goes on to say that 'there was some fear the King might take another wife'.[33] This is nearly three months before Anne Boleyn's arrest and connected to a paragraph containing news of her miscarriage as well as the first mention of Jane Seymour. Chapuys ties the events together, whether consciously or not. The three women were very intertwined during 1536. Anne replaced one and was replaced by another. Anne had been lady-in-waiting to Katherine, and Jane had been lady-in-waiting to Anne, and Katherine before her. The three were in each other's lives for years but 1536 was the crux and only one would survive to the end of the year.

Anne Boleyn was arrested at Greenwich Palace on 2 May 1536 on charges of adultery, incest, and treason. She was imprisoned in the royal apartments at the Tower of London, which had been refurbished for her coronation just three years earlier. William Kingston, the Constable of the Tower, was responsible for Anne's imprisonment, and he reported back to Thomas Cromwell on everything she said and did, feeding back information from the ladies who served her at this time. These ladies included Anne's aunt, Lady Boleyn, and the wife of the Constable of the Tower, Lady Kingston. Cromwell was able to use Anne's loose tongue and fear to help form the case against her. Kingston's first letter to Cromwell described how Anne reacted when she arrived at the Tower under arrest, that she asked 'Mr. Kingston, shall I go into a dungeon?' to which he responded that 'no, Madam. You shall go into the lodging you lay in at your coronation'. Anne declared that 'It is too good for me … Jesu have mercy on me'.[34] There has been quite a lot of debate over this comment, as to whether Anne was admitting to adultery, or some other unknown sin. Maybe she believed that she had not been as nice or humble to the king as she should have been. Anne also asked Kingston 'shall I die without justice?' to which he replied that 'the poorest subject the king hath, hath justice' and Anne is reported to have laughed at this reply.[35] Anne had seen the king's 'justice', seen first-hand the way he treated Katherine of Aragon, his own daughter Mary, his old friend Sir Thomas More, and Bishop John Fisher, and must have known that she would get little real justice at the king's hands.

The indictment against Anne Boleyn presented at her trial on 15 May 1536 named five men who she was said to have had sexual relations with, including her own brother, George, along with Henry Norris, Francis Weston, William Brereton, and Mark Smeaton. George Boleyn was arrested on the same day as his sister, on 2 May, along with Henry Norris. Mark Smeaton had already been arrested on 30 April and questioned by Thomas Cromwell. It was his confession which led to Anne's own arrest, and quite possibly the implication of Henry Norris and George Boleyn. There have been suggestions Smeaton may have been tortured to gain a confession from him, as he was the only commoner. Anne's own ramblings in the Tower, due to her own fear of the situation in which she found herself, led directly to the arrest of Francis Weston on 4 or 5 May, alongside William Brereton. In the same letter where the Constable of the Tower William Kingston reported on Anne's arrival at the Tower, dated 3 May, he reported that Anne spoke to Weston 'because he did love her kinswoman … [she] said he loved not his wife, and he made answer to her again that he loved one in her house better than them both. And the Queen said, who is that? It is yourself'.[36] This seems to have given Cromwell enough probable cause to arrest Weston as well, though it may have just been the usual courtly love taking place in the queen's household. Sarah Gristwood discusses courtly love in Anne's household in her book *The Tudors in Love*. Baldassare Castiglione, the Italian Renaissance author of *The Book of the Courtier*, declared that the courtly woman's 'contradictory task' was to 'come just to certain limits, but not to pass them', and Andreas Capellanus in the twelfth century declared that 'once suspicion about a lover is entertained, jealousy and the feeling of love grow'.[37] It was a difficult line for a woman to tread, and it is quite possible that Henry VIII saw some of Anne Boleyn's comments to have overstepped the line and demonstrated a deeper relationship with other men.

Norris, Weston, Brereton, and Smeaton were tried in Westminster Hall on 12 May 1536, and they were condemned to death by the traditional punishment for traitors – hanging, drawing, and quartering. The sentences would be commuted to beheading, even for Smeaton, perhaps as a reward for his confession. Two other men who were arrested, Thomas Wyatt and Richard Page, were never tried and would be released after Anne's execution. It is possible that they were arrested to 'prove' the guilt of the others, never intending for them to be tried, but to demonstrate the legality of the process, and that proper investigation of the charges was carried out. Anne and George were tried in the Great Hall at the Tower of London on 15 May. The indictment claimed that:

> … queen Anne has been the wife of Henry VIII for three years and more, she, despising her marriage, and entertaining malice against the King, and following daily her frail and carnal lust, did falsely and traitorously procure by base conversations and kisses, touchings, gifts, and other infamous incitations, divers of the King's daily and familiar servants to be her adulterers and concubines.[38]

The idea was to make the accusations as lurid as possible, to ruin Anne's reputation completely. Words like 'despising', 'malice' and 'traitorously' are very negative, about as bad as you can get, and aimed at her relationship with the king, painting Anne in the worst light possible in her actions against the king, which was treason. The indictment also portrayed Anne as being the one who incited the others to adultery; that she was the puppet master behind their actions, again defiling her reputation. The most damaging charge in the indictment, however, was not the sexual encounters, but in planning and conspiring the king's death, that Anne:

> … conspired the death and destruction of the King, the Queen often saying she would marry one of them as soon as the King died, and affirming that she would never love the King in her heart.[39]

The suggestion that Anne Boleyn said that she would marry one of her lovers when the king died may well have come from her conversation with Henry Norris just days before her arrest, reported to Cromwell by William Kingston during Anne's imprisonment in the Tower. Anne talked a lot during her time in the Tower, trying to figure out exactly why she had been arrested and what had led her to this. She was not being told things to escalate her fear and encourage her to incriminate herself. Anne related a conversation she had on either 29 or 30 April 1536 with Henry Norris:

> For I asked him why he did not go through with his marriage, and he made answer he would tarry a time. Then I said, You look for dead men's shoes, for if aught come to the king but good, you would look to have me. And he said if he should have any such thought, he would his head were off.[40]

This would condemn them both under the 1534 Treason Act for imagining the king's death. Norris immediately recognised the import of the exchange as he responded that if he had a thought like that 'he would his head were off'. Anne Boleyn was becoming reckless in her fear and anxiety over her relationship with the king, and her tongue ran away with her. In having this conversation with Norris, Anne 'had unwittingly handed her enemies the means with which to destroy her'.[41] There was a familiar conversation also with the musician Mark Smeaton which Anne revealed while in the Tower. On 29 April 1536, just days before her arrest, Anne came across Smeaton looking despondent and when asked why he looked so sad, Smeaton responded 'it was no matter' to which Anne replied 'you may not look to have me speak to you as I should do to a noble man, because ye be an inferior person'. In response to this reproving comment, Smeaton said 'a look sufficeth me'.[42] Anne put Smeaton in his place, but this familiar conversation, suggestive of feelings at least on Smeaton's part, would condemn them both.

At her trial, Anne Boleyn was sentenced to be taken 'to the green within the Tower, and there to be burned or beheaded as shall please the King'.[43] In cases of treason, women who were found guilty were sentenced to be burned, whereas men were sentenced to be hung, drawn, and quartered. However, in Anne's trial, the king was given an option of the method of execution, which prompted a 'bemused murmur among the judges' as giving the king a choice was 'most improper and irregular in court judgements'.[44] The king, in the end, decided Anne would die by beheading – not by the traditional English axe, but a French sword, more commonly used on the Continent. There was an additional intrigue in her brother George's trial. He was handed a piece of paper detailing a conversation between Anne Boleyn and his wife, Jane Boleyn, and told not to read it out but just say yes or no as to whether the comments detailed on the paper had been made. George, in defiance of instructions, read the paper out, stating that 'he would not in this point arouse any suspicion which might prejudice the King's issue'.[45] This condemned him utterly, though he probably already knew he would not escape death. Despite this, he defended himself so well that 'several of those present wagered 10 to 1 that he would be acquitted'.[46] George Boleyn, like the other men, was sentenced to be hung, drawn, and quartered, sentences which would all later be commuted to beheading with an axe.

George Boleyn, Henry Norris, Francis Weston, William Brereton, and Mark Smeaton were all beheaded on Tower Hill on 17 May. Anne Boleyn was beheaded privately on Tower Green within the Tower of London two days later, on 19 May 1536. On the scaffold, Anne made a speech, later written down in John Foxe's *Book of Martyrs*, that she would not speak of what she was accused, but also refused to admit her guilt:

> Good Christian people! I am come hither to die, for according to the law, and by the law, I am judged to death; and therefore I will speak nothing against it. I come hither to accuse no man, not to speak any thing of that whereof I am accused and condemned to die; but I pray God save the king, and send him long to reign over you, for a gentler, or a more merciful prince was there never; and to me he was ever a good, a gentle, and a sovereign lord. And if any person will meddle of my cause, I require them to judge the best. And thus I take my leave of the world, and of you all, and I heartily desire you all to pray for me. O Lord have mercy on me! To God I commend my soul.[47]

The speech was, in many ways, very traditional, praising the king and praying for his long life, accepting the fate she had been given. However, there is a sly comment about the charges against her when she asks people to 'judge the best'. She knew people would be talking about her and asks people to consider what has happened and whether it was true, all in that single line. Chapuys reported that 'no person ever showed greater willingness to die' but that 'there are some who murmur at the mode of procedure against her and the others'.[48] Despite some of the hatred that Anne had received during her rise to power and her short reign, the people did not fully believe the veracity of the charges against her. Although Henry VIII had exhibited almost tyrannical characteristics at earlier points in his reign, this is the moment where the full force of his power and will is exerted. It was just seventeen days from Anne Boleyn's arrest to her death, and Henry VIII would become betrothed to his third wife, Jane Seymour, the following day, and married before the month was out.

On 24 May, the Bishop of Faenza, who had written about believing Anne Boleyn had faked her final pregnancy, did not seem to know that Henry VIII was already betrothed to Jane Seymour. He wrote that 'the Imperialists have offered the king of England the queen of Hungary as a wife'.[49] It does not appear that Henry VIII ever considered another woman as his third wife, especially not a foreign match. What drew Henry to Jane Seymour is that she was so different to Anne Boleyn – she was thought to be more compliant and submissive, less outspoken and political than her predecessor. Henry also liked to meet and get to know women before he married them. The only one of his wives he did not know before he married her was Anne of Cleves, and that marriage was the shortest. She was not what the king expected or wanted and he was disappointed.

Henry VIII married his third wife, Jane Seymour, on 30 May 1536. The king, of course, believed Jane was his first true wife, as his previous two marriages had been annulled and his children declared illegitimate. At this time, Henry did not have a legitimate child or an heir to the throne. He had two illegitimate daughters and an illegitimate son who would die in July 1536. Beverley Murphy describes Fitzroy, age 17, as having 'departed this world as he had entered it, in quiet obscurity', and he left no children or heirs to 'recommend him to posterity'.[50] He died on 23 July 1536 at St James's Palace in London, leaving behind his widow, Mary Howard, Duchess of Richmond and Somerset, daughter of Thomas Howard, 3rd Duke of Norfolk, and cousin of the recently executed Anne Boleyn. On the very day that Fitzroy died, Chapuys wrote to Charles V that the king 'has no hope that the duke of Richmond can live long, whom he certainly intended to make his successor, and but for his illness, would have got him declared so by parliament'.[51] Perhaps Henry VIII would have declared Fitzroy his successor had he survived and Jane Seymour had not given birth to a live son the following year. The same day as Chapuys wrote this letter, he wrote another to say that he had 'just this moment heard that the duke of Richmond died this morning; not a bad thing for the interests of the Princess'.[52] Chapuys was very focused on what would benefit Lady Mary, whom he still called princess, and he believed that Fitzroy's death could only be a positive thing for Mary in terms of the succession. There are not really any accounts of what happened at Fitzroy's deathbed, but he was buried first at Thetford Priory in Norfolk and, when that was dissolved in 1539, his remains were moved to the Church of St Michael the Archangel at Framlingham in Suffolk, one of the seats of the Duke of Norfolk. His tomb can still be seen there today. Fitzroy is buried among the Howard relatives of his wife rather than the royal relatives of his father, which is perhaps a little unusual, but he was an illegitimate son rather than the heir. The king's only son, Henry Fitzroy, was dead, and his daughters, Mary and Elizabeth, declared illegitimate. The pressure was all on Jane to make it happen and provide the king with a son and heir.

While Anne Boleyn was under arrest in the Tower, Henry VIII was courting Jane Seymour in preparation for their marriage. It was said that 'to cover the affection he has for the said Semel he has lodged her seven miles hence ... and says publicly that he has no desire in the world to get married again unless he is constrained by his subjects to do so'.[53] The speed of their betrothal and marriage so quickly after Anne's death told people that Henry had not meant it when he said this. He acted as though his experiences so far with his wives had turned him off marrying again, but he needed to remarry to get a son and heir. His people probably expected him to remarry. He did already have another wife in mind before Anne was even arrested, in hopes of begetting a male heir to succeed him on the throne. The king did not want the fact that he had already chosen another wife to be common knowledge in case it prejudiced the case against Anne and turned people against him and Jane. It was not the best start to a marriage, made in Anne Boleyn's blood on the scaffold legend says, as Jane Seymour was choosing her wedding outfit.

Jane Seymour would go on to provide the king with a son, the future Edward VI, but she would die within weeks of her son's birth, and Edward himself would die at the age of just 15. At the time of Edward's death, all of his possible heirs were women, and he would be succeeded by three women inturn – Lady Jane Grey (or Queen Jane), Mary I, and Elizabeth I. It would be Anne Boleyn's daughter, Elizabeth, who would be considered to be the most successful of the Tudor monarchs, so it could be said that the 'Great Matter' was worth pursuing in that sense. The children of Katherine of Aragon, Anne Boleyn, and Jane Seymour by Henry VIII would all rule England in their own right, but the Tudor dynasty would not last as all three would fail to produce issue, leaving the crown to the Scottish Stuart dynasty, the descendants of Henry VIII's sister, Margaret, who had married the Scots king, James IV.

These three women at the centre of the 'Great Matter' – Katherine of Aragon, Anne Boleyn, and Jane Seymour – were all as close to the crown as they could get as wives of the monarch. The historian Lacey Baldwin Smith has said that 'the closer the proximity to the crown, the greater the danger'.[54] This was certainly true in the case of Anne Boleyn, who was beheaded, but also for Katherine of Aragon. She was in danger and may have faced execution had she not had the backing of her nephew, the powerful Charles V, Holy Roman Emperor. Anne Boleyn had no such protection. Jane Seymour provided the king with a son, which would have been a protection of sorts for her had she not died soon after the birth. Had she not provided the king with a son, she could have found herself in as much danger as Anne Boleyn had been and faced a similar fate. The 'Great Matter' had women at its centre. Although we often put the focus on Henry VIII, it was Katherine of Aragon, Anne Boleyn, Jane Seymour, and the future Mary I and Elizabeth I, whose lives were most directly affected.

Chapter 11

Aftermath and Lessons

Anne Boleyn's execution on 19 May 1536 was a watershed in England and it marked the first judicial execution of a crowned and anointed king or queen. Others had been killed in battle, like Richard III, or in suspicious circumstances, like Richard II and Henry VI. But these were men. Anne Boleyn's execution set a new and dangerous precedent for both women and royals. There would be multiple other royal executions in the sixteenth century including Katherine Howard, Lady Jane Grey (or Queen Jane), and Mary, Queen of Scots, leading to the execution of Charles I at the culmination of the English Civil War in 1649. The importance of the 'Great Matter' and Anne Boleyn's fall and execution cannot be understated. These were events that changed the face of England forever and opened up new questions about the power of the monarch, which would endure across the centuries.

The Victorian historian James Froude wrote that, by the time of Elizabeth I, Anne Boleyn's daughter, it was a point of 'honour and loyalty' to believe in Anne's innocence in the crimes of which she was accused, that 'of all abominable crimes committed by tyrannical princes there was never one more base or cowardly than Anne's execution'.[1] Fairly early on, it seems that the charges against Anne were in doubt and that, with her daughter on the throne, people could be more open about it. The Strickland sisters also portrayed Anne as an enchanting and tragic heroine, but acknowledged her faults, too:

> There is no name in the annals of female royalty over which the enchantments of poetry and romance have cast such bewildering spells as that of Anne Boleyn. Her wit, her beauty, and the striking vicissitudes of her fate, combined with the peculiar mobility of her character, have invested her with an interest not commonly excited by a woman, in whom vanity and ambition were the leading traits.[2]

Anne Boleyn's image was undergoing a revival under Victorians like Froude and the Stricklands, and Queen Victoria seemed to have a great interest herself in Anne Boleyn. It was during Victoria's reign that excavations were carried out in the Chapel of St Peter ad Vincula at the Tower of London where Anne, Katherine Howard, Lady Jane Grey, and many others were buried after their executions, and their burial places were marked by the stones which you can see today. However, these stones are unlikely to mark the exact spots where the remains actually lie. John Guy and Julia Fox state that 'none of Henry's queens is etched into the popular imagination so deeply as is Anne [Boleyn]'.[3] This is absolutely true. The number of books written about Anne far outstrips works on any of Henry VIII's other wives.

Thomas Wyatt, rumoured to have been involved with Anne Boleyn prior to her relationship with the king, summed up the events of May 1536 poignantly in a poem. He was arrested for adultery with Anne but would never be tried, would survive the events and be released from the Tower, and accepted back at court. However, five men and one woman did not survive and were judicially murdered:

Who list his wealth and ease retain,
Himself let him unknown contain.
Press not too fast in at that gate
Where the return stands by disdain,
For sure, *circa Regna tonat*.

The high mountains are blasted oft
When the low valley is mild and soft.
Fortune with Health stands at debate.
The fall is grievous from aloft
And sure, *circa Regna tonat*.

These bloody days have broken my heart.
My lust, my youth did them depart,
And blind desire of estate.
Who hastes to climb seeks to revert.
Of truth, *circa Regna tonat*.

The bell tower showed me such a sight,
That in my head sticks day and night.
There did I learn out of a grate,
For all favour, glory, or might,
That yet, *circa Regna tonat.*

By proof, I say, there did I learn:
Wit helpeth not defence too yerne,
Of innocence to plead or prate.
Bear low, therefore, give God the stern,
For sire, *circa Regna tonat.*[4]

It is a haunting exploration of the dangers of ambition and lust. There is also a sense of survivor's guilt which comes through because Wyatt survived when his friends did not, and he may well have been able to see in the distance as the men died on Tower Hill, from his cell in the Bell Tower. No one expected that a queen of England could be executed, but Henry VIII had changed the laws of the country and made sure that he had complete power over Church and State. The Treason Act 1534 which was meant to protect Anne Boleyn and her children, had in fact been what had condemned her. 'Circa Regna tonat' translates as 'thunder rolls around the throne'.[5] An alternative translation of 'around the throne he thunders' has also been suggested.[6] This meant that Wyatt saw the events of May 1536 play out at close quarters, under threat of execution himself. Whether you believe that Anne Boleyn and Thomas Wyatt had a relationship or were in love, it still must have been devastating for him, as he grew up close to the Boleyn family seat and would have known the men who were killed as well. The poem really shows his despair and sense of loss at what had happened.

As for Anne Boleyn herself, Eric Ives says that Anne 'had been a remarkable woman. She would remain a remarkable woman even in a century which produced many of great note. There were few others who rose from such beginnings to a crown, and none contributed to a revolution as far-reaching as the English Reformation'.[7] Anne Boleyn is often the one who the focus is on during the 'Great Matter', because of her role in obtaining the annulment, influencing the king, and as a catalyst for the Break with Rome. But it is also important not to forget Katherine of Aragon. She was England's queen for twenty-four years. Katherine fought for her position and that of her daughter, and although Henry VIII and Anne Boleyn committed to each other probably around 1527, Katherine of Aragon was still in Henry's life and resident in his palaces until 1531. It was Katherine who was losing her title and position, and although she is often seen as the wife who failed to give Henry a son, she was stubborn, pious, and driven by her conscience to do what she believed was right. Henry VIII and Anne Boleyn had been up against someone formidable. Although Katherine had died alone, having not seen her husband or daughter for nearly five years, her popularity lived on and, ironically, it was her death that enabled the king to bring down the woman who replaced her – Anne Boleyn.

By the end of 1536, Jane Seymour was the only queen in England. There had been two queens in England for three years between 1533 and 1536, and a queen and a queen-in-waiting for seven years before that. Henry VIII had exiled Katherine of Aragon, who died alone at Kimbolton Castle in Cambridgeshire at the beginning of the year. Anne Boleyn had been found guilty of adultery, incest, and treason just five months after the death of Katherine, and executed, along with five men including her own brother. If Jane felt uncomfortable or scared at the thought of becoming queen, particularly to this king, then it is not at all surprising. Henry had ruthlessly rid himself of his first two queens – one abandoned and exiled, and the other executed on suspicious charges. There is no evidence that Jane Seymour fell pregnant before the beginning of 1537 with the pregnancy which would result in the birth of Prince Edward. There have been some suggestions that Jane may have been pregnant in the summer of 1536, which could explain the shotgun wedding at the end of May, but that she subsequently miscarried. David Loades reports that one observer in Rome thought that Henry VIII had married a woman already six months pregnant by him.[8] This seems inexplicable. Had Jane been six months pregnant on her marriage, it would likely have been visible and certainly commented on, but there is nothing in the contemporary sources to support this. The Imperial ambassador Chapuys wrote to Charles V on 12 August 1536 and reported that the king had told Thomas Cromwell that he felt he was growing old and 'doubted whether he should have any child by the Queen'.[9] Whether this was a sign that Jane had already miscarried, or the king's frustration that she was not yet pregnant is not stated, though the latter seems the most likely, given the lack of evidence for the former. Elizabeth Norton says that there was a hope that Jane was pregnant in autumn 1536, but that this had proven to be false.[10] There is no real evidence in the contemporary sources for the theory that Jane was pregnant prior to the beginning of 1537 so it seems likely that she only had the one pregnancy by the king, probably conceiving around January 1537.

The pregnancy seems to have proceeded smoothly. A public announcement was not immediately made but Jane did tell Henry VIII and her physician, though rumours soon started to spread through the court. Things could not be kept quiet for long. Thomas Howard, 3rd Duke of Norfolk, uncle to the former queen, Anne Boleyn, seems to have been told by the king in March 1537 of Jane's pregnancy as he responded that the news was 'as much rejoiced as anything that ever I saw'.[11] Perhaps he found it difficult to stomach that his own niece had failed to produce a son for the king, yet there was so much hope that Jane Seymour would. About a month later in a letter to Honor Grenville, Lady Lisle, John Husee reported that 'it is said the Queen is with child, Jesu send her a prince'.[12] So there were letters spreading the news across England before any official announcement was made. The baby quickened, meaning it moved for the first time in Jane's belly, on 27 May 1537, which was Trinity Sunday. It was at this point that a public announcement was made, and a Te Deum sung to celebrate the news.[13] Jane began to wear her gowns unlaced as the pregnancy progressed to accommodate her growing stomach, and plans were made for her lying-in at Hampton Court Palace where the child, hopefully a son, would be born.

When Jane went into labour on 9 October 1537, everyone, especially the king, hoped it would finally be a prince and a male heir. However, the labour seemed to be a long one and on 11 October there was a procession to pray for the queen's safe delivery, as she was still in labour, as related by the chronicler Charles Wriothesley:

> This yeare, the 11th daie of October, Anno 1537, and the 29th yeare of the raigne of King Henrie the Eight, being Thursdaie, their was a solempne generall procession in London, with all the orders of friars, preistes, and clarkes going in all copes, the major and aldermen, with all the craftes of the

> cittie, following in their liveries, which was donne to praye for the Queene that was then in labour of chielde. And the morrow after, being Fridaie and the eaven of Sinet Edward, sometime King of Englande, at tow of the blocke in the morning the Queene [was] delivered of a man chielde at Hampton Court beside Kingston.[14]

Jane Seymour finally gave birth to a son, Prince Edward, later Edward VI, at Hampton Court Palace on 12 October 1537. Henry VIII must have been elated and considered that all of his actions in displacing Katherine of Aragon, executing Anne Boleyn, and breaking with the Roman Catholic Church, were justified to bring him to this moment. A celebratory *Te Deum* was sung. The official announcement of the birth read as follows:

> By the provision of God, Our Lady St Mary and the glorious martyr St George, on the 12th day of October, the feast of Sr Wilfrid and the vigil of St Edward which was on the Friday, about two o'clock in the morning, was born at Hampton Court Edward, son to King Henry VIII.[15]

The fact that the baby was born on the vigil of St Edward perhaps informed the name of the child. It is also possible that Jane chose Hampton Court herself for the birth as it had recently been renovated, including the addition of the Queen's Gallery.[16] Perhaps Henry VIII ruled out Greenwich as a possible birthplace, since he had been disappointed there twice already with the births of Princess Mary in 1516 and then Princess Elizabeth in 1533. Since they were both born at Greenwich, perhaps that was considered to be an unlucky place to birth a son. The sixteenth century was a very superstitious age. Hampton Court proved to be a place both of celebration and mourning.

Jane Seymour was well enough to receive guests on the day of the christening of her son, 15 October, but fell ill soon after. She clung to life for a further week as physicians worked to save her life, but they would fail. Jane Seymour died at Hampton Court Palace on 24 October 1537. This was possibly due to puerperal fever or a retained placenta; both have been suggested as possible causes, as has poor hygiene which could have led to an infection. Jane would not be Henry VIII's only wife to die of childbirth complications. Katherine Parr would also die in childbed in September 1548 after Henry VIII's death, with her only child, Mary, who does not seem to have long outlived her. Henry VIII wrote to Francis I of France after Prince Edward's birth and Jane Seymour's death that:

> I have so cordially received the congratulations, which, by this bearer and by your letters, you have made me for the son which it has pleased God to give me, that I desire nothing more than an occasion by the success of your good desires to make the like. Notwithstanding, Divine Providence has mingled my joy with the bitterness of the death of her who brought me this happiness.[17]

Henry VIII would ultimately be buried beside Jane Seymour in St George's Chapel at Windsor Castle on his own death in January 1547. There is a detailed account of what happened after Jane's death:

> Immediately upon this heavy news the King ordained the duke of Norfolk, High Marshal, and Sir Wm. Pawlet, Treasurer of the Household, to see to her burial; and he himself retired to a solitary place to pass his sorrows. The aforesaid councillors then sent for Garter and other of the Office of Arms to show precedents. First the wax-chandler did his office, taking out the entrails 'with searing, balming, spicing, and trammeling in cloth,' then the plumber leaded, soldered, and chested; and her entrails were honourably interred in the chapel. Friday, 26 Oct., there was provided in the chamber of presence a hearse with 21 tapers about it, &c., and the corpse conveyed, in honourable wise, from the place where she died, and laid beneath the hearse. All the ladies and gentlewomen 'put off their rich apparel, doing on their mourning habit and white kerchers hanging over their heads and shoulders,' and there knelt about the hearse during mass afore noon and Dirige after; there was also a watch kept nightly until the last day of the month.[18]

Lady Mary, the king's eldest daughter, acted as chief mourner, having been welcomed back to court the previous year. Jane Seymour would be buried in St George's Chapel at Windsor on 13 November 1537, her body having been conveyed there from Hampton Court:

> The chief mourner followed the corpse, having her train borne by the viscountess Rochforde, and assisted by lady Fraunces, the countesses of Oxford, Derby (widow), Rutland, Bath, and Southampton, and lady Margaret Howard. The corpse being passed under the hearse, a Dirige began in which

> the lessons were read by the prelates in turn (named) and that finished, the nobility went to the Castle. Describes solemn watch that night and services next day, after which the 'offering of the palles began' i.e., ladies Bray, Dawbeney, Morley and Cobham offered one each, ladies Margaret Howard, and Marg. Gray two each, the countesses of Southampton, Bath, Sussex, Rutland, Oxford, and Derby three each, lady Fraunces four, and the lady Mary, who was lead between the dukes of Norfolk and Suffolk, seven. That done, the mourners went to the Castle where they were sumptuously provided for, and the corpse was solemnly buried and all finished by 12 o'clock that day.[19]

We have far more information about Jane Seymour's funeral than any of Henry's other wives as she was the only one who died a respectable death while still queen. Katherine of Aragon died in exile as Princess Dowager of Wales, Anne Boleyn and Katherine Howard were executed, Anne of Cleves died in the reign of Mary I having never remarried after the annulment of her marriage, and Katherine Parr died as dowager queen, having remarried to someone considered beneath her. None were afforded a royal burial, though Anne of Cleves is buried in Westminster Abbey. Between Jane Seymour's death and his own, Henry would marry a further three times. One son was not enough. Henry himself had been the 'spare' growing up. His elder brother, Arthur, was the heir, until his early death at the age of 15. Henry thus became the Prince of Wales and heir to the English throne in 1502. He was therefore very aware of the need for more than one son to secure the succession.

Henry VIII married Anne of Cleves in 1540, but the marriage was annulled six months later on the grounds of non-consummation. Henry never seemed to take to Anne, complaining about her looks, though the 'Flander's Mare' epithet is a later invention. Katherine Howard was Henry's fifth wife, the cousin of Anne Boleyn, who he also married in 1540, very shortly after the annulment of the Cleves marriage. The same day that Henry VIII married Katherine at Oatlands Palace, on 28 July 1540, his great servant and orchestrator of the 'Great Matter', Thomas Cromwell, was executed. This was because his enemies on the council had persuaded the king that Cromwell was a heretic and traitor. It is often pointed out that Cromwell's execution aligned with the end of the Cleves marriage and that this was likely connected, even that Cromwell had been 'indiscreet about [the king's] sexual performance'.[20] It was a collection of different accusations, both religious and political, that Cromwell's enemies persuaded the king were true. Katherine herself was then executed just a year and a half after her wedding, on charges of adultery and treason, like her cousin, Anne Boleyn. Executed alongside Katherine Howard on 13 February 1542 was Jane Boleyn, Viscountess Rochford, one of her ladies-in-waiting, accused of aiding and abetting Katherine's adultery. Jane had served all of Henry VIII's first five wives from Katherine of Aragon to Katherine Howard and had seen all of the changes in the lives of those involved in the 'Great Matter' at close quarters. Her own life ended on the scaffold like her notorious sister-in-law, Anne Boleyn. It is sometimes said that it was on Jane's evidence that both Anne and George Boleyn were executed, but there is no evidence for this. Henry VIII's sixth and final wife was the widowed Katherine Parr, whom he married in 1543, and she outlasted him, dying in 1548.

Henry VIII and Jane Seymour's son would become Edward VI on Henry VIII's death on 28 January 1547. His reign would not be without controversy. As Edward was still in his minority when his father died, his uncle, Edward Seymour, became Lord Protector and Duke of Somerset. In 1549 there were two simultaneous rebellions – Kett's Rebellion in Norfolk and the Western Rebellion in the West Country – which were brutally crushed. This same year, Edward VI's younger maternal uncle, Thomas Seymour, was executed on charges of treason, and his elder uncle and Lord Protector, Edward Seymour, was removed from office, to be executed in 1552.[21] Edward would himself die aged just 15 on 6 July 1553, the same age as Henry's brother and his own uncle, Arthur, fifty-two years earlier. This paved the way for the succession crisis between his Protestant cousin and nominated successor, Lady Jane Grey, and his Catholic half-sister, Mary I, who was the rightful heir by the will of Henry VIII and the Second Succession Act of 1544.

This succession crisis is important to look at as a lesson of Henry VIII's quest for an heir. He was so determined to have a son but, when that son died before attaining his majority and without having an heir of his own, all of the remaining possible heirs were female. This is exactly what Henry had been trying to avoid. Henry VIII's will and the Second Succession

Act of 1544 stated that the line of succession would be Prince Edward and his heirs, then Princess Mary and hers, then Princess Elizabeth and hers. Neither Mary nor Elizabeth were made legitimate by their father, but they were restored to the line of succession. How much this was due to the influence of their final stepmother, Katherine Parr, is unclear, though it seems likely that she did have a hand in influencing the king. Linda Porter says that the improvement in the fortunes of her stepdaughters was 'welcomed wholeheartedly' by Katherine.[22] She certainly seems to have done her best to restore the king's daughters to his good graces, and to form a family unit with their brother, Edward.

After Henry VIII's children, if they all died without issue, the line of succession was to pass to the children of Henry's younger sister, Mary, the former queen of France and Duchess of Suffolk. Henry had rejected the line of his elder sister, Margaret, queen of Scotland, whose son was James V of Scotland. James had failed to turn up to a meeting with Henry in York in 1541 when he was on progress with his fifth wife, Katherine Howard, which upset Henry. James had then died in 1542, just a year after the meeting was supposed to happen, but the regency council for the baby Mary, Queen of Scots had refused to agree to the marriage of Mary to Prince Edward to unite England and Scotland, instead sending her overseas with the intent for her to marry the French Dauphin, who would become Francis II. Mary would indeed be his queen. All of this Scottish defiance no doubt had an influence on Henry VIII's decision to reject Margaret's line from the English succession. However, it would eventually be Margaret's line that would triumph when, in 1603, James VI of Scotland became James I of England.

The line of Henry's younger sister, Mary Tudor, included the Grey family. Lady Jane Grey was the granddaughter of Mary Tudor, through her daughter, Frances Brandon, who had married Henry Grey, who was created 1st Duke of Suffolk under Edward VI. It was Lady Jane who Edward VI nominated as his successor in his *Devise for the Succession* of 1553, drafted before his death.[23] The original draft of the *Devise* said, 'L Janes heires male', meaning that the throne would be left to a male heir, but when Edward realised that he was dying, Jane was newly married and not yet pregnant. She would not have a son before Edward VI died, and so the *Devise* had to be changed:

> For lakke of issu of my body to the L Franceses heires masles, if she have any such issu before my death, to the L Jane and her heires masles, to the L Katerins heires masles, to the L Maries heires masles, to the heires masles of the daughters which she shall have hereafter, then to the L Margets heires masles. For lakke of such issu, to heires masles of the L Janes daughters, to heires male of the L Katerins daughters and so forth til you come to the L Margets daughters heires masles.[24]

The first step was unlikely at the time – that Lady Jane Grey's mother, Frances, would have a son. Then the line passed to Lady Jane herself and her male heirs, then to the male heirs of Jane's sisters, Katherine and Mary Grey, then to the male heirs of any other daughters that Frances Grey might have. If those lines all failed, then the line would pass to the male heirs of Margaret Clifford, the daughter of Frances Grey's sister, Eleanor Clifford, Countess of Cumberland. If that line also failed, then it would go through the sons of the daughters of each of these women. Edward VI really covered his bases in outlining his idea for the succession, determined to exclude any possibility of either of his half-sisters succeeding to the throne.

The religious consequences would echo across the century as well, with Henry VIII's children each taking a different path through the turmoil which resulted from the 'Great Matter' and the Henrician Reformation. Henry's son, Edward VI, went down the route of further reform and Protestantism. Mary I then tried to undo that with her Catholic Counter-Reformation, and Elizabeth attempted to find a middle way with her Religious Settlement in 1559. The consequences of these years of the 'Great Matter' were far-reaching – monasteries destroyed, and wealth confiscated, and rebellions such as the Pilgrimage of Grace arising out of the want for traditional and conservative religion to be restored. Popular figures were brought down, imprisoned or executed, including Katherine of Aragon, Thomas Wolsey, Thomas More, and John Fisher. It is important to place these wider events like the Break with Rome into the context of the period, including the 'Great Matter' and examine how these events effected the people at the centre in different ways. Understanding the personal helps to understand the political, and vice versa. Henry VIII's 'Great Matter' and his constant quest for a male heir destroyed many lives and changed the face of England forever. His belief that a woman could not rule in England would be disproved by both of his daughters as Mary I followed by Elizabeth I proved that women could wield power, some more successfully than others. The 'Great Matter' is often condensed down into these massive over-arching changes that transformed England, but it is also important not to forget the effect it had on the people who were closest to it – Katherine of Aragon, Anne Boleyn, Princess Mary, Princess Elizabeth, Thomas Wolsey, and Thomas Cromwell. They were queens, mothers, daughters, advisers, and powerful men. But their lives were all irrevocably changed by Henry VIII in his quest for a male heir.

Epilogue

Henry VIII's quest for an heir was long and tumultuous. It resulted in the first ever execution of a queen of England in one of the most surprising and sudden coups in English history. Right to the end, no one truly expected Henry to go through with it. Anne Boleyn was Henry VIII's great obsession, but also his great tragedy. Her execution paved the way for the royal executions that would follow, including Henry's fifth wife, Katherine Howard, in 1542, another queen consort. Executions of queens regnant would follow with Lady Jane Grey executed by Mary I in 1554 and Mary, Queen of Scots by Elizabeth I in 1587. These executions then paved the way for the execution of the English king, Charles I, in 1649 at the height of the English Civil War. Henry VIII's 'Great Matter' had far-reaching political consequences into the following century and beyond.

The changing perception of the people involved in the 'Great Matter' – kings, queens, advisers, and courtiers – is important. Today, we see Henry VIII as a tyrant and wife-killer, but when he began his 'Great Matter' he was a handsome and highly eligible man and king. He had already displayed some tyrannical tendencies prior to this, specifically in the case of Edward Stafford, 3rd Duke of Buckingham, who was executed in 1521.[1] These tendencies would only increase throughout the 'Great Matter', leading to the image of Henry VIII that we recognise today, painted so ably by Hans Holbein and showing the king in an all-powerful stance.

Katherine of Aragon was a much-respected wife and queen, pitied towards the end of her life, abandoned and alone. During her time as queen, she had many books dedicated to her, including *De institutione feminae christianae* (*The Education of a Christian Woman*) by Juan Luis Vives, which was published in 1524. There were very positive references to her in the 1529 version of the text, when her star was waning and her patronage was not guaranteed, but these were then changed in later editions. The dedication 'unto the quenes good grace' was dropped from the 1541 edition and instead it was addressed to 'the most gracious princesse Katharine of Englande'.[2] The change in status is explicit, that Katherine was not, and never had been, queen of England but was a princess as the wife of Prince Arthur. Katherine of Aragon's posthumous status would change again when her daughter, Mary I, came to the throne in 1553 and she reinstated her parents' marriage and her own legitimacy in her first parliament. William Shakespeare portrayed Katherine as 'non-threatening' and a 'pious, learned, and domesticated woman' which was more widely celebrated in this period – the end of the Tudors and the beginning of the Stuarts.[3] Katherine of Aragon was held up almost as an ideal, in comparison to Anne Boleyn.

Anne Boleyn was one of the most controversial people of the Tudor age. She remains divisive today, nearly 500 years after her death. Anne was not popular during her rise and queenship in England, and she was not much talked about for a long time after her death, largely due to fear and a desire to forget. Her daughter, Elizabeth I, respected and remembered her mother privately, but also had an effigy of her mother at her own coronation in January 1559, and portraits of her recreated, and even her image in a ring she wore, known today as the Chequers ring. Other sitters for the second portrait in the ring have been suggested, including Katherine Parr, though this seems unlikely, given their relationship did not end on the best note, despite Katherine's influence on Elizabeth's education and in her relationship with her father. Elizabeth was far more likely to keep her mother close to her, despite her execution and ignominy. As Tracy Borman says, the ring was 'a poignant symbol of the private reverence in which [Elizabeth] held her late mother throughout her long life'.[4] When the ring is closed the portraits inside almost touch, a very intimate gesture from a daughter to her mother. Even once his third wife, Jane Seymour, provided Henry VIII with a son and heir in 1537 – Prince Edward, later Edward VI – he was still determined that he needed a spare. He was himself a second son with an older brother who had died to enable him to become king. His mother, Elizabeth of York, had lost at least one other son, Prince Edmund, in infancy, along with two daughters, Elizabeth and Katherine. There was no guarantee that Prince Edward would survive to become king. Henry wanted to protect the succession as much as he could. He married a further three times, to Anne of Cleves in 1540, to Katherine Howard, also in 1540, and to Katherine Parr in 1543. There would not be any more children born to the king from these final three marriages. No other wife would be married to the king as long as Katherine of Aragon had been or provoke the obsession and devotion that he showed to Anne Boleyn. In fact, Henry VIII's last five marriages combined would not last as long as his first marriage. But it was beside his third wife, Jane Seymour, the mother of his son and heir, that Henry would choose to be buried, in St George's Chapel at Windsor Castle. Unfortunately, Jane and Henry's son, Edward VI, would die young, and Henry's daughters, Mary I and Elizabeth I, would both go on to rule as England's first regnant queens. Henry VIII did not believe a woman could rule, but his own daughters by the woman he abandoned and the woman he executed during this pivotal period proved him wrong.

Katherine of Aragon and Anne Boleyn are often pitted against each other as rivals, but the two had more in common than is often accepted. Thomas Cromwell and Anne Boleyn are often said to have been allies and even friends because of their shared faith in the reformed religion. However, there is little evidence to substantiate this, and more to suggest that they worked together while it was necessary but turned against each other when it became a life-or-death situation. Thanks to the fantastic, combined, work of Kate McCaffrey, Dr Owen Emmerson, and Alison Palmer, we now know that three of the pivotal people in the 'Great Matter' actually owned a copy of the same devotional printed Book of Hours from *c.*1527 – Katherine of Aragon, Anne Boleyn, and Thomas Cromwell. They are often seen as figures divided, but in a single book, we can see that they also had things in common.[5] This is a glimpse into the personal worlds of these important people at a pivotal time in the history of the 'Great Matter'. In 1527, Henry VIII was just beginning to pursue his annulment from Katherine of Aragon, Anne Boleyn was emerging onto the political scene because of her romantic entanglement with the king, and Thomas Cromwell was working his way up in the household of Cardinal Wolsey which gave him entry to court. One of the biggest shocks to come out of the king's 'Great Matter' was the execution of the first English queen – 'Anne's rise had been unthinkable and her end unspeakable'.[6] They echoed down the centuries and explain why we are still so fascinated with the Tudors today.

It was the women who were at the centre of the 'Great Matter', much as the focus tends to be on Henry VIII and the upheaval of religion in England. It is five queens whose lives were most affected by the events of this period of English history – Katherine of Aragon, Anne Boleyn, Jane Seymour, Mary I, and Elizabeth I. Katherine of Aragon was supplanted and died alone in exile, abandoned by her husband and forbidden to see her daughter. Anne Boleyn was made queen of England in an incredible rise and then became the first English queen to be executed in a tumultuous fall. Jane Seymour was also elevated to the position of queen, then died finally giving the king the son he so desperately craved, perhaps preventing the king tiring of her and assuring her place in his affections. The future Mary I went from being the assumed heir to the throne, beloved by her parents, to being separated from her mother, forced to serve her half-sister, and then her mother dying having not been able to see her for four years. The future Elizabeth I lost her mother at the age of 2, the daughter of an adulteress and traitor, tainted for the rest of her life, but determined to remember and honour that mother in her own private ways. Their trials and fears shaped how these women reacted to events throughout their lives, stemming from Henry VIII's quest for a male heir.

The 'Great Matter' was a longer period than it is often thought to be, bookended by the births of two sons in 1519 and 1537, one illegitimate and one legitimate. These eighteen years saw three women become queens of England and die, and the births of two future English monarchs, Elizabeth I and Edward VI. It is the most important period of the Tudor dynasty, with massive religious and political change, which shaped what England and, by extension the United Kingdom, is today. Henry VIII's 'Great Matter' was 'doomed by an extraordinary convergence of international political forces whose combined power he could not overcome'.[7] Had it happened at a different time, the king may well have been successful in gaining an annulment from the Pope and marrying Anne Boleyn much sooner. Perhaps that could have resulted in a son and spared Anne the fate that she eventually suffered. The position and connections of Katherine of Aragon, her familial relationship to the Holy Roman Emperor, Charles V, and the devotion of Imperial ambassador Eustace Chapuys, meant that getting an annulment was never going to be easy for Henry VIII. He was challenged, and it resulted in the fall of one minister, the rise and subsequent execution of another, and the execution of a queen, as well as the upending of the religion of England and tightening of the treason laws. Nothing would ever be the same in England again.

Notes

Introduction

1. Lloyd, Carol Ann, *The Tudors by Numbers: The Stories and Statistics Behind England's Most Infamous Royal Dynasty* (2023) p.21.
2. Gairdner, James, 'A Supposed Conspiracy against Henry VII', *Transactions of the Royal Historical Society* (1904) p.187.
3. 'Letter from de Puebla to Ferdinand and Isabella of Spain 11 January 1500', *Calendar of State Papers: Spain*, Vol.1, 1485–1509, no.249 (1862).
4. Froude, James, *The Divorce of Catherine of Aragon* (2015) p.19.
5. Thurston, Herbert, 'The Canon Law of the Divorce', *The English Historical Review* (1904) p.632.
6. 'Leviticus 20:21', *King James Bible*, https://www.kingjamesbibleonline.org/Leviticus-Chapter-20/.
7. 'Deuteronomy 25:5', *King James Bible*, https://www.kingjamesbibleonline.org/Deuteronomy-Chapter-25/.
8. Travitsky, Betty, 'Reprinting Tudor History: The Case of Catherine of Aragon', *Renaissance Quarterly* (1997) p.172.

Chapter 1 – Roots of Dissatisfaction

1. 'Treaty between England and Spain, ratified by Ferdinand and Isabella 27–28 March 1489', *Calendar of State Papers: Spain*, Vol.1, 1485–1509, no.34 (1862).
2. McElroy, Amy, *Women's Lives in the Tudor Era* (2024) p.25.
3. 'Treaty between England and Spain, ratified by Ferdinand and Isabella 27–28 March 1489', *Calendar of State Papers: Spain*, Vol.1, 1485–1509, no.34 (1862).
4. Licence, Amy, *Catherine of Aragon: An Intimate Life of Henry VIII's True Wife* (2016) p.66.
5. Tremlett, Giles, *Catherine of Aragon: Henry's Spanish Queen* (2011) p.74.
6. Thurston, Herbert, 'The Divorce of Henry VIII', *Studies: An Irish Quarterly Review* (1932) p.56.
7. Fox, Julia, *Sister Queens: Katherine of Aragon and Juana, Queen of Castile* (2011) p.65.
8. Ibid, p.66.
9. Licence, Amy, *Catherine of Aragon: An Intimate Life of Henry VIII's True Wife* (2016) p.116.
10. Tremlett, Giles, *Catherine of Aragon: Henry's Spanish Queen* (2010) p.89.
11. Licence, Amy, *Catherine of Aragon: An Intimate Life of Henry VIII's True Wife* (2016) p.119.
12. 'Depositions as to Katherine of Aragon's marriage with Prince Arthur', *Letters and Papers of Henry VIII*, Vol.4, 1524–1530, no.5774 (1875).
13. Ibid.
14. Ibid.
15. Tremlett, Giles, *Catherine of Aragon: Henry's Spanish Queen* (2010) p.96.
16. Licence, Amy, *Catherine of Aragon: An Intimate Life of Henry VIII's True Wife* (2016) pp.135–136.

17. Tremlett, Giles, *Catherine of Aragon: Henry's Spanish Queen* (2010) p.102.
18. Williams, Patrick, *Katharine of Aragon* (2013) p.123.
19. 'Letter from Ferdinand and Isabella to de Puebla 12 May 1502', *Calendar of State Papers: Spain*, Vol.1, 1485–1509, no.319 (1862).
20. Tremlett, Giles, *Catherine of Aragon: Henry's Spanish Queen* (2010) p.104.
21. 'Instructions given to the Duque de Estrada 10 May 1502', *Calendar of State Papers: Spain*, Vol.1, 1485–1509, no.317 (1862).
22. 'Letter from Isabella I of Castile to De Puebla 11 April 1503', *Calendar of State Papers: Spain*, Vol.1, 1485–1509, no.359 (1862).
23. 'Letter from Isabella I of Castile to Duque de Estrada 11 and 12 April 1503', *Calendar of State Papers: Spain*, Vol.1, 1485–1509, no.360 (1862).
24. Ibid.
25. Williams, Patrick, *Katharine of Aragon* (2013) p.133.
26. 'Letter from Katherine of Aragon to Ferdinand II of Aragon 9 March 1509', *Calendar of State Papers: Spain*, Supplement to Vol.1 & 2, Queen Katherine & Intended Marriage of Henry VII to Queen Juana, no.3 (1868).
27. Ibid.
28. 'Words pronounced at the wedding of Henry VIII and Katherine Princess of Wales', *Calendar of State Papers: Spain*, Vol.2, 1509–1525, no.17 (1866).
29. 'The Coronation 24 June 1509', *Letters and Papers of Henry VIII*, Vol.1, 1509–1514, no.82 (1920).
30. 'Letter from Henry VIII to Margaret of Savoy 27 June 1509', *Letters and Papers of Henry VIII*, Vol.1, 1509–1514, no.84 (1920).
31. Licence, Amy, *Catherine of Aragon: An Intimate Life of Henry VIII's True Wife* (2016) p.213.
32. 'Letter from Diego Fernandez to Ferdinand II of Aragon 25 May 1510', *Calendar of State Papers: Spain*, Supplement to Vol.1 & 2, Queen Katherine & Intended Marriage of Henry VII to Queen Juana, no.7 (1868).
33. Ibid.
34. Licence, Amy, *Catherine of Aragon: An Intimate Life of Henry VIII's True Wife* (2016) p.217.
35. 'Letter from Katherine of Aragon to Ferdinand II of Aragon 27 May 1510', *Letters and Papers of Henry VIII*, Vol.1, 1509–1514, no.473 (1920).
36. 'Letter from Diego Fernandez to Ferdinand II of Aragon 25 May 1510', *Calendar of State Papers: Spain*, Supplement to Vol.1 & 2, Queen Katherine & Intended Marriage of Henry VII to Queen Juana, no.7 (1868).
37. 'Account of the Christening of Henry, Duke of Cornwall 5 January 1511', *Letters and Papers of Henry VIII*, Vol.1, 1509–1514, no.670 (1920).
38. McElroy, Amy, *Women's Lives in the Tudor Era* (2024) p.79.
39. 'Account of the Tourney on the Birth of a Prince 12 February 1511', *Letters and Papers of Henry VIII*, Vol.1, 1509–1514, no.698 (1920).
40. Dewhurst, John, 'The Alleged Miscarriages of Catherine of Aragon and Anne Boleyn', *Medical History* (1984) p.51.
41. Hall, Edward, *Hall's Chronicle* (1809) p.519.
42. Licence, Amy, *Catherine of Aragon: An Intimate Life of Henry VIII's True Wife* (2016) p.228.
43. Scarisbrick, J. J., *Henry VIII* (1988) p.150.
44. Dewhurst, John, 'The Alleged Miscarriages of Catherine of Aragon and Anne Boleyn', *Medical History* (1984) p.49.
45. Ibid, p.50.

46. Earenfight, Theresa, *Catherine of Aragon: Infanta of Spain, Queen of England* (2021) p.116.
47. 'Receipt of letter through Duke of Ferrara 8 October 1513', *Calendar of State Papers: Venice*, Vol.2, 1509–1519, no.329 (1867).
48. 'Letter from Nicolo di Favri of Treviso to Franceso Gradenigo 30 October 1514 dated 24 September 1514', *Calendar of State Papers: Venice*, Vol.2, 1509–1519, no.505 (1867).
49. 'Letter from Andrea Badoer to the State 8 January 1515 dated December 1514', *Calendar of State Papers: Venice*, Vol.2, 1509–1519, no.555 (1867).
50. Holinshed, Raphael, *Holinshed's Chronicle of England, Scotland, and Ireland, Volume 3* (1807) p.607.
51. 'Letter from Sebastian Giustinian to Council of Ten 24 February 1516', *Calendar of State Papers: Venice*, Vol.2, 1509–1519, no.691 (1867).
52. 'Account of the Christening of the Princess Mary 21 February 1516', *Letters and Papers of Henry VIII*, Vol.2, 1515–1518, no.1573 (1864).
53. Ibid.
54. 'Letter from Sebastian Giustinian to Council of Ten 24 February 1516', *Calendar of State Papers: Venice*, Vol.2, 1509–1519, no.691 (1867).
55. 'Letter from Henry VIII to Cardinal Wolsey 1 July 1518', *Letters and Papers of Henry VIII*, Vol.2, 1515–1518, no.4279 (1864).
56. 'Letter from Sebastian Giustinian to the Signory 10 November 1518', *Calendar of State Papers: Venice*, Vol.2, 1509–1519, no.1103 (1867).
57. Licence, Amy, *Catherine of Aragon: An Intimate Life of Henry VIII's True Wife* (2016) p.280.
58. Williams, Patrick, *Katharine of Aragon* (2014) p.9.

Chapter 2 – The Mistress and the Son

1. Williams, Patrick, *Katharine of Aragon* (2014) p.9.
2. Rabow, Jerry, *Henry VIII and his Rabbis: How the King Relied on Jewish Law to End His First Marriage – and Why He Failed* (2025) p.43.
3. Murphy, Beverley, *Bastard Prince: Henry VIII's Lost Son* (2001) p.3.
4. Loades, David, *The Six Wives of Henry VIII* (2010) p.30.
5. Fraser, Antonia, *The Six Wives of Henry VIII* (2002) p.103.
6. Rabow, Jerry, *Henry VIII and his Rabbis: How the King Relied on Jewish Law to End His First Marriage – and Why He Failed* (2025) p.43.
7. Wooding, Lucy, *Tudor England: A History* (2022) p.176.
8. 'Letter from Henry VIII to Thomas Wyatt 5 April 1538', *Letters and Papers of Henry VIII*, Vol.13 Pt.1, Jan–Jul 1538, no.679 (1892).
9. Hart, Kelly, *The Mistresses of Henry VIII* (2011) pp.76–77.
10. Barnwell, E. L. *Perrot Notes* (1867) p.40.
11. Hart, Kelly, *The Mistresses of Henry VIII* (2011) p.77.
12. Murphy, Beverley, *Bastard Prince: Henry VIII's Lost Son* (2001) p.5.
13. Loades, David, *The Six Wives of Henry VIII* (2010) p.28.
14. Lindsey, Karen, *Divorced, Beheaded Survived: A Feminist Reinterpretation of the Wives of Henry VIII* (1995) p.40.
15. Rabow, Jerry, *Henry VIII and his Rabbis: How the King Relied on Jewish Law to End His First Marriage – and Why He Failed* (2025) p.43.
16. Fraser, Antonia, *The Six Wives of Henry VIII* (2002) p.102.
17. Herbert of Cherbury, *The History of England Under Henry VIII* (1870) p.270.
18. Ibid.

19. 'Affairs of the realm under Cardinal Wolsey', *Letters and Papers of Henry VIII*, Vol.4, 1524–1530, no.5750 (1875).
20. Sylvester, R. S. (ed.), More, Thomas, *The History of King Richard III* (1976) p.62.
21. 'Letter from Antonio Giustinian and Antonio Surian to the Signory 4 June 1519', *Calendar of State Papers: Venice*, Vol.2, 1509–1519, no.1230 (1867).
22. Murphy, Beverley, *Bastard Prince: Henry VIII's Lost Son* (2001) p.31.
23. Ibid.
24. Wooding, Lucy, *Henry VIII* (2015) p.128.
25. Ibid.
26. Fraser, Antonia, *The Six Wives of Henry VIII* (2002) p.132.
27. Wooding, Lucy, *Tudor England: A History* (2022) p.176.
28. Fraser, Antonia, *The Six Wives of Henry VIII* (2002) p.133.
29. Wooding, Lucy, *Henry VIII* (2015) p.128.
30. Loades, David, *The Six Wives of Henry VIII* (2010) p.37.
31. Duncan, J. & Derrett, M., 'Henry Fitzroy and Henry VIII's "Scruple of Conscience"', *Renaissance News* (1963) p.1.
32. Ibid, p.5.
33. Lindsey, Karen, *Divorced, Beheaded Survived: A Feminist Reinterpretation of the Wives of Henry VIII* (1995) p.60.
34. Rabow, Jerry, *Henry VIII and his Rabbis: How the King Relied on Jewish Law to End His First Marriage – and Why He Failed* (2025) p.43.
35. Fraser, Antonia, *The Six Wives of Henry VIII* (2002) p.185.
36. 'Letter from Campeggio to Sanga 28 October 1528', *Letters and Papers of Henry VIII*, Vol.4, 1524–1530, no.4881 (1875).
37. Murphy, Beverley, *Bastard Prince: Henry VIII's Lost Son* (2001) p.87.
38. Ibid, pp.85–86.
39. Ibid, pp.134–135.
40. Ibid, p.139.
41. 'Letter from Eustace Chapuys to Charles V 24 November 1533' *Letters and Papers of Henry VIII*, Vol.6, 1533, no.1460 (1882).
42. Murphy, Beverley, *Bastard Prince: Henry VIII's Lost Son* (2001) p.143.
43. Fraser, Antonia, *The Six Wives of Henry VIII* (2002) p.37.
44. 'Letter from Chapuys to Charles V 19 May 1536', *Letters and Papers of Henry VIII*, Vol.10, Jan–Jun 1536, no.908 (1887).
45. Murphy, Beverley, *Bastard Prince: Henry VIII's Lost Son* (2001) p.213.
46. Duncan, J. & Derrett, M., 'Henry Fitzroy and Henry VIII's "Scruple of Conscience"', *Renaissance News* (1963) p.8.
47. Ibid.
48. Ibid, p.3.
49. Ibid, p.4.
50. Fuller, Thomas, *The Church History of Britain from the Birth of Jesus Christ Until the Year M.DC.XLVIII*, Vol.3 (1845) p.232.
51. Murphy, Beverley, *Bastard Prince: Henry VIII's Lost Son* (2001) p.243.
52. Hackett, Francis, *Henry the VIII: The Personal History of a Dynast and His Wives* (1945) p.104.

Chapter 3 – Enter the Boleyns

1. 'Letter from George Throckmorton to Henry VIII, undated', *Letters and Papers of Henry VIII*, Vol.12, Pt.2, Jul–Dec 1537, no.952 (1891).
2. Rabow, Jerry, *Henry VIII and his Rabbis: How the King Relied on Jewish Law to End His First Marriage – and Why He Failed* (2025) p.44.
3. Ibid, p.47.
4. Hart, Kelly, *The Mistresses of Henry VIII* (2011) p.56.
5. Jones, Philippa, *The Other Tudors: Henry VIII's Mistresses and Bastards* (2010) p.16.
6. Wilkinson, Josephine, *Mary Boleyn: The True Story of Henry VIII's Favourite Mistress* (2010) p.65.
7. Weir, Alison, *Mary Boleyn: 'The Great and Infamous Whore'* (2011) pp.109, 136.
8. Murphy, Beverley, *Bastard Prince: Henry VIII's Lost Son* (2001) p.4.
9. Ibid, pp.4–5.
10. Dunn, Wendy J., *Henry VIII's True Daughter: Catherine Carey, a Tudor Life* (2023) p.20.
11. Rabow, Jerry, *Henry VIII and his Rabbis: How the King Relied on Jewish Law to End His First Marriage – and Why He Failed* (2025) p.44.
12. Murphy, Beverley, *Bastard Prince: Henry VIII's Lost Son* (2001) p.5.
13. Dunn, Wendy J., *Henry VIII's True Daughter: Catherine Carey, a Tudor Life* (2023) p.20.
14. Rabow, Jerry, *Henry VIII and his Rabbis: How the King Relied on Jewish Law to End His First Marriage – and Why He Failed* (2025) p.46.
15. Guy, John and Fox, Julia, *Hunting the Falcon: Henry VIII, Anne Boleyn and the Marriage That Shook Europe* (2023) p.95.
16. 'Letter from Bishop of Faenza to the Prothonotary Ambrogio 10 March 1536', *Letters and Papers of Henry VIII*, Vol.10, Jan–Jun 1536, no.450 (1887) & Guy, John and Fox, Julia, *Hunting the Falcon: Henry VIII, Anne Boleyn and the Marriage That Shook Europe* (2023) n.23, p.452.
17. Bruce, Marie Louise, *Anne Boleyn* (1975) p.23.
18. Wilkinson, Josephine, *Mary Boleyn: The True Story of Henry VIII's Favourite Mistress* (2010) p.38.
19. Hackett, Francis, *Henry the VIII: The Personal History of a Dynast and His Wives* (1945) p.157.
20. Dunn, Wendy J., *Henry VIII's True Daughter: Catherine Carey, a Tudor Life* (2023) p.15.
21. Weir, Alison, *Mary Boleyn: 'The Great and Infamous Whore'* (2011) p.68.
22. Ibid, p.69.
23. 'Letter from Anne Boleyn to Thomas Boleyn c.1513', in Norton, Elizabeth, *Anne Boleyn: In Her Own Words and the Words of Those Who Knew Her* (2011) p.25.
24. Emmerson, Owen and McCaffrey, Kate, *Becoming Anne: Connections, Culture, Court* (2022) p.62.
25. Norton, Elizabeth, *Anne Boleyn: Henry VIII's Obsession* (2009) p.18.
26. 'Letter from Margaret of Austria to Thomas Boleyn *c.*1513' in Norton, Elizabeth, *Anne Boleyn: In Her Own Words and the Words of Those Who Knew Her* (2011) p.25.
27. Emmerson, Owen and Ridgway, Claire, *The Boleyns of Hever Castle* (2021) p.63.
28. Dr Owen Emmerson and Natalie Grueninger revealed this information in their *The Making of a Queen: Anne Boleyn 1501–1522* online event in March 2025.
29. Hall, Edward, *Hall's Chronicle* (1809) p.631.
30. 'Richard Gibson's accounts for Revels held 29 Dec and 1 Jan 13 Hen. VIII', *Letters and Papers of Henry VIII*, Vol.3, 1519–1523, no.2 (1867).

31. Credit to Owen Emmerson and Natalie Grueninger for bringing this to light and to James Taffe for his initial question on the subject, see note 28, above.
32. Ives, Eric, *The Life and Death of Anne Boleyn* (2005) p.37.
33. 'Letter from Northumberland to Thomas Cromwell 13 May 1536', *Letters and Papers of Henry VIII*, Vol.10, Jan–Jun 1536, no.864 (1887).
34. Ives, Eric, *The Life and Death of Anne Boleyn* (2005) p.166.
35. Cavendish, George, The Life of Cardinal Wolsey (1890) p.48.
36. Ibid.
37. Ibid.
38. Ibid, p.51.
39. Ibid, p.54.
40. Ives, Eric, *The Life and Death of Anne Boleyn* (2005) p.65.
41. Wyatt, Thomas, 'Whoso List to Hunt', in Norton, Elizabeth, *Anne Boleyn: In Her Own Words and the Words of Those Who Knew Her* (2011) p.34.
42. Wyatt, Thomas, 'If Waker care; if sudden pale colour', in Norton, Elizabeth, *Anne Boleyn: In Her Own Words and the Words of Those Who Knew Her* (2011) p.34.
43. Ibid.
44. Duncan, J. & Derrett, M., 'Henry Fitzroy and Henry VIII's "Scruple of Conscience"', *Renaissance News* (1963) p.8.
45. Cavendish, George, The Life of Cardinal Wolsey (1890) p.48.
46. Licence, Amy, *Anne Boleyn: Adultery, Heresy, Desire* (2017) p.161.
47. Ibid.
48. Guy, John and Fox, Julia, *Hunting the Falcon: Henry VIII, Anne Boleyn and the Marriage That Shook Europe* (2023) p.124.
49. Borman, Tracy, *Anne Boleyn and Elizabeth I: The Mother and Daughter Who Changed History* (2023) p.15.
50. Ibid, p.16.
51. Vatican Archives, ref. Vat.lat.3731.pt.A.
52. Starkey, David, *Six Wives: The Queens of Henry VIII* (2004) p.278.
53. Duncan, J. & Derrett, M., 'Henry Fitzroy and Henry VIII's "Scruple of Conscience"', *Renaissance News* (1963) p.1.
54. Starkey, David, *Six Wives: The Queens of Henry VIII* (2004) p.273; Lindsey, Karen, *Divorced, Beheaded, Survived: A Feminist Reinterpretation of the Wives of Henry VIII* (1995) p.57.
55. Denny, Joanna, *Anne Boleyn: A New Life of England's Tragic Queen* (2004) p.57; Loades, David, *The Boleyns: The Rise and Fall of a Tudor Family* (2011) p.79.
56. Warnicke, Retha, *The Rise and Fall of Anne Boleyn* (2008) p.78.
57. 'Love Letter 4 from Henry VIII to Anne Boleyn', in Norton, Elizabeth, *Anne Boleyn: In Her Own Words and the Words of Those Who Knew Her* (2011) p.42.
58. Bernard, G. W., *Anne Boleyn: Fatal Attractions* (2011) p.25.

Chapter 4 – Agreement to Marry

1. Emmerson, Owen & Ridgway, Claire, *The Boleyns of Hever Castle* (2021) p.73.
2. Adams, Tracy, '"Ma seulle mestres": The Myth of the Coquettish Anne Boleyn', *The Court Historian* (2024) p.196.
3. Guy, John & Fox, Julia, *Hunting the Falcon: Henry VIII, Anne Boleyn and the Marriage That Shook Europe* (2023) p.123.

4. Ives, Eric, *The Life and Death of Anne Boleyn* (2005) pp.86–87.
5. Denny, Joanna, *Anne Boleyn: A new life of England's tragic Queen* (2008) p.97.
6. 'Love Letter 5 from Henry VIII to Anne Boleyn', in Norton, Elizabeth, *Anne Boleyn: In Her Own Words and the Words of Those Who Knew Her* (2011) p.42.
7. Chaucer, Geoffrey, edited by Nicholas, Harris, *Chaucer's Romaunt of the Rose, Troilus and Creseide, and the Minor Poems* (1846) p.131.
8. Erickson, Carolly, *Mistress Anne* (1984) p.108.
9. Adams, Tracy, '"Ma seulle mestres": The Myth of the Coquettish Anne Boleyn', *The Court Historian* (2024) p.195.
10. Ibid, p.198.
11. Borman, Tracy, *Henry VIII and the Men Who Made Him* (2020) p.148.
12. Emmerson, Owen & Ridgway, Claire, *The Boleyns of Hever Castle* (2021) p.73.
13. Borman, Tracy, *Henry VIII and the Men Who Made Him* (2020) p.148.
14. 'Letter from Chapuys to Charles V 15 February 1533', *Calendar of State Papers: Spain*, Vol.4 Pt.2, 1531–1533, no.1048 (1882).
15. Ives, Eric, *The Life and Death of Anne Boleyn* (2005) p.88.
16. Emmerson, Owen & Ridgway, Claire, *The Boleyns of Hever Castle* (2021) p.76; 'The Subsidy 20 March 1527', *Letters and Papers of Henry VIII*, Vol.4, 1524–1530, no.2972 (1875).
17. Emmerson, Owen, McCaffrey, Kate & Palmer, Alison, *Catherine and Anne: Queens, Rivals, Mothers* (2023) p.40.
18. 'Letter from Wolsey to Ghinucci and Lee 1 August 1527', *Letters and Papers of Henry VIII*, Vol.4, 1524–1530, no.3327 (1875).
19. 'Letter from Wolsey to Henry VIII 5 July 1527', *Letters and Papers of Henry VIII*, Vol.4, 1524–1530, no.3231 (1875).
20. Thomas, Melita, *The King's Pearl: Henry VIII and His Daughter Mary* (2019) p.109.
21. 'Proposed bull of dispensation for Henry VIII', *Letters and Papers of Henry VIII*, Vol.4, 1524–1530, no.3686 (1875).
22. Ibid.
23. Pole, Reginald, *Defense of the Unity of the Church* (1965) p.185.
24. Adams, Tracy, '"Ma seulle mestres": The Myth of the Coquettish Anne Boleyn', *The Court Historian* (2024) p.195.
25. Ives, Eric, *The Life and Death of Anne Boleyn* (2005) p.96.
26. 'Letter from Gardiner and Casale to Wolsey 13 April 1528', *Letters and Papers of Henry VIII*, Vol.4, 1524–1530, no.4167 (1875).
27. 'Love Letter 14 from Henry VIII to Anne Boleyn', in Norton, Elizabeth, *Anne Boleyn: In Her Own Words and the Words of Those Who Knew Her* (2011) p.45.
28. 'Love Letter 1 from Henry VIII to Anne Boleyn', in Norton, Elizabeth, *Anne Boleyn: In Her Own Words and the Words of Those Who Knew Her* (2011) p.41.
29. 'Love Letter 10 from Henry VIII to Anne Boleyn', in Norton, Elizabeth, *Anne Boleyn: In Her Own Words and the Words of Those Who Knew Her* (2011) pp.43–44.
30. 'Love Letter 2 from Henry VIII to Anne Boleyn', in Norton, Elizabeth, *Anne Boleyn: In Her Own Words and the Words of Those Who Knew Her* (2011) p.41.
31. 'Love Letter 6 from Henry VIII to Anne Boleyn', in Norton, Elizabeth, *Anne Boleyn: In Her Own Words and the Words of Those Who Knew Her* (2011) p.43.
32. 'Love Letter 16 from Henry VIII to Anne Boleyn', in Norton, Elizabeth, *Anne Boleyn: In Her Own Words and the Words of Those Who Knew Her* (2011) p.45.

33. 'Love Letter 3 from Henry VIII to Anne Boleyn', in Norton, Elizabeth, *Anne Boleyn: In Her Own Words and the Words of Those Who Knew Her* (2011) p.41.
34. 'Love Letter 12 from Henry VIII to Anne Boleyn', in Norton, Elizabeth, *Anne Boleyn: In Her Own Words and the Words of Those Who Knew Her* (2011) p.44.
35. 'Letter from Du Bellay to Montmorency', *Letters and Papers of Henry VIII*, Vol.4, 1524–1530, no.4440 (1875).
36. 'Letter from Du Bellay to Montmorency', *Letters and Papers of Henry VIII*, Vol.4, 1524–1530, no.4542 (1875).
37. Ibid.
38. Emmerson, Owen & Ridgway, Claire, *The Boleyns of Hever Castle* (2021) p.80.
39. 'Love Letter 3 from Henry VIII to Anne Boleyn', in Norton, Elizabeth, *Anne Boleyn: In Her Own Words and the Words of Those Who Knew Her* (2011) p.41.
40. Guy, John & Fox, Julia, *Hunting the Falcon: Henry VIII, Anne Boleyn and the Marriage That Shook Europe* (2023) p.127.
41. Ives, Eric, *The Life and Death of Anne Boleyn* (2005) p.86.
42. Norton, Elizabeth, *Anne Boleyn: Henry VIII's Obsession* (2009) p.50.
43. Ibid.
44. Guy, John & Fox, Julia, *Hunting the Falcon: Henry VIII, Anne Boleyn and the Marriage That Shook Europe* (2023) p.128.
45. Bernard, G. W., *Anne Boleyn: Fatal Attractions* (2011) p.31.
46. Emmerson, Owen & Ridgway, Claire, *The Boleyns of Hever Castle* (2021) p.68.
47. Bernard, G. W., *Anne Boleyn: Fatal Attractions* (2011) p.31.
48. Emmerson, Owen & Ridgway, Claire, *The Boleyns of Hever Castle* (2021) p.80.
49. 'Love Letter 6 from Henry VIII to Anne Boleyn', in Norton, Elizabeth, *Anne Boleyn: In Her Own Words and the Words of Those Who Knew Her* (2011) p.43.
50. Emmerson, Owen, McCaffrey, Kate & Palmer, Alison, *Catherine and Anne: Queens, Rivals, Mothers* (2023) p.40.
51. Hadwin, J. F., 'Leviticus, Deuteronomy and Henry VIII', *Journal of Ecclesiastical History* (2019) p.488.

Chapter 5 – Divorce Versus Annulment

1. Thurston, Herbert, 'The Divorce of Henry VIII', *Studies: An Irish Quarterly Review* (1932) p.55.
2. Hadwin, J. F., 'Leviticus, Deuteronomy and Henry VIII', *Journal of Ecclesiastical History* (2019) p.488.
3. Ibid, p.489.
4. 'Leviticus 20:21', *King James Bible*, https://www.kingjamesbibleonline.org/Leviticus-Chapter-20/.
5. Duncan, J. & Derrett, M., 'Henry Fitzroy and Henry VIII's "Scruple of Conscience"', *Renaissance News* (1963) p.2.
6. Hadwin, J. F., 'Leviticus, Deuteronomy and Henry VIII', *Journal of Ecclesiastical History* (2019) p.494.
7. 'Deuteronomy 25:5', *King James Bible*, https://www.kingjamesbibleonline.org/Deuteronomy-Chapter-25/.
8. Hadwin, J. F., 'Leviticus, Deuteronomy and Henry VIII', *Journal of Ecclesiastical History* (2019) p.489.

9. Rabow, Jerry, *Henry VIII and his Rabbis: How the King Relied on Jewish Law to End His First Marriage – and Why He Failed* (2025) p.78.
10. Murphy, Virginia, 'The Literature and Propaganda of Henry VIII's First Divorce', in MacCulloch, Diarmaid (ed.) *The Reign of Henry VIII: Politics, Policy and Piety* (1995) p.136.
11. Hadwin, J. F., 'Leviticus, Deuteronomy and Henry VIII', *Journal of Ecclesiastical History* (2019) p.504.
12. Ibid, p.489.
13. Williams, Patrick, *Katharine of Aragon* (2014) p.9.
14. Travitsky, Betty, 'Reprinting Tudor History: The Case of Catherine of Aragon', *Renaissance Quarterly* (1997) p.166.
15. Duncan, J. & Derrett, M., 'Henry Fitzroy and Henry VIII's "Scruple of Conscience"', *Renaissance News* (1963) p.2.
16. 'Letter from Inigo de Mendoza to Charles V 18 May 1527', *Calendar of State Papers: Spain*, Vol.3 Pt.2, 1527–1529, no.69 (1877).
17. Rabow, Jerry, *Henry VIII and his Rabbis: How the King Relied on Jewish Law to End His First Marriage – and Why He Failed* (2025) p.86.
18. 'A conditional dispensation for the King's Majesty from the bishop of Rome', *Letters and Papers of Henry VIII*, Vol.4, 1524–1530, no.3686 (1875).
19. 'Letter from Clement VII to Cardinal Wolsey 8 July 1529', *Letters and Papers of Henry VIII*, Vol.4, 1524–1530, no.5759 (1875).
20. Rabow, Jerry, *Henry VIII and his Rabbis: How the King Relied on Jewish Law to End His First Marriage – and Why He Failed* (2025) p.74.
21. Duncan, J. & Derrett., M, 'Henry Fitzroy and Henry VIII's "Scruple of Conscience"', *Renaissance News* (1963) p.9.
22. 'Letter from Gardiner and Casale to Wolsey on 13 April 1528', *Letters and Papers of Henry VIII*, Vol.4, 1524–1530, no.4167 (1875).
23. Ibid.
24. Thurston, Herbert, 'The Canon Law of the Divorce', *The English Historical Review* (1904) p.633.
25. Ibid.
26. Thurston, Herbert, 'The Divorce of Henry VIII', *Studies: An Irish Quarterly Review* (1932) p.66.
27. Guy, John & Fox, Julia, *Hunting the Falcon: Henry VIII, Anne Boleyn and the Marriage That Shook Europe* (2023) pp.176–177.
28. Thurston, Herbert, 'The Canon Law of the Divorce', *The English Historical Review* (1904) p.633.
29. Ibid.
30. 'Letter from Ferdinand of Aragon to De Rojas on 20 August 1503', *Calendar of State Papers: Spain*, Vol.1, 1485–1509, no.370 (1862).
31. Thurston, Herbert, 'The Canon Law of the Divorce', *The English Historical Review* (1904) p.639.
32. Thurston, Herbert, 'The Divorce of Henry VIII', *Studies: An Irish Quarterly Review* (1932) p.65.
33. Thurston, Herbert, 'The Canon Law of the Divorce', *The English Historical Review* (1904) p.637.
34. Ibid, p.640.

35. Pocock, Nicholas, *Records of the Reformation: The Divorce 1527–1533*, Vol.1 (1870) pp.184–186.
36. Thurston, Herbert, 'The Canon Law of the Divorce', *The English Historical Review* (1904) p.640.
37. Ibid, p.643.
38. Rabow, Jerry, *Henry VIII and his Rabbis: How the King Relied on Jewish Law to End His First Marriage – and Why He Failed* (2025) p.93.
39. Cavendish, George, *The Life of Cardinal Wolsey* (1890) pp.116–117.
40. Rabow, Jerry, *Henry VIII and his Rabbis: How the King Relied on Jewish Law to End His First Marriage – and Why He Failed* (2025) p.94.
41. 'Letter from Inigo de Mendoza to Charles V on 18 November 1528', *Calendar of State Papers: Spain*, Vol.3 Pt.2, 1527–1529, no.586 (1877).
42. Guy, John & Fox, Julia, *Hunting the Falcon: Henry VIII, Anne Boleyn and the Marriage That Shook Europe* (2023) p.466.
43. Rabow, Jerry, *Henry VIII and his Rabbis: How the King Relied on Jewish Law to End His First Marriage – and Why He Failed* (2025) p.92.
44. Hadwin, J. F., 'Leviticus, Deuteronomy and Henry VIII', *Journal of Ecclesiastical History* (2019) p.487.
45. Rabow, Jerry, *Henry VIII and his Rabbis: How the King Relied on Jewish Law to End His First Marriage – and Why He Failed* (2025) p.72.
46. Wooding, Lucy, *Henry VIII* (2015) p.163.
47. 'Letter from Eustace Chapuys to Charles V 24 November 1533', *Letters and Papers of Henry VIII*, Vol.6, 1533, no.1460 (1882).

Chapter 6 – The Fall of Thomas Wolsey

1. Roberts, Phil, *Cardinal Wolsey: For King and Country* (2022) p.114.
2. Starkey, David, *The Reign of Henry VIII: Personalities and Politics* (2002) p.38.
3. Ibid.
4. Borman, Tracy, *Henry VIII and the Men Who Made Him* (2020) p.88.
5. Ibid.
6. Cavendish, George, *The Life of Cardinal Wolsey* (1890) p.24.
7. Hall, Edward, *Hall's Chronicle* (1809) p.583.
8. Roberts, Phil, *Cardinal Wolsey: For King and Country* (2022) p.115.
9. Ibid.
10. Borman, Tracy, *Henry VIII and the Men Who Made Him* (2020) p.147.
11. Ives, Eric, *The Life and Death of Anne Boleyn* (2005) p.65.
12. Cavendish, George, *The Life of Cardinal Wolsey* (1890) p.54.
13. Ibid, p.56.
14. Ibid, pp.135–136.
15. Wilkinson, Josephine, *Anne Boleyn: The Young Queen to Be* (2011) p.96.
16. Murphy, Virginia, 'The Literature and Propaganda of Henry VIII's First Divorce', in MacCulloch, Diarmaid (ed.) *The Reign of Henry VIII: Politics, Policy and Piety* (1995) p.135.
17. Wilkinson, Josephine, *Anne Boleyn: The Young Queen to Be* (2011) p.97.
18. Denny, Joanna, *Anne Boleyn: A new life of England's tragic Queen* (2008) p.109.
19. Ibid, p.110.

20. 'Letter from Wolsey to Henry VIII 1 July 1527', *Letters and Papers of Henry VIII*, Vol.4, 1524–1530, no.3217 (1875).
21. Ibid.
22. 'Letter from Anne Boleyn to Cardinal Wolsey', in Norton, Elizabeth, *Anne Boleyn: In Her Own Words and the Words of Those Who Knew Her* (2011) pp.47–48.
23. Ibid.
24. 'Letter from Anne Boleyn to Cardinal Wolsey *c.* July 1528', in Norton, Elizabeth, *Anne Boleyn: In Her Own Words and the Words of Those Who Knew Her* (2011) p.48.
25. Ibid.
26. 'Letter from Anne Boleyn to Cardinal Wolsey c.1529' in Norton, Elizabeth, *Anne Boleyn: In Her Own Words and the Words of Those Who Knew Her* (2011) p.49.
27. Ives, Eric, *The Life and Death of Anne Boleyn* (2005) p.102.
28. 'Love Letter 13 from Henry VIII to Anne Boleyn' in Norton, Elizabeth, *Anne Boleyn: In Her Own Words and the Words of Those Who Knew Her* (2011) pp.44–45.
29. Ibid.
30. Ives, Eric, *The Life and Death of Anne Boleyn* (2005) p.102.
31. Thurston, Herbert, 'The Canon Law of the Divorce', *The English Historical Review* (1904) p.633.
32. 'Letter from Sanga to Cardinal Campeggio 29 May 1529', *Letters and Papers of Henry VIII*, Vol.4, 1524–1530, no.5604 (1875).
33. Cavendish, George, *The Life of Cardinal Wolsey* (1890) pp.116–117.
34. Wooding, Lucy, *Henry VIII* (2015) p.159.
35. Ibid.
36. Starkey, David, *The Reign of Henry VIII: Personalities and Politics* (2002) p.81.
37. Wooding, Lucy, *Henry VIII* (2015) p.159.
38. Roberts, Phil, *Cardinal Wolsey: For King and Country* (2022) p.137.
39. 'Letter from de Vaux to Montmorency 10 November 1530', *Letters and Papers of Henry VIII*, Vol.4, 1524–1530, no.6720 (1875).
40. 'Letter from Francis Bryan to Henry VIII 21 November 1530', *Letters and Papers of Henry VIII*, Vol.4, 1524–1530, no.6733 (1875).
41. Ibid.
42. Ibid.
43. 'Letter from Eustace Chapuys to Charles V 27 November 1530', *Letters and Papers of Henry VIII*, Vol.4, 1524–1530, no.6738 (1875).
44. Ibid.
45. Cavendish, George, *The Life of Cardinal Wolsey* (1890) pp.230–231.
46. Ibid, pp.231–232.
47. Ibid, p.54.
48. Bernard, G. W., 'The Fall of Wolsey Reconsidered', *Journal of British Studies* (1996) p.277.
49. Ibid, p.310.

Chapter 7 – A Second Marriage

1. Guy, John and Fox, Julia, *Hunting the Falcon: Henry VIII, Anne Boleyn and the Marriage That Shook Europe* (2023) p.236.
2. Harpsfield, Nicholas, *A Treatise on the Pretended Divorce Between Henry VIII and Catharine of Aragon* (1878) pp.234–235.
3. Ibid, p.26.

4. Lloyd, Carol Ann, *The Tudors by Numbers: The Stories and Statistics Behind England's Most Infamous Royal Dynasty* (2023) p.107.
5. 'Letter from Eustace Chapuys to Charles V 16 June 1533', *Calendar of State Papers, Spain,* Vol.14, 1531–1533, no.1081 (1882).
6. 'Nicholas Udall's verse in the coronation procession of Anne Boleyn', in Norton, Elizabeth, *Anne Boleyn: In Her Own Words and the Words of Those Who Knew Her* (2011) pp.136–137.
7. Biedermann, Hans, *The Wordsworth Dictionary of Symbolism* (1996) p.333.
8. Ibid, p.380.
9. Ives, Eric, *The Life and Death of Anne Boleyn* (2005) p.221.
10. Hall, Edward, *Hall's Chronicle* (1809) p.805.
11. Borman, Tracy, *Anne Boleyn and Elizabeth I: The Mother and Daughter Who Changed History* (2023) p.3.
12. Ibid, pp.150–151.
13. Hall, Edward, *Hall's Chronicle* (1809) p.806.
14. 'Letter from Eustace Chapuys to Charles V 15 September 1536', *Letters and Papers, Foreign and Domestic, Henry VIII,* Vol.6, 1533, No.1125 (1882).
15. Ibid.
16. Ives, Eric, *The Life and Death of Anne Boleyn* (2005) p.184.
17. Dewhurst, John, 'The Alleged Miscarriages of Catherine of Aragon and Anne Boleyn', *Medical History* (1984) p.54.
18. Bruce, Marie Louise, *Anne Boleyn* (1975) p.251.
19. 'Letter from Eustace Chapuys to Charles V 28 January 1534', *Letters and Papers, Foreign and Domestic, Henry VIII,* Vol.7, 1534, No.114 (1883).
20. 'Letter from George Taylor to Lady Lisle 27 April 1534', *Letters and Papers, Foreign and Domestic, Henry VIII,* Vol.7, 1534, No.556 (1883).
21. 'Instructions to my lord of Rochford, whom the King now sends to the French king July 1534', *Letters and Papers, Foreign and Domestic, Henry VIII,* Vol.7, 1534, No.958 (1883).
22. 'Letters from Eustace Chapuys to Charles V 27 September 1534', *Letters and Papers, Foreign and Domestic, Henry VIII,* Vol.7, 1534, No.1193 (1883).
23. Jones, Philippa, *The Other Tudors: Henry VIII's Mistresses and Bastards* (2010) p.241.
24. Ibid.
25. Hart, Kelly, *The Mistresses of Henry VIII* (2011) p.121.
26. Licence, Amy, *The Six Wives and Many Mistresses of Henry VIII: The Women's Stories* (2015) p.257.
27. Ibid, p.122.
28. 'Letter from Eustace Chapuys to Charles V 25 February 1535', *Letters and Papers, Foreign and Domestic, Henry VIII,* Vol.8, Jan–Jul 1535, No.263 (1885).
29. 'Letter from William Kingston to Lord Lisle 24 June 1535', *Letters and Papers, Foreign and Domestic, Henry VIII,* Vol.8, Jan–Jul 1535, No.919 (1885).
30. Neale, J. E., *Queen Elizabeth I* (1957) p.5.
31. Whitley, Catrina Banks and Kramer, Kyra, 'A New Explanation for the Reproductive Woes and Midlife Decline of Henry VIII', *The Historical Journal* (2010) p.828.
32. Ibid, pp.833–834.
33. 'Letter from William Kingston to Lord Lisle on 18 April 1534', *Letters and Papers, Foreign and Domestic, Henry VIII,* Vol.7, 1534, No.509 (1883).
34. Borman, Tracy, *Anne Boleyn and Elizabeth I: The Mother and Daughter Who Changed History* (2023) p.57.

35. Wyatt, George, *Extracts from the Life of the Virtuous, Christian, and Renowned Queen Anne Boleigne* (1817) p.18.
36. 'Letter from Eustace Chapuys to Charles V 13 October 1534', *Letters and Papers, Foreign and Domestic, Henry VIII*, Vol.7, 1534, No.1257 (1883).
37. Fenton, Charlie, *Jane Parker: The Downfall of Two Tudor Queens?* (2021) p.17.
38. Wyatt, George, *Extracts from the Life of the Virtuous, Christian, and Renowned Queen Anne Boleigne* (1817) p.18.
39. Ibid.
40. 'Act of Succession 1534', in Gee, Henry & Hardy, John William (eds.), *Documents Illustrative of English Church History* (1914) pp.232–243.
41. Ibid.
42. Ibid.
43. Ibid.
44. Foxe, John, *Actes and Monuments*, Vol.4 (1838) p.658.
45. 'Treason Act 1534', in Gee, Henry & Hardy, John William (eds.), *Documents Illustrative of English Church History* (1914) pp.247–251.
46. Ibid.
47. 'Treason Act 1351', *The National Archives*.
48. 'Treason Act 1534', in Gee, Henry & Hardy, John William (eds.), *Documents Illustrative of English Church History* (1914) pp.247–251.

Chapter 8 – Thomas Cromwell and the English Reformation

1. MacCulloch, Diarmaid, *Thomas Cromwell: A Revolutionary Life* (2018) p.1.
2. Starkey, David, *The Reign of Henry VIII: Personalities and Politics* (2002) p.83.
3. Emmerson, Owen, McCaffrey, Kate & Palmer, Alison, *Catherine and Anne: Queens, Rivals, Mothers* (2023) p.43.
4. Ibid, p.59.
5. Emmerson, Owen, 'Make or Mar', in *Thomas Cromwell: Beyond Wolf Hall* [online lecture series] (2024).
6. Angus, Caroline, *The Private Life of Thomas Cromwell* (2022) p.9.
7. Ibid, p.21.
8. Emmerson, Owen, 'Nothing Spoken Against My Lord', in *Thomas Cromwell: Beyond Wolf Hall* [online lecture series] (2024).
9. 'Letter from Eustace Chapuys to Granvelle 21 November 1535', *Letters and Papers of Henry VIII*, Vol.9, Aug–Dec 1535, no.862 (1886).
10. Murphy, Beverley, *Bastard Prince: Henry VIII's Lost Son* (2001) p.146.
11. Submission of the Clergy Act 1533, *Acts of the English Parliament*, 1533 c.19, https://www.legislation.gov.uk/aep/Hen8/25/19/contents.
12. 'Letter from Eustace Chapuys to Charles V 19 May 1534', *Letters and Papers of Henry VIII*, Vol.7, 1534, no.690 (1883).
13. 'Letter from Eustace Chapuys to Granvelle 21 November 1535', *Letters and Papers of Henry VIII*, Vol.9, Aug–Dec 1535, no.862 (1886).
14. Ives, Eric, *The Life and Death of Anne Boleyn* (2005) p.207.
15. Angus, Caroline, *The Private Life of Thomas Cromwell* (2022) p.87.
16. MacCulloch, Diarmaid, *Thomas Cromwell: A Revolutionary Life* (2018) p.113.
17. Ibid, p.115.
18. Wyatt, George, *Extracts from the Life of the Virtuous, Christian, and Renowned Queen Anne Boleigne* (1817) p.18.

19. Ives, Eric, *The Life and Death of Anne Boleyn* (2005) p.309.
20. 'Letter from Eustace Chapuys to Granvelle 21 November 1535', *Letters and Papers of Henry VIII*, Vol.9, Aug–Dec 1535, no.862 (1886).
21. Paul, Joanne, *Thomas More: A Life and Death in Tudor England* (2025) p.407.
22. Ibid.
23. 'Treason Act 1534' in Gee, Henry & Hardy, John William (eds.), *Documents Illustrative of English Church History* (1914) pp.247–251.
24. Loades, David, *Thomas Cromwell: Servant to Henry VIII* (2014) p.112.
25. Elton, G. R., *England under the Tudors* (2006) p.139.
26. 'Letter from Bishop of Faenza to M. Ambrogio 22 June 1535', *Letters and Papers of Henry VIII*, Vol.9, Jan–Jul 1535, no.909 (1885).
27. 'Trial of Sir Thomas More July 1535', *Letters and Papers of Henry VIII*, Vol.8, Jan–Jul 1535, no.974 (1885).
28. Ibid.
29. Paul, Joanne, *Thomas More: A Life and Death in Tudor England* (2025) p.430.
30. 'Trial of Sir Thomas More July 1535', *Letters and Papers of Henry VIII*, Vol.9, Jan–Jul 1535, no.974 (1885).
31. Paul, Joanne, *Thomas More: A Life and Death in Tudor England* (2025) p.432.
32. Angus, Caroline, *The Private Life of Thomas Cromwell* (2022) p.131.
33. 'Letter from Bishop of Faenza to M. Ambrogio 4 July 1535', *Letters and Papers of Henry VIII*, Vol.9, Jan–Jul 1535, no.985 (1885).
34. Ibid.
35. 'Letter from Thomas More to Margaret Roper 5 July 1535', *Letters and Papers of Henry VIII*, Vol.9, Jan–Jul 1535, no.988 (1885).
36. 'Account of Sir Thomas More 6 July 1535 [MS. Bibl. Nat., Paris. Castelnau's Memoirs]', *Letters and Papers of Henry VIII*, Vol.9, Jan–Jul 1535, no.996 (1885).
37. Wilson, Derek, *In the Lion's Court: Power, Ambition, and Sudden Death in the Reign of Henry VIII* (2002) p.456.
38. Angus, Caroline, *The Private Life of Thomas Cromwell* (2022) p.166.
39. MacCulloch, Diarmaid, *Thomas Cromwell: A Revolutionary Life* (2018) p.315.
40. Schofield, John, *The Rise and Fall of Thomas Cromwell: Henry VIII's Most Faithful Servant* (2012) p.61.
41. Borman, Tracy, *Henry VIII and the Men Who Made Him* (2020) pp.219–220.
42. Schofield, John, *The Rise and Fall of Thomas Cromwell: Henry VIII's Most Faithful Servant* (2012) p.61.
43. Starkey, David, *The Reign of Henry VIII: Personalities and Politics* (2002) p.84.
44. Ban, Joseph, D., 'English Reformation: Product of King or Minister?', *Church History* (1972) p.197.
45. Starkey, David, *The Reign of Henry VIII: Personalities and Politics* (2002) p.84.
46. Angus, Caroline, *The Private Life of Thomas Cromwell* (2022) p.xi.
47. Borman, Tracy, *Henry VIII and the Men Who Made Him* (2020) pp.205–206.
48. Carlton, Charles, 'Thomas Cromwell: A Study in Interrogation', *Albion* (1973) p.116.

Chapter 9 – Princess Mary and the Rivalry

1. 'Letter from Eustace Chapuys to Charles V 29 January 1536', *Letters and Papers of Henry VIII*, Vol.10, Jan–Jun 1536, no.199 (1887).

2. 'Report of England made by Giovanni Michiel, late Ambassador to Queen Mary and King Philip, to the Venetian Senate 13 May 1557', *Calendar of State Papers: Venice*, Vol.6, 1555–1558, no.884 (1877).
3. Ibid.
4. 'Letter from Eustace Chapuys to Charles V 29 January 1536', *Letters and Papers of Henry VIII*, Vol.10, Jan–Jun 1536, no.199 (1887).
5. Thomas, Melita, *The King's Pearl: Henry VIII and His Daughter Mary* (2019) p.175.
6. 'Letter from Eustace Chapuys to Charles V 27 September 1534', *Letters and Papers of Henry VIII*, Vol.7, 1534, no.1193 (1883).
7. 'Letter from Eustace Chapuys to Charles V 23 September 1534', *Calendar of State Papers: Spain*, Vol.5, Pt.1, 1534–1535, no.90 (1886).
8. Travitsky, Betty, 'Reprinting Tudor History: The Case of Catherine of Aragon', *Renaissance Quarterly* (1997) p.166.
9. Edwards, John, *Mary I: The Daughter of Time* (2018) p.13.
10. Thomas, Melita, *The King's Pearl: Henry VIII and His Daughter Mary* (2019) p.120.
11. Edwards, John, *Mary I: The Daughter of Time* (2018) p.14.
12. Ives, Eric, *The Life and Death of Anne Boleyn* (2005) p.197.
13. Jones, Philippa, *The Other Tudors: Henry VIII's Mistresses and Bastards* (2010) p.240.
14. 'Letter from Eustace Chapuys to Charles V 6 December 1533', *Letters and Papers of Henry VIII*, Vol.6, 1533, no.1501 (1882).
15. Ibid.
16. Ives, Eric, *The Life and Death of Anne Boleyn* (2005) p.198.
17. Thomas, Melita, *The King's Pearl: Henry VIII and His Daughter Mary* (2019) p.139.
18. 'Letter from Eustace Chapuys to Charles V 16 December 1533', *Letters and Papers of Henry VIII*, Vol.6, 1533, no.1528 (1882).
19. Ibid.
20. Ibid.
21. Whitelock, Anna, *Mary Tudor: Princess, Bastard, Queen* (2009) p.55.
22. 'Letter from Eustace Chapuys to Charles V 16 December 1533', *Letters and Papers of Henry VIII*, Vol.6, 1533, no.1528 (1882).
23. 'Letter from Eustace Chapuys to Charles V 23 June 1534', *Letters and Papers of Henry VIII*, Vol.7, 1534, no.871 (1883).
24. Ives, Eric, *The Life and Death of Anne Boleyn* (2005) p.198.
25. 'Letter from Eustace Chapuys to Charles V 23 December 1533', *Letters and Papers of Henry VIII*, Vol.6, 1533, no.1558 (1882).
26. Ibid.
27. Whitelock, Anna, *Mary Tudor: Princess, Bastard, Queen* (2009) p.57.
28. Ibid.
29. 'Letter from Eustace Chapuys to Charles V 11 February 1534', *Letters and Papers of Henry VIII*, Vol.7, 1534, no.171 (1883).
30. Ibid.
31. 'Letter from Eustace Chapuys to Charles V 7 March 1534', *Letters and Papers of Henry VIII*, Vol.7, 1534, no.296 (1883).
32. Ives, Eric, *The Life and Death of Anne Boleyn* (2005) p.198.
33. 'Letter from Eustace Chapuys to Charles V 1 July 1536', *Letters and Papers of Henry VIII*, Vol.11, July–Dec 1536, no.7 (1888).
34. 'Letter from Eustace Chapuys to Charles V 10 February 1536', *Letters and Papers of Henry VIII*, Vol.10, Jan–Jun 1536, no.282 (1887).

35. Ibid.
36. 'Letter from Eustace Chapuys to Charles V 21 January 1536', *Letters and Papers of Henry VIII*, Vol.10, Jan–Jun 1536, no.141 (1887).
37. Ibid.
38. 'Letter from Eustace Chapuys to Charles V 29 January 1536', *Letters and Papers of Henry VIII*, Vol.10, Jan–Jun 1536, no.199 (1887).
39. 'Letter from Eustace Chapuys to Charles V 19 May 1536', *Letters and Papers of Henry VIII*, Vol.10, Jan–Jun 1536, no.908 (1887).
40. Ibid.
41. Ibid.
42. Murphy, Beverley, *Bastard Prince: Henry VIII's Lost Son* (2001) p.146.
43. 'Letter from Princess Mary to Secretary Cromwell 1536' from Cotton MS Otho C.X. fol.263b, in Wood, Mary Anne Everett, *Letters of Royal and Illustrious Ladies of Great Britain* (1846) pp.250–252.
44. 'The Princess Mary's Submission', *Letters and Papers of Henry VIII*, Vol.10, Jan–Jun 1536, no.1137 (1887).
45. Whitelock, Anna, *Mary Tudor: Princess, Bastard, Queen* (2009) p.90.
46. Hunt, Alice, 'The Monarchical Republic of Mary I', *The Historical Journal* (2009) p.568.

Chapter 10 – The Year of Three Queens

1. 'Letter from Edmund Bedingfield to Cromwell 5 January 1536', *Letters and Papers of Henry VIII*, Vol.10, Jan–Jun 1536, no.28 (1887).
2. Ibid.
3. Ibid.
4. 'Letter from Eustace Chapuys to Charles V 9 January 1536', *Letters and Papers of Henry VIII*, Vol.10, Jan–Jun 1536, no.59 (1887).
5. 'Will of Katherine of Aragon', *Letters and Papers of Henry VIII*, Vol.10, Jan–Jun 1536, no.40 (1887).
6. Ibid.
7. 'Letter from Cromwell to Gardiner and Wallop 8 January 1536', *Letters and Papers of Henry VIII*, Vol.10, Jan–Jun 1536, no.54 (1887).
8. Vergil, Polydore, *Anglica Historia* (2005) Chapter XXVII, https://philological.cal.bham.ac.uk/polverg/27eng.html.
9. Licence, Amy, *Catherine of Aragon: An Intimate Life of Henry VIII's True Wife* (2016) p.495.
10. Tremlett, Giles, *Catherine of Aragon: Henry's Spanish Queen* (2011) p.422.
11. 'Letter from Eustace Chapuys to Charles V 21 January 1536', *Letters and Papers of Henry VIII*, Vol.10, Jan–Jun 1536, no.141 (1887).
12. Williams, Patrick, *Katharine of Aragon* (2014) p.381.
13. Licence, Amy, *Catherine of Aragon: An Intimate Life of Henry VIII's True Wife* (2016) p.496.
14. Tremlett, Giles, *Catherine of Aragon: Henry's Spanish Queen* (2011) p.424.
15. Guy, John and Fox, Julia, *Hunting the Falcon: Henry VIII, Anne Boleyn and the Marriage That Shook Europe* (2023) p.341.
16. 'Letter from Eustace Chapuys to Charles V 29 January 1536', *Letters and Papers of Henry VIII*, Vol.10, Jan–Jun 1536, no.199 (1887).
17. Williams, Patrick, *Katharine of Aragon* (2014) p.9.

18. Guy, John and Fox, Julia, *Hunting the Falcon: Henry VIII, Anne Boleyn and the Marriage That Shook Europe* (2023) p.341.
19. Weir, Alison, *The Lady in the Tower: The Fall of Anne Boleyn* (2009) p.18.
20. 'Letter from Eustace Chapuys to Charles V 10 February 1536', *Letters and Papers of Henry VIII*, Vol.10, Jan–Jun 1536, no.282 (1887).
21. Ibid.
22. Ibid.
23. Dewhurst, John, 'The Alleged Miscarriages of Catherine of Aragon and Anne Boleyn', *Medical History* (1984) p.54.
24. Neale, J. E. *Queen Elizabeth I* (1957) p.5.
25. Wyatt, George, *Extracts from the Life of the Virtuous, Christian, and Renowned Queen Anne Boleigne* (1817), p.19.
26. 'Letter from Bishop of Faenza to Prothonotary Ambrogio 10 March 1536', *Letters and Papers of Henry VIII*, Vol.10, Jan–Jun 1536, no.450 (1887).
27. 'Letter from Dr Ortiz to the Empress 22 March 1536', *Letters and Papers of Henry VIII*, Vol.10, Jan–Jun 1536, no.528 (1887).
28. Wriothesley, Charles, *A Chronicle of England During the Reigns of the Tudors* (1875) p.33.
29. Grueninger, Natalie, *The Final Year of Anne Boleyn* (2022) p.133.
30. Ibid.
31. 'Letter from Eustace Chapuys to Charles V 29 January 1536', *Letters and Papers of Henry VIII*, Vol.10, Jan–Jun 1536, no.199 (1887).
32. 'Letter from Eustace Chapuys to Charles V 10 February 1536', *Letters and Papers of Henry VIII*, Vol.10, Jan–Jun 1536, no.282 (1887).
33. Ibid.
34. 'Letter from William Kingston to Thomas Cromwell 3 May 1536', *Letters and Papers of Henry VIII*, Vol.10, Jan–Jun 1536, no.793 (1888).
35. Ibid.
36. Ibid.
37. Gristwood, Sarah, *The Tudors in Love: The Courtly Code Behind the Last Medieval Dynasty* (2021) p.176.
38. 'Trial Documents of Anne Boleyn and Lord Rochford', *Letters and Papers of Henry VIII*, Vol.10, Jan–Jun 1536, no.876 (1888).
39. Ibid.
40. 'Letter from William Kingston to Thomas Cromwell 3 May 1536', *Letters and Papers of Henry VIII*, Vol.10, Jan–Jun 1536, no.793 (1888).
41. Grueninger, Natalie, *The Final Year of Anne Boleyn* (2022) p.156.
42. 'Letter from William Kingston to Cromwell undated May 1536', *Letters and Papers of Henry VIII*, Vol.10, Jan–Jun 1536, no.793 (1888).
43. 'Trial Documents of Anne Boleyn and Lord Rochford', *Letters and Papers of Henry VIII*, Vol.10, Jan–Jun 1536, no.876 (1888).
44. Day, Chris; Gosling, Daniel; Johnston, Neil & Roger, Euan, *A History of Treason: The Bloody History of Britain Through the Stories of its Most Notorious Traitors* (2022) pp.114–115.
45. 'Letter from Eustace Chapuys to Charles V 19 May 1536', *Letters and Papers of Henry VIII*, Vol.10, Jan–Jun 1536, no.908 (1887).
46. Ibid.
47. Foxe, John, *Actes and Monuments* (1838) p.135.

48. 'Letter from Eustace Chapuys to Charles V 19 May 1536', *Letters and Papers of Henry VIII*, Vol.10, Jan–Jun 1536, no.908 (1887).
49. 'Letter from Bishop of Faenza to Mons. Ambrogio 24 May 1536' *Letters and Papers of Henry VIII*, Vol.10, Jan–Jun 1536, no.956 (1887).
50. Murphy, Beverley A., *Bastard Prince: Henry VIII's Lost Son* (2001) p.213.
51. 'Letter from Eustace Chapuys to Charles V 23 July 1536', *Letters and Papers of Henry VIII*, Vol.11, Jul–Dec 1536, no.147 (1888).
52. 'Letter from Eustace Chapuys to Granvelle 23 July 1536', *Letters and Papers of Henry VIII*, Vol.11, Jul–Dec 1536, no.148 (1888).
53. 'Letter from Eustace Chapuys to Charles V 19 May 1536', *Letters and Papers of Henry VIII*, Vol.10, Jan–Jun 1536, no.908 (1887).
54. Smith, Lacey Baldwin, 'English Treason Trials and Confessions in the Sixteenth Century', *Journal of the History of Ideas* (1954) p.472.

Chapter 11 – Aftermath and Lessons

1. Froude, James, *The Divorce of Catherine of Aragon* (2015) p.8.
2. Strickland, Agnes, *Lives of the Queens of England, Volume II* (1909) p.176.
3. Guy, John and Fox, Julia, *Hunting the Falcon: Henry VIII, Anne Boleyn and the Marriage That Shook Europe* (2023) p.xxxii.
4. Wyatt, Thomas, 'Innocentia Veritas Viat Fides Circumdederunt me inimici mei', in Norton, Elizabeth, *Anne Boleyn: In Her Own Words and the Words of Those Who Knew Her* (2011) p.237.
5. Weir, Alison, *The Lady in the Tower: The Fall of Anne Boleyn* (2009) p.291.
6. Walker, Greg, *Writing Under Tyranny: English Literature and the Henrician Reformation* (2005) p.290.
7. Ives, Eric, *The Life and Death of Anne Boleyn* (2005) p.359.
8. Loades, David, *The Seymours of Wolf Hall: A Tudor Family Story* (2015) p.71.
9. 'Letter from Eustace Chapuys to Charles V 12 August 1536', *Letters and Papers of Henry VIII*, Vol.11, Jul–Dec 1536, no.285 (1888).
10. Norton, Elizabeth, *Jane Seymour: Henry VIII's True Love* (2009) p.99. 11. 'Letter from Duke of Norfolk to Henry VIII 24 March 1537', *Letters and Papers of Henry VIII*, Vol.12 Pt.1, Jan–May 1537, no.709 (1890).
11. 'Letter from Duke of Norfolk to Henry VIII 24 March 1537', *Letters and Papers of Henry VIII*, Vol.12 Pt.1, Jan–May 1537, no.709 (1890).
12. 'Letter from John Husee to Lady Lisle 30 April 1537', *Letters and Papers of Henry VIII*, Vol.12 Pt.1, Jan–May 1537, no.1069 (1890).
13. Johnston, Carol-Ann, *Jane Seymour: An Illustrated Life* (2023) p.110.
14. Wriothesley, Charles, *A Chronicle of England During the Reigns of the Tudors*, Vol.1 (1875) pp.65–66.
15. 'Birth and Christening of Prince Edward', *Letters and Papers of Henry VIII*, Vol.12 Pt.2, Jun–Dec 1537, no.911 (1891).
16. Johnston, Carol-Ann, *Jane Seymour: An Illustrated Life* (2023) pp.119–120.
17. 'Letter from Henry VIII to Francis I 24 October 1537', *Letters and Papers of Henry VIII*, Vol.12 Pt.2, Jun–Dec 1537, no.972 (1891).
18. 'A remembrance of the interment of Queen Jane, mother of Edward VI', *Letters and Papers of Henry VIII*, Vol.12 Pt.2, Jun–Dec 1537, no.1060 (1891).
19. Ibid.

20. MacCulloch, Diarmaid, *Thomas Cromwell: A Revolutionary Life* (2018) p.524.
21. Harrison, Helene, *Tudor Executions: From Nobility to the Block* (2024) chapters 7 and 8 for the executions of Thomas and Edward Seymour, pp.103–137.
22. Porter, Katherine, *Katherine the Queen: The Remarkable Life of Katherine Parr, the Last Wife of Henry VIII* (2010) p.194.
23. Edward VI, *Devise for the Succession* (1553).
24. Ibid.

Epilogue

1. Harrison, Helene, *Tudor Executions: From Nobility to the Block* (2024) chapter 2 for the execution of the Duke of Buckingham, pp.18–34.
2. Travitsky, Betty, 'Reprinting Tudor History: The Case of Catherine of Aragon', *Renaissance Quarterly* (1997) p.167.
3. Ibid, p.170.
4. Borman, Tracy, *Anne Boleyn and Elizabeth I: The Mother and Daughter Who Changed History* (2023) p.1.
5. You can read about the discoveries in the books: Emmerson, Owen, McCaffrey, Kate & Palmer, Alison, *Catherine and Anne: Queens, Rivals, Mothers* (2023) and Emmerson, Owen & McCaffrey, Kate, *Holbein's Hidden Gem: Rediscovering Thomas Cromwell's Lost Book* (2023).
6. Emmerson, Owen and Ridgway, Claire, *The Boleyns of Hever Castle* (2021) p.101.
7. Rabow, Jerry, *Henry VIII and his Rabbis: How the King Relied on Jewish Law to End His First Marriage – and Why He Failed* (2025) p.196.

Bibliography

Primary Sources

Archives

Acts of the English Parliament. Legislation.gov.uk, https://www.legislation.gov.uk/aep.

Calendar of State Papers, Spain. Edited by Pascual de Gayangos. London: Her Majesty's Stationery Office 1882. British History Online, https://www.british-history.ac.uk/search/series/cal-state-papers--spain.

Calendar of State Papers Relating to English Affairs in the Archives of Venice. Edited by Rawdon Brown. London: Her Majesty's Stationery Office 1867. British History Online, https://archive.british-history.ac.uk/search/series/cal-state-papers--venice.

Letters and Papers, Foreign and Domestic, Henry VIII. Edited by James Gairdner. London: Her Majesty's Stationery Office 1864–1920. British History Online, http://www.british-history.ac.uk/letters-papers-hen8/.

Treason Act 1351. The National Archives, https://www.legislation.gov.uk/aep/Edw3Stat5/25/2.

Vatican Archives, ref. Vat.lat.3731.pt.A, https://digi.vatlib.it/view/MSS_Vat.lat.3731.pt.A.

Online

Edward VI, *Devise for the Succession*, Luminarium Encyclopedia Project (1553) https://luminarium.org/encyclopedia/edward6devise.htm.

Vergil, Polydore, *The Anglica Historia of Polydore Vergil A.D. 1485–1537*, Dana J. Sutton (ed.), Library of Humanistic Texts at the Philological Museum of University of Birmingham's Shakespeare Institute (2005) http://www.philological.bham.ac.uk/polverg/.

Printed

Barnwell, E. L., *Perrot Notes, or Some Account of the Various Branches of the Perrot Family* (London: J. Russell Smith, 1867).

Cavendish, George, *The Life of Cardinal Wolsey* (London: George Routledge and Sons Limited, 1890).

Chaucer, Geoffrey, *Chaucer's Romaunt of the Rose, Troilus and Creseide and the Minor Poems* (London: William Pickering, 1846).

Foxe, John (Townsend, George ed.), *Actes and Monuments of these Latter and Perillous Days, Touching Matters of the Church* (London: Seeley, Burnside and Seeley, 1838).

Fuller, Thomas, *The Church History of Britain from the Birth of Jesus Christ Until the Year M. DC.XLVIII* (Oxford: Oxford University Press, 1845).

Gee, Henry & Hardy, William (eds.), *Documents Illustrative of English Church History* (London: Macmillan, 1914).

Hall, Edward (Ellis, Henry ed.), *Hall's Chronicle; Containing the History of England During the Reign of Henry the Fourth and the Succeeding Monarchs to the End of the Reign of*

Henry VIII, in Which are Particularly Described the manners and Customs of Those Periods (London: J. Johnson, 1809).

Harpsfield, Nicholas, *A treatise on the pretended divorce between Henry VIII and Catharine of Aragon* (London: Camden Society, 1878).

Henry VIII (Phillips, J. O. ed.), *Love Letters of Henry VIII to Anne Boleyn* (London: Merchant Books, 2009).

Herbert of Cherbury, *The History of England Under Henry VIII* (London: Alexander Murray, 1870).

Holinshed, Raphael, *Holinshed's Chronicle of England, Scotland, and Ireland, Volume 3* (London: J. Johnston, 1807).

Hume, Martin, *The Chronicle of King Henry VIII of England, Being a Contemporary Record of Some of the Principal Events of the Reigns of Henry VIII and Edward VI* (London: G. Bell & Sons, 1889).

Norton, Elizabeth, *Anne Boleyn: In Her Own Words and the Words of Those Who Knew Her* (Stroud: Amberley Publishing, 2011).

Parker, Matthew, *Correspondence of Matthew Parker, D.D.: Archbishop of Canterbury: comprising letters written by and to him, from A.D. 1535 to his death, A.D. 1575* (Cambridge: Cambridge University Press, 1853).

Pocock, Nicholas, *Records of the Reformation: The Divorce 1527–1533* (Oxford: Clarendon Press, 1870).

Pole, Reginald, *Defense of the Unity of the Church* (Pine Beach NJ: Newman Press, 1965).

Sander, Nicholas, *Rise and Growth of the Anglican Schism* (London: Burns and Oates, 1877).

Strickland, Agnes, *Lives of the Queens of England from the Norman Conquest, Volume II* (London: George Bell & Sons, 1909).

Sylvester, R. S. (ed.), More, Thomas, *The History of King Richard III* (New Haven: Yale University Press, 1976).

Wood, Mary Anne Everett (ed.), *Letters of Royal and Illustrious Ladies of Great Britain, from the commencement of the twelfth century to the close of the reign of Queen Mary, Volume II* (London: Henry Colburn, 1846).

Wriothesley, Charles, *A Chronicle of England During the Reigns of the Tudors, from A.D. 1485 to 1559, Volume I* (London: The Camden Society, 1875).

Wyatt, George, *Extracts from the Life of the Virtuous, Christian, and Renowned Queen Anne Boleigne* (London: Richard and Arthur Taylor, Shoe Lane, 1817).

Secondary Sources

Books

Angus, Caroline, *Planning the Murder of Anne Boleyn* (Barnsley: Pen and Sword History, 2024).

Angus, Caroline, *The Private Life of Thomas Cromwell* (Barnsley: Pen and Sword History, 2022).

Bennett Connolly, Sharon, *Heroines of the Tudor World* (Stroud: Amberley Publishing, 2024).

Biedermann, Hans, *The Wordsworth Dictionary of Symbolism* (Ware: Wordsworth Editions, 1996).

Bolland, Charlotte, *Six Lives: The Stories of Henry VIII's Queens* (London: National Portrait Gallery, 2024).

Borman, Tracy, *Anne Boleyn and Elizabeth I: The Mother and Daughter Who Changed History* (London: Hodder & Stoughton, 2023).

Borman, Tracy, *Henry VIII and the Men Who Made Him* (New York: Grove Press, 2020).

Borman, Tracy, *The Private Lives of the Tudors: Uncovering the secrets of Britain's greatest dynasty* (London: Hodder & Stoughton, 2016).

Bruce, Marie Louise, *Anne Boleyn* (London: Pan Books Ltd, 1975).

Carradice, Phil, *Rebellion Against Henry VIII: The Rise and Fall of a Dynasty* (Barnsley: Pen and Sword History, 2022).

Darsie, Heather R., *Katharine of Aragon, Spanish Princess: 'I Am Not as Simple as I May Seem'* (Stroud: Amberley Publishing, 2025).

Day, Chris; Gosling, Daniel; Johnston, Neil; & Roger, Euan, *A History of Treason: The Bloody History of Britain Through the Stories of its Most Notorious Traitors* (London: John Blake Publishing, 2022).

Denny, Joanna, *Anne Boleyn: A New Life of England's Tragic Queen* (London: Piatkus Books, 2008).

Dunn, Wendy J., *Henry VIII's True Daughter: Catherine Carey, a Tudor Life* (Barnsley: Pen and Sword History, 2023).

Earenfight, Theresa, *Catherine of Aragon: Infanta of Spain, Queen of England* (University Park: Pennsylvania State University Press, 2021).

Edwards, John, *Mary I: The Daughter of Time* (London: Penguin Books, 2018).

Elton, G. R., *England under the Tudors* (London: Routledge, 2006).

Emmerson, Owen & McCaffrey, Kate, *Becoming Anne: Connections, Culture, Court* (Exeter: Jigsaw Publishing, 2022).

Emmerson, Owen; McCaffrey, Kate; & Palmer, Alison, *Catherine and Anne: Queens, Rivals, Mothers* (Exeter: Jigsaw Publishing, 2023).

Emmerson, Owen & Ridgway, Claire, *The Boleyns of Hever Castle* (Almeria: MadeGlobal Publishing, 2021).

Erickson, Carolly, *Mistress Anne* (New York: St Martin's Press, 1984).

Fenton, Charlie, *Jane Parker: The Downfall of Two Tudor Queens?* (Alresford: Chronos Books, 2021).

Fletcher, Catherine, *The Divorce of Henry VIII: The Untold Story from Inside the Vatican* (New York: Palgrave Macmillan, 2012).

Fox, Julia, *Jane Boleyn: The Infamous Lady Rochford* (London: Weidenfeld & Nicolson, 2007).

Fox, Julia, *Sister Queens: Katherine of Aragon and Juana, Queen of Castile* (London: Weidenfeld & Nicolson, 2011).

Fraser, Antonia, *The Six Wives of Henry VIII* (London: Phoenix, 2002).

Friedmann, Paul, *Anne Boleyn* (Stroud: Amberley Publishing, 2010).

Froude, James, *The Divorce of Catherine of Aragon* (Scotts Valley, CA: CreateSpace Independent Publishing Platform, 2015).

Gristwood, Sarah, *Game of Queens: The Women Who Made Sixteenth Century Europe* (London: Oneworld Publications, 2016).

Gristwood, Sarah, *The Tudors in Love: The Courtly Code Behind the Last Medieval Dynasty* (London: OneWorld Publications, 2011).

Grueninger, Natalie, *The Final Year of Anne Boleyn* (Barnsley: Pen and Sword History, 2022).

Guy, John, *The Children of Henry VIII* (Oxford: Oxford University Press, 2013).

Guy, John & Fox, Julia, *Hunting the Falcon: Henry VIII, Anne Boleyn and the Marriage That Shook Europe* (London: Bloomsbury Publishing, 2023).

Gwyn, Peter, *The King's Cardinal: The Rise and Fall of Thomas Wolsey* (London: Barrie & Jenkins Ltd, 1990).

Hackett, Francis, *Henry the VIII: The Personal History of a Dynast and His Wives* (New York: Liveright Publishing Corporation, 1945).
Harrison, Helene, *The Many Faces of Anne Boleyn: Interpreting Image and Perception* (Barnsley: Pen and Sword History, 2025).
Harrison, Helene, *Tudor Executions: From Nobility to the Block* (Barnsley: Pen and Sword History, 2024).
Hart, Kelly, *The Mistresses of Henry VIII* (Stroud: The History Press, 2011).
Heath, Richard, *Henry VIII and Charles V: Rival Monarchs, Uneasy Allies* (Barnsley: Pen and Sword History, 2023).
Hutchinson, Robert, *Thomas Cromwell: The Rise and Fall of Henry VIII's Most Notorious Minister* (London: Phoenix, 2008).
Ives, Eric, *The Life and Death of Anne Boleyn* (Oxford: Blackwell Publishing Ltd, 2005).
Johnston, Carol-Ann, *Jane Seymour: An Illustrated Life* (Barnsley: Pen and Sword History, 2023).
Jones, Philippa, *The Other Tudors: Henry VIII's Mistresses and Bastards* (London: New Holland Publishers, 2010).
Licence, Amy, *Anne Boleyn: Adultery, Heresy, Desire* (Stroud: Amberley Publishing, 2017).
Licence, Amy, *Catherine of Aragon: An Intimate Life of Henry VIII's True Wife* (Stroud: Amberley Publishing, 2016).
Licence, Amy, *In Bed with the Tudors: The Sex Lives of a Dynasty from Elizabeth of York to Elizabeth I* (Stroud: Amberley Publishing, 2012).
Licence, Amy, *The Six Wives and Many Mistresses of Henry VIII: The Women's Stories* (Stroud: Amberley Publishing, 2015).
Licence, Amy, *Tudor Roses: From Margaret Beaufort to Elizabeth I* (Stroud: Amberley Publishing, 2022).
Lindsey, Karen, *Divorced, Beheaded, Survived: A Feminist Reinterpretation of the Wives of Henry VIII* (Cambridge MA: Da Capo Press, 1995).
Lipscomb, Suzannah, *1536: The Year That Changed Henry VIII* (Oxford: Lion Hudson plc, 2009).
Lloyd, Carol Ann, *The Tudors by Numbers: The Stories and Statistics Behind England's Most Infamous Royal Dynasty* (Barnsley: Pen and Sword History, 2023).
Loades, David, *The Boleyns: The Rise and Fall of a Tudor Family* (Stroud: Amberley Publishing, 2011).
Loades, David, *Henry VIII* (Stroud: Amberley Publishing, 2011).
Loades, David, *The Seymours of Wolf Hall: A Tudor Family Story* (Stroud: Amberley Publishing, 2015).
Loades, David, *The Six Wives of Henry VIII* (Stroud: Amberley Publishing, 2010).
Loades, David, *Thomas Cromwell: Servant to Henry VIII* (Stroud: Amberley Publishing, 2014).
Loades, David, *The Tudor Queens of England* (London: Continuum UK, 2009).
MacCulloch, Diarmaid (ed.), *The Reign of Henry VIII: Politics, Policy and Piety* (New York: Palgrave Macmillan, 1995).
MacCulloch, Diarmaid, *Thomas Cromwell: A Revolutionary Life* (New York: Viking, 2018).
Mackay, Lauren, *Inside the Tudor Court: Henry VIII and his Six Wives Through the Eyes of the Spanish Ambassador* (Stroud: Amberley Publishing, 2015).
Martin, Claire, *Heirs of Ambition: The Making of the Boleyns* (Cheltenham: The History Press, 2023).

Matusiak, John, *Martyrs of Henry VIII: Repression, Defiance, Sacrifice* (Cheltenham: The History Press, 2019).
McElroy, Amy, *Women's Lives in the Tudor Era* (Barnsley: Pen and Sword History, 2024).
Morris, Sarah & Grueninger, Natalie, *In the Footsteps of the Six Wives of Henry VIII* (Stroud: Amberley Publishing, 2016).
Murphy, Beverley A., *Bastard Prince: Henry VIII's Lost Son* (Stroud: Sutton Publishing Limited, 2001).
Neale, J. E., *Queen Elizabeth I* (New York: Doubleday & Co., 1957).
Norton, Elizabeth, *Anne Boleyn: Henry VIII's Obsession* (Stroud: Amberley Publishing, 2009).
Norton, Elizabeth, *The Boleyn Women: The Tudor Femmes Fatales Who Changed English History* (Stroud: Amberley Publishing, 2013).
Norton, Elizabeth, *Jane Seymour: Henry VIII's True Love* (Stroud: Amberley Publishing, 2010).
Paranque, Estelle, *Thorns, Lust and Glory: The Betrayal of Anne Boleyn* (London: Ebury Press, 2024).
Paul, Joanne, *Thomas More: A Life and Death in Tudor England* (London: Penguin Michael Joseph, 2025).
Porter, Linda, *Katherine the Queen: The Remarkable Life of Katherine Parr, the Last Wife of Henry VIII* (New York: St Martin's Press, 2010).
Rabow, Jerry, *Henry VIII and His Rabbis: How the King Relied on Jewish Law to End His First Marriage – and Why He Failed* (Stroud: Amberley Publishing, 2025).
Roberts, Phil, *Cardinal Wolsey: For King and Country* (Barnsley: Pen and Sword History, 2022).
Scarisbrick, J. J., *Henry VIII* (London: Methuen London Ltd, 1988).
Schofield, John, *Thomas Cromwell: Henry VIII's Most Faithful Servant* (Stroud: The History Press, 2012).
Smith, Lacey Baldwin, *Anne Boleyn: The Queen of Controversy* (Stroud: Amberley Publishing, 2013).
Starkey, David, *The Reign of Henry VIII: Personalities and Politics* (London: Random House, 2002).
Starkey, David, *Six Wives: The Queens of Henry VIII* (London: Vintage, 2004).
Thomas, Melita, *1000 Tudor People* (Llanelli: Graffeg Publishing, 2024).
Thomas, Melita, *The King's Pearl: Henry VIII and His Daughter Mary* (Stroud: Amberley Publishing, 2019).
Tremlett, Giles, *Catherine of Aragon: Henry's Spanish Queen* (London: Faber and Faber Limited, 2010).
Vasoli, Sandra, *Anne Boleyn's Letter from the Tower: New Updated Edition* (Gwynedd Valley, PA: GreyLondon Press, 2023).
Walker, Greg, *Writing Under Tyranny: English Literature and the Henrician Reformation* (Oxford: Oxford University Press, 2005).
Warnicke, Retha, *The Rise and Fall of Anne Boleyn* (Cambridge: Cambridge University Press, 2008).
Weir, Alison, *Children of England: The Heirs of King Henry VIII* (London: Pimlico, 1997).
Weir, Alison, *Henry VIII: King and Court* (London: Vintage, 2008).
Weir, Alison, *The Lady in the Tower: The Fall of Anne Boleyn* (London: Jonathan Cape, 2009).
Weir, Alison, *Mary Boleyn: 'The Great and Infamous Whore'* (London: Jonathan Cape, 2011).
Weir, Alison, *The Six Wives of Henry VIII* (London: Pimlico, 1997).
Whitelock, Anna, *Mary Tudor: Princess, Bastard, Queen* (New York: Random House, 2009).

Wiesner-Hanks, Merry E., *Women and Gender in Early Modern Europe* (Cambridge: Cambridge University Press, 2008).
Wilkinson, Josephine, *Anne Boleyn: The Young Queen to Be* (Stroud: Amberley Publishing, 2011).
Wilkinson, Josephine, *Mary Boleyn: The True Story of Henry VIII's Favourite Mistress* (Stroud: Amberley Publishing, 2010).
Williams, Patrick, *Katharine of Aragon* (Stroud: Amberley Publishing, 2014).
Wilson, Derek, *In the Lion's Court: Power, Ambition, and Sudden Death in the Reign of Henry VIII* (New York: St Martin's Press, 2002).
Wooding, Lucy, *Henry VIII*, 2nd ed. (Abingdon: Routledge, 2015).
Wooding, Lucy, *Tudor England: A History* (New Haven, CT: Yale University Press, 2022).

Articles

Adams, Tracy, '"Ma seulle mestres": The Myth of the Coquettish Anne Boleyn', *The Court Historian*, Vol. 29, No. 3 (2024) pp.194–210.
Ban, Joseph D., 'English Reformation: Product of King or Minister?', *Church History*, Vol. 41, No. 2 (1972) pp.186–197.
Bernard, G. W., 'The Fall of Anne Boleyn', *English Historical Review*, Vol. 106, No. 420 (1991) pp.584–610.
Bernard, G. W., 'The Fall of Wolsey Reconsidered', *Journal of British Studies*, Vol. 35, No. 3 (1996) pp.277–310.
Carlton, Charles, 'Thomas Cromwell: A Study in Interrogation', *Albion*, Vol. 5, No. 2 (1973) pp.116–127.
Costa, Alexandra de, 'The King's Great Matter: Writing Under Censure at Syon Abbey 1532–1534', *The Review of English Studies*, Vol. 62, No. 253 (2011) pp.15–29.
Dewhurst, John, 'The Alleged Miscarriages of Catherine of Aragon and Anne Boleyn', *Medical History*, Vol. 28 (1984) pp.49–56.
Duncan, J. & Derrett, M., 'Henry Fitzroy and Henry VIII's "Scruple of Conscience"', *Renaissance News*, Vol. 61, No. 1 (1963) pp.1–9.
Gairdner, James, 'New Lights on the Divorce of Henry VIII', *The English Historical Review*, Vol. 11, No. 44 (1896) pp.673–702.
Gairdner, James, 'A Supposed Conspiracy Against Henry VII', *Transactions of the Royal Historical Society*, Vol. 18 (1904) pp.157–194.
Hadwin, J. F., 'Katherine of Aragon and the Veil', *Journal of Ecclesiastical History*, Vol. 66, No. 3 (2015) pp.509–523.
Hadwin, J. F., 'Leviticus, Deuteronomy and Henry VIII', *Journal of Ecclesiastical History*, Vol. 70, No. 3 (2019) pp.487–506.
Hunt, Alice, 'The Monarchical Republic of Mary I', *The Historical Journal*, Vol. 52, No. 3 (2009) pp.557–572.
Ives, Eric, 'Anne Boleyn and the Early Reformation in England: The Contemporary Evidence', *The Historical Journal*, Vol. 37, No. 2 (1994) pp.389–400.
Ives, Eric, 'Anne Boleyn on Trial Again', *Journal of Ecclesiastical History*, Vol. 62, No. 4 (2011) pp.763–777.
Ives, Eric, 'Faction at the Court of Henry VIII: The Fall of Anne Boleyn', *History*, Vol. 57, No. 190 (1972) pp.169–188.
Ives, Eric, 'The Fall of Anne Boleyn Reconsidered', *English Historical Review*, Vol. 107, No. 424 (1992) pp.651–664.

Ives, Eric, 'Tudor Dynastic Problems Revisited', *Historical Research*, Vol. 81, No. 212 (2008) pp.255–279.

Levine, Mortimer, 'Henry VIII's Use of His Spiritual and Temporal Jurisdiction in His Great Causes of Matrimony, Legitimacy, and Succession', *The Historical Journal*, Vol. 10, No. 1 (1967) pp.3–10.

Marius, Richard C., 'Henry VIII, Thomas More, and the Bishop of Rome', *Albion*, Vol. 10 (1978) pp.89–107.

Smith, Lacey Baldwin, 'English Treason Trials and Confessions in the Sixteenth Century', *Journal of the History of Ideas*, Vol. 15, No. 4 (1954) pp.471–498.

Smith, Preserved, 'German Opinion of the Divorce of Henry VIII', *The English Historical Review*, Vol. 27, No. 108 (1912) pp.671–681.

Thornley, I.D., 'The Treason Legislation of Henry VIII (1531–1534)', *Transactions of the Royal Historical Society*, Vol. 11 (1917) pp.87–123.

Thurston, Herbert, 'The Canon Law of the Divorce', *The English Historical Review*, Vol. 19, No. 76 (1904) pp.632–645.

Thurston, Herbert, 'The Divorce of Henry VIII', *Studies: An Irish Quarterly Review*, Vol. 21, No. 81 (1932) pp.55–72.

Travitsky, Betty S., 'Reprinting Tudor History: The Case of Catherine of Aragon', *Renaissance Quarterly*, Vol. 50, No. 1 (1997) pp.164–174.

Walker, Greg, 'Rethinking the Fall of Anne Boleyn', *The Historical Journal*, Vol. 45, No. 1 (2002) pp.1–29.

Warnicke, Retha, 'The Eternal Triangle and Court Politics: Henry VIII, Anne Boleyn and Sir Thomas Wyatt', *Albion*, Vol. 18, No. 4 (1986) pp.565–579.

Warnicke, Retha, 'The Fall of Anne Boleyn: A Reassessment', *History*, Vol. 70, No. 228 (1985) pp.1–15.

Whitley, Catrina Banks, 'A New Explanation for the Reproductive Woes and Midlife Decline of Henry VIII', *The Historical Journal*, Vol. 53, No. 4 (2010) pp.827–848.

Zimmerman, T.C. Price, 'A Note on Clement VII and the Divorce of Henry VIII', *The English Historical Review*, Vol. 82, No, 324 (1967) pp.548–552.

Other Resources

Emmerson, Owen, *Thomas Cromwell: Beyond Wolf Hall* [online lecture series] (2024).

King James Bible. https://www.kingjamesbibleonline.org/.

National Archives Currency Converter 1270–2017. The National Archives. https://www.nationalarchives.gov.uk/currency-converter/#.

Index

Dear Reader,

We hope you [illegible] this book [illegible]

[illegible]

You can [illegible]

[illegible]

[illegible]

We [illegible]

Thank you!